Nine Professional Conversations to Change Our Schools

Nine Professional Conversations to Change Our Schools

A Dashboard of Options

William A. Sommers, PhD, and
Diane P. Zimmerman, PhD

Foreword by Andy Hargreaves

CORWIN
A SAGE Publishing Company

FOR INFORMATION:

Corwin

A SAGE Company

2455 Teller Road

Thousand Oaks, California 91320

(800) 233-9936

www.corwin.com

SAGE Publications Ltd.

1 Oliver's Yard

55 City Road

London EC1Y 1SP

United Kingdom

SAGE Publications India Pvt. Ltd.

B 1/I 1 Mohan Cooperative Industrial Area

Mathura Road, New Delhi 110 044

India

SAGE Publications Asia-Pacific Pte. Ltd.

3 Church Street

#10-04 Samsung Hub

Singapore 049483

Publisher: Arnis Burvikovs

Development Editor: Desirée A. Bartlett

Editorial Assistant: Eliza Riegert

Production Editor: Tori Mirsadjadi

Copy Editor: Amy Hanquist Harris

Typesetter: C&M Digitals (P) Ltd.

Proofreader: Gretchen Treadwell

Indexer: Beth Nauman-Montana

Cover Designer: Candice Harman

Marketing Manager: Nicole Franks

Printed in the United States of America

Library of Congress Cataloging-in-Publication Data

Names: Sommers, William A., author. | Zimmerman, Diane P., author.

Title: Nine professional conversations to change our schools : a dashboard of options / William A. Sommers, Ph.D.,and Diane P. Zimmerman, Ph.D.

Description: Thousand Oaks, California : Corwin, 2018. | Includes bibliographical references and index.

Identifiers: LCCN 2018000794 | ISBN 9781506398488 (pbk. : alk. paper)

Subjects: LCSH: Teachers—Professional relationships—United States. | Communication in education—United States. | Educational change—United States.

Classification: LCC LB1775.2 .S686 2018 | DDC 371.102/2—dc23 LC record available at https://lccn.loc.gov/2018000794

This book is printed on acid-free paper.

SFI label applies to text stock

18 19 20 21 22 10 9 8 7 6 5 4 3 2 1

DISCLAIMER: This book may direct you to access third-party content via Web links, QR codes, or other scannable technologies, which are provided for your reference by the author(s). Corwin makes no guarantee that such third-party content will be available for your use and encourages you to review the terms and conditions of such third-party content. Corwin takes no responsibility and assumes no liability for your use of any third-party content, nor does Corwin approve, sponsor, endorse, verify, or certify such third-party content.

CONTENTS

FOREWORD

In life, unless you're driving a car, avoidance is rarely an effective strategy. Avoiding the school bully will only delay the inevitable beating that will one day come your way. Avoiding dull or difficult colleagues will make completing any task with them all the harder when the time eventually comes. And avoiding persistent school problems that everyone knows about—the parents who get extra favors for their child from the principal, the teacher who is not pulling his or her weight, or the budget that never quite adds up—creates a gradual corrosion of trust that eats away at a community from within.

But coming at problems head on rarely moves a school forward either. Confronting persistent absenteeism or chronic underperformance has to be dealt with directly at some point, of course, but most of the time, haranguing and hectoring people into compliance have few chances of success. Talking *at* people won't get you far as a colleague or a principal, and avoiding talking to people at all will get you equally depressing results. Bad communication and no communication are the doom-loops that determine organizational decline.

So the answer to making improvement in almost anything has to be talking *with* people, not at them—all kinds of people, including ones you can't stand. This is the art of conversation (talking with), and it belongs not just at dinner parties or at gatherings of political fund raisers, but it is at the heart of effective organizational life. In this book, Sommers and Zimmerman make accessible the art of professional conversations.

In the last twenty years or so, we have learned a lot about the value of professional collaboration in teaching—about sharing resources and ideas, giving moral support on a bad day, planning and brainstorming together, and even taking joint responsibility for the same classes. Mainly, working together beats trying to do everything yourself. But not all professional collaboration is effective. A big part of professional collaboration is rooted in talk and words. But talk isn't always productive. The griping curmudgeon who lurks in the back corner of every meeting, the verbally incontinent colleague who rarely gets anything done, the pointy-headed pseudo-academic who wants to turn every issue into a theoretical debate for its own sake, the network meetings that go around in circles, or the purveyors of pleasantries who will skirt around all the important issues for fear of giving offense—these are the characters who provide little or no inspiration for the idea that more conversation will lead to better outcomes for students.

More collaboration is better than no collaboration. And some conversation is invariably better than none. But from this pretty low baseline of effective collegial practice, what we need to know next and now is which ways of collaborating are better than others. This is what Michael O'Connor and I call *collaborative professionalism*—collaborating together more professionally by using honesty, protocols, and rigor; and being more collaborative as professionals so that people build relationships as well as just completing tasks.

The same point applies to the Nine Professional Conversations described in this book. The issue is not to have more or less of it, but to determine and design forms of professional conversations that are most engaging and productive for the people involved and most valuable for the students who will benefit. This is the secret sauce of Zimmerman and Sommers's insightful and practical book *Nine Professional Conversations to Change Our Schools*.

The authors aren't the first to enter the field of professional conversation; indeed, they draw from many experts. They draw from advocates of reflective or mindful conversations that draw people out, encourage them to explore key problems and dilemmas, listen respectfully to others, and eventually determine solutions together. They take a fresh look at ways to handle difficult, challenging, or hard conversations; coach leaders and colleagues about how to talk tough; and raise difficult subjects in a respectful but nonetheless clear and direct way about underperformance or insufficiently high expectations. Finally, there are those who are persuaded by the value of data, evidence, or outside expertise to inform, provoke, or challenge existing and sometimes overly comfortable assumptions about how things must be and can only be. The authors stress that this outside information should inform professional learning; anything short of that wastes time.

In the wider community of educators, advocates of these approaches often fall into separate camps—supportive, challenging, or clinically evidence-driven. This book brings them all together. They are complementary skills sets, not competing ones, each having its time and place and needing to belong to a wider repertoire on which leaders, colleagues, consultants, and staff developers can draw at any time. In clear language and building on their years of experience as highly effective leaders in education, Zimmerman and Sommers take the reader through these different approaches, show them what they look like and what impact they can have, and then provide very clear tools and protocols along with illustrative examples that will help teacher leaders and school leaders put them into practice.

John Dewey taught us that we don't have to and shouldn't make a choice between work and play or theory and experience—that each involves the other. The same is true of the approaches to professional conversation. They all have their place. They all overlap. Sommers and Zimmerman's helpful book shows just what this abiding and practical philosophy will mean for conducting positive professional conversations in real schools; and it demonstrates how to confront professional issues head on and take actions to support learning. After all, we are not driving cars—we are educating the next generation.

Andy Hargreaves
Boston College
January 2018

REFERENCE

Hargreaves, A., & O'Connor, M. (2018). *Collaborative professionalism*. Thousand Oaks, CA: Corwin.

ACKNOWLEDGMENTS

I am not interested in how children behave when they know the answer to something. I am interested in how they behave when they don't know the answer. —Art Costa

Art Costa has been a mentor, colleague, and friend to both of us for over 35 years. Bill thanks Art for reigniting his passion for education when he was ready to give up. When the student is ready, a teacher appears—Art showed up in his life at the right time, and he is eternally grateful. Diane is also forever grateful for the way he encouraged her at every step of the way to create knowledge legacies.

Sometimes those who challenge you teach you best. —Unknown

Bob Garmston joined Art Costa in the development of Cognitive Coaching. Diane and Bob, in particular, have enjoyed a lifelong, intellectual friendship. They continuously challenge each other's thinking and look for knowledge gaps that need filling. Bill honors Bob as one of the great storytellers of all time. His use of stories as a teaching strategy is unsurpassed.

All learning begins when our comfortable ideas turn out to be inadequate. —John Dewey

The Learning Omnivores are a small but dedicated group of voracious learners that have come together to learn from each other. Some of the experts who have worked with our group include: Peter Block, David Berliner, Gene Glass, Andy Hargreaves, David Hyerle, George Lakoff, Linda Lambert, Barbara McAfee, David Perkins, Stevie Ray, Jon Saphier, Edgar Schein, Richard Sheridan, Stan Slap, Tony Wagner, David Whyte, Pat Wolfe, and Yong Zhao.

Knowledge is like a garden. . . . If it is not cultivated, it cannot be harvested. —African proverb

Mary Oberg was dedicated to excellence and brought Bill and Diane back again and again to make sure every teacher got a chance to participate in Cognitive Coaching training. She pursued excellence and communicated that vision to others. Her dedication to inner-city youth was never ending. Sadly, as this book went to print she passed away, and we lost one of our greatest fans. We will miss her inquiring mind and dedication to excellence for all kids and colleagues.

And . . .

Ellie Drago-Severson receives as special acknowledgment for her seminal work in adult development in schools. She is a person of integrity, and her honest feedback on this book was extremely helpful.

Arnis Burvikovs and **Dan Alpert** of Corwin encouraged us to write this book and guided us along the way with their keen insight.

Colton Fitzgerald, from Urban Luck Design, developed our graphic, adjusting to our constant iterations and thought development. Youth like him are our future.

Thanks From Bill

Marney Wamsley was my third principal. My first two, a Marine Corp colonel and a college wrestler, both taught me power, courage, and political savvy. Marney modeled and taught me humanity, thoughtfulness, and the power of community. I am forever grateful.

> *If your walking isn't your preaching, there is no point walking anywhere to preach.* —St. Francis of Assisi

Diane Zimmerman taught me, coached me, and, when necessary, confronted me. Thank you for making me a better teacher, student, leader, and person. Our learning conversations over the years continue to provide new perspectives. We always create new ways of teaching and learning while we merge theory and practice.

> *The things that matter most should never be at the mercy of the things that matter least.* —Goethe

I got to learn from **Jane Stevenson** in three schools. In addition to being a caring, committed teacher and principal, her reflective thought process always produces better decisions for students. I believe we are the best administrative team in the country. I am grateful for her honest feedback over the years.

> *You don't learn from the event. You learn from reflecting on the event.* —Judy Arin-Krupp

As a business agent for the union, **Skip Olsen** became a learning colleague I could have never imagined. We taught school leadership together, worked for ten years on a state professional development project, and continue to collaborate on books, websites, and our "learning omnivore" seminars. He is my bricoleur buddy.

Put yourself in the place of most potential. —DeWitt Jones

There are so many others who have contributed to my learning. Although not an exhaustive list, they include (but are not limited to) Don Anderson, Angeles Arrien, Michael Ayers, Suzanne Bailey, Betty Burks, Shirley Hord, Yvette Jackson, Barbara Lawson, Jim Lewis, Keith Olsen, Dennis Peterson, Ron Petrich, Stevie Ray, Frank Wagner, Pat Wolfe, and Jennifer York-Barr. Thank you for your gifts that helped me become better.

Thanks From Diane

I wish to acknowledge my husband, Rich Zimmerman, who puts up with my long hours dedicated to writing.

I'd also like to thank the following intellectual friends by their communities—without you, I would not be the person I am today. Your dedication to educational excellence continues to inspire and renew my hope. In this book, you will find your stories interwoven with mine.

Coauthors—Bob Garmston, Art Costa, Linda Lambert, Mary Gardner, Bill Sommers, and Jim Roussin.

Cognitive Coaching—Laura Lipton, Bruce Wellman, Peg Leidens, Bill Baker, Barb Lawson, Kay Coleman, Judy Gottschalk, Marlene Honerman, Mary Oberg, and Lynn Sawyer.

Fairfield-Suisun Unified—Agnes Johnson, Kathy Deignan, Ursula Kudszus, and Rosa Washington.

Davis Joint Unified School District—Everyone! For helping me "come of age" as a leader and especially those who mentored me from the top down as administrators (Floyd Fenocchio, Darrel Taylor, and Leo Masson), from the bottom up as teachers (Ellie Bonner, Mark Cary, Terry Clark, and Elinor Olsen), and from the side (Norm Enfield, Judy Davis, Bev Maul, Barbara Wells, and Connie Coughran).

Old Adobe Union School District—Once again, everyone! But in particular Patsy Knight, Carol Henderson, Tracy McClure, Kim Harper, Adrienne Lofton, Mary Lavezzoli, and Saundra Parret.

Visual Thinking Strategies—Philip Yenawine and Oren Slozberg.

Children's Museum of Sonoma County—Collette Michaud.

PUBLISHER'S ACKNOWLEDGMENTS

Corwin gratefully acknowledges the contributions of the following reviewers:

Lyne Ssebikindu, Principal
Crump Elementary School
Cordova, TN

Jessica Brown, Math Interventionist
Achilles Elementary School
Hayes, VA

Brigitte Tennis, Junior High Headmistress
Stella Schola Middle School
Redmond, WA

Joyce Sager, Middle School Special Education Teacher
Litchfield Middle School
Gadsden, AL

ABOUT THE AUTHORS

William A. Sommers, PhD, of Austin, Texas, continues to be a learner, teacher, principal, author, leadership coach, and consultant. Bill has come out of retirement multiple times to put theory into practice as a principal.

Bill has been a consultant for Cognitive Coaching, Adaptive Schools, brain research, poverty, habits of mind, conflict management, and classroom management strategies. He was also on the board of trustees of the National Staff Development Council (now called Learning Forward) for five years and also served as president of that group.

Bill is the former executive director for Secondary Curriculum and Professional Learning for Minneapolis Public Schools and has been a school administrator for more than thirty-five years. He has been a senior fellow for the Urban Leadership Academy at the University of Minnesota and has served as an adjunct faculty member at Texas State University, Hamline University, University of St. Thomas, St. Mary's University, Union Institute, and Capella University. In addition, he has been a program director for an adolescent chemical dependency treatment center and on the board of a halfway house for twenty years.

Bill has coauthored more than ten books, including *Living on a Tightrope: A Survival Handbook for Principals*; *Being a Successful Principal: How to Ride the Wave of Change Without Drowning*; *Reflective Practice to Improve Schools* (now in the third edition as *Reflective Practice for Renewing Schools*); *A Trainer's Companion*; *Energizing Staff Development Using Video Clips*; *Leading Professional Learning Communities*; *Guiding Professional Learning Communities*; *Principal's Field Manual*; and an e-book, *Habits of Mind Teacher's Companion* (in the second edition). Bill has also coauthored chapters in several other books.

In January 2016, Bill and his colleague Skip Olsen launched the website www.learningomnivores.com, which includes educational posts, new rules, and book reviews.

Bill is a practitioner who integrates theory into leading and facilitating schools. He continues to coach school leaders, as he has done for over thirty years.

Courtesy of UC Davis Library

Diane P. Zimmerman, PhD, lives in Suisun Valley, California, on a sixty-acre ranch with her husband Rich and their two dogs. She retired as a superintendent of schools after a thirty-six-year career in education, where she perfected her skills in the art of the conversation, dialogue, coaching, conflict management, and leadership development. She has reinvented herself as a writer and consultant, focusing specifically on investing human capital.

Diane has worked as a teacher, speech therapist, program manager, and assistant director of special education. She served as a principal in Davis, California, for thirteen years before being promoted to assistant superintendent for human resources. In 2002, she began a nine-year appointment as a superintendent of Old Adobe Union School District. She prides herself in having moved the district's teachers from contentious union interactions to productive, interest-based relations. Together with her teachers, she forged a knowledge partnership to build a robust and successful writing program. Together, they set the highest standards possible for their school district and demonstrated that when a community works together they create knowledge legacies.

She has coauthored four books on leadership. Two argue for building professional capital—*Cognitive Capital: Investing in Teacher Quality* and *Liberating Leadership Capacity: Pathways to Wisdom. From Lemons to Lemonade: Resolving Problems in Meetings, Workshops, and PLCs* expands the leadership paradigm to include all participants. Her real passion is writing about how to build communities of collective efficacy. Her articles regularly appear in the *Journal of Staff Development.* In 1998, she obtained her PhD in human and organizational development from the Fielding Graduate Institute. She has taught college courses at Sacramento State and Sonoma State Universities.

Diane is involved in her local community organizations, helped to build the Children's Museum of Sonoma County, and serves on the Petaluma Education Foundation. Most recently, she joined the board of Watershed, a nonprofit organization dedicated to bringing Visual Thinking Strategies to all classrooms. She also serves on the University of California, Davis, Library Leadership Board, working to reenvision libraries. She smiles and says, "Who would have guessed that our first job would be building the best wine library in the world, and in the course of this, we would get to taste amazing wines?"

A Dedication

Join us, Bill and Diane, to consider the possibilities of professional conversations in real time in schools with a story from Diane Zimmerman's years as a principal. We dedicate this story to teachers and staffs everywhere who are brave enough to confront truths. We invite others to commit to do the same. Here is Diane's story, which is fractal of this book in that the narrative contains so much more than first meets the eye. Indeed, you may want to reread this section after you have read the book.

In this suburban school district, teachers have been complaining about chronic bullying; the counselor suggested that the staff explore what teachers observe in the moment of bullying. More specifically, she wanted them to identify what they could control—what behavioral triggers they noted and how they responded. The topic of bullying had cycled on and off staff meeting agendas, with no real action taken, so Diane decided to set aside an hour for the staff to explore this bullying problem in more depth and organized the time around the counselor's unanswered query.

As the teachers talked, not surprisingly they exhibited a large repertoire of responses. Some teachers had finely tuned observation systems and intervened at the first instance of "mean" behavior. Others stayed out of student interactions until they could ignore them no longer. As the teachers talked, it became evident that the teachers who intervened early and had a repertoire of interventions were the most effective at reducing bullying behaviors.

One teacher, clearly an outlier, had the most layered set of responses, all designed to encourage the students to self-monitor. First, she constantly monitored voice tone, and if she heard sarcasm or put-downs, she'd stop what she was doing and look toward the offending students. If this was not enough, she prompted the students with a simple inquiry, "What is going on here?" This signaled that the teacher was watching and often stopped the behavior. If that didn't work, the next step was to move closer and remind the students, "Remember, treat others as you wish to be treated. Please focus on (the task)." Or finally, the teacher would call attention to the students at the center of the altercation with a more specific inquiry: "Briana and Jackson, do I need to talk with you?" What was unstated but clear to the students was an embedded command: Stop the behavior, or we'll be in conversation about it.

Diane reflects, "I was amazed that some teachers could dip into consciousness to find such nuanced responses, which may have been unconscious until they became spoken. What was most amazing to observe was how teachers who had limited repertoire engaged in inquiry to learn more about successful moves." Collectively, teachers decided that they could do much more to stop bullying in the school. They decided to follow up at the next staff meeting with a reflection-on-action conversation to check in to hear how teachers were changing practices. And the principal now had some new ways to expand conversations with teachers who made excessive referrals to the office.

The big aha moment for many was that by looking for antecedent behaviors and intervening early, they could change the culture of the entire school. Furthermore, it became clear that when conversations raise consciousness about a gap in knowledge, the professionals continue to puzzle and observe behaviors and make changes long after the initial conversation.

This is just one small example that demonstrates if we just listen, we can learn so much more from our teachers. We owe it to our profession to open the doors to create a culture of open access in which we build knowledge, coherence, and legacies, which are then passed on to a new generation of teachers.

*Those that understand how conversation works—no matter their ages—
need to step up and pass on what they know. . . . This is the wrong time
to step back.*

—Sherry Turkel, *Reclaiming Conversations*, 2015

*We recommend that educators . . . keep evolving the complexity of
collaborative professionalism beyond conversation or meetings to deeper
forms of dialogue, feedback, and inquiry.*

—Andy Hargreaves, *Collaborative Professionalism*, 2018

INTRODUCTION

The belief in the collective capacity of teachers to foster student growth and learning is vital for the health of our schools. School cultures are dynamic and complex and deserve careful attention and dedication to positive system-level interventions. Incremental change models that seek "one right program" or that privilege the textbook and force fidelity insult the intellectual capacity of the professionals. Instead of mandates, changing the way professionals converse is essential.

Teachers need to be given quality time to interact with each other about the practice of teaching and to determine how they support student learning. Furthermore, they need support in developing the skills for meaningful, professional conversations. Moving from incidental sharing to deep, meaningful conversations is critical. Indeed, collective efficacy, the single most important factor in school achievement, cannot occur without this valuable intervention—the introduction of Nine Professional Conversations to a school faculty. Each conversation in this book is designed to improve the efficacy beliefs of teachers and the faculty as a whole. These conversations are a necessary starting place. With tenacity and persistence, those that embark on this journey can bring positive change to a school system.

Nothing is more important than listening to the professionals with whom you work. However, as we listened as school administrators, we were discouraged by what we were told. Over our careers, we both heard far too many disenfranchised comments from teachers:

- *I tried to share things with others when I started teaching, but nobody listened, so I stopped talking in staff meetings.* —Retiring teacher
- *This charter school is consumed by all the extracurricular activities we offer. We never have time to talk about what I love, the teaching of writing. I feel so alone.* —Early-career teacher
- *Yes, you can share this information at a staff meeting, but do not give me credit. My colleagues will tease me mercilessly about being a "know-it-all."* —Late-career high school teacher
- *My district invested in training teacher leaders in a new approach to mathematics. It was so gratifying to work with others and learn from experts. But when I went back to my school, the principal always made*

excuses, putting discussion of this to another day. The school year ended, and it was forgotten. —Late-career elementary teacher

These comments know no boundaries. They came from all levels, preK–12. They came from schools identified as the "best in town" and schools that have struggled to raise standards despite the byproducts of poverty. They came from schools with charismatic and well-liked leaders, as well as from those with less-respected administrators. These comments demonstrate teaching can be a very isolating profession. In fact, the term, *the silo effect* is now commonly used to describe this isolation. The point is this: Professional conversations cannot be left to happenstance; they require careful thought about how to build communities of shared practice. This book tells "how to" break down the barriers to professional conversations.

> Professional conversations cannot be left to happenstance; they require careful thought about how to build communities of shared practice. This book tells "how to" break down the barriers to professional conversations.

Just what are *professional conversations*? Let us begin with a counterexample from a popular charter school—a delightful elementary school, rich in extracurricular activities organized around the garden. The problem is not this enrichment; indeed, one might argue that every school should have a garden. The problem is that this one enrichment focus consumes all available conversational time. Coordination, maintenance, learning strands, and schedules consume staff meetings, grade-level meetings, and more than their fair share of professional development days. Yes, the staff does arrive at some discussions of curriculum integration, and for those with a passion for the garden, the conversations can shift to a deep professional level. The problem is that the staff vested in the garden is small in number, yet the passions of this small group dominate all professional conversations. This unilateral dominance is not healthy, nor does it promote the kind of professional conversations that we promote in this book.

Professional conversations require group commitment to work together to improve all practices, not just a narrow band of interests. Over time, these conversations need to touch on all problems of practice, from classroom management to how metacognitive conversations in mathematics or literacy can also inform other content areas. Everyone needs to be involved and to know how he or she contributes to the collective belief that "this school makes a difference for all students."

The good news is that we do not need to break down these barriers in the traditional way through mandates or edicts. What is needed is the invitation to talk about what matters most. It turns out that a simple invitation will open most doors. From time to time throughout this book, we will invite the reader to pause and reflect. We invite you to also think about what matters most.

Reflection

iStock.com/BlackJack3D

A Place to Pause

- Think about your professional life. What do you reflect on daily?
- What parts of your work bring you passion?
- What do you puzzle about?
- What do you wish for?

The questions are endless. The key is that these conversations are public and become part the regular professional conversations within a school. When teachers have open access to each other's thinking, they find more in common than what draws them apart. They find that colleagues they thought they did not like have amazing stories to tell, and as a whole, they gain new appreciation for the deep well of knowledge secretly held by each teacher.

As authors, when we first started having these kinds of conversations almost forty years ago, we started with simple invitations. We used program quality reviews and accreditations to frame smaller conversations that mattered about some element of curriculum, whether it was more interdepartmental integration or better grade-level congruence. The responses we got were a great antidote to the previous discouraging quotes. This book is full of scenarios that describe more of these successes. We pulled a few comments here to make a point and to invite you to hope:

- *That was the best staff development day we have ever had. It is the first time the entire school has ever talked about how we can work together to build a more robust curriculum.* —Former principal who returned to teaching
- *The questions we explored as a staff have changed how I think about teaching. I ask more questions now and wait longer to develop more nuanced, reflective options.* —Mid-career teacher
- *This coaching session was amazing. I talk about baseball in this deep way, but I have never had a conversation with my principal like this.* —Mid-career teacher
- *I pride myself in working with difficult people, but today, something happened that I still do not understand. When those two teachers started*

arguing so loudly, I thought the collaboration would end. Instead, you invited the entire group to listen more deeply, captured the disagreement, and then miraculously, the two teachers in conflict looked at each other and started laughing. The day went without a hitch. —Outside consultant

While much of this book could also apply to all conversations, the focus is on professional conversations—those that happen as part of our daily work life, whether they are in one-to-one interactions or in larger groups such as meetings or workshops. We draw from our rich repertoire of experience with coaching and facilitating to describe frameworks that can be used as conversational anchor points. Time in schools is a limited resource and not to be wasted. So by making the conversational patterns explicit, as this book does, and working together to accelerate learning, educators will not only learn new ways of conversing, but how to make collaboration and professional learning more efficient, satisfying, and beneficial to student learning.

Each conversation has a specific structure that promotes effective communication on the Professional Conversation Arc—the Dashboard of Options— from least directive to most directive. The aim of these Nine Professional Conversations is to assist groups in setting conditions for creating their own best future. In the bid for improvement, however, those in power easily fall prey to directive approaches, not realizing that compliance is only surface deep. Yet the evidence is clear: When people think for themselves, they learn. The conversations outlined here provide ways to support thinking as part of the conversational processes that facilitate complex problem solving and deep learning.

The linguistics of conversation has a fractal pattern in that the message repeats, iterates outward, and returns in varying patterns. This type of pattern is self-reinforcing and creates new paths of understanding that sustain and expand interest. Likewise, professional conversations should also sustain and expand interests. The magic of a fractal is that it allows for great diversity within clear boundaries. Furthermore, the conversational patterns when repeated are adopted and applied by all members. Bill, for example, tells a story about how a university supervisor noticed that the lead teacher had better results in his work with student teachers. When the supervisor commented on this, the lead teacher told how Bill's coaching had informed his practice as a lead teacher. He remarked, "Bill asks me questions about my plans and then reflects with me about the lesson. I started to ask my student teachers the same kinds of questions, and it has made a huge difference." By modeling constructive, self-replicating patterns of communication, leaders or group members become role models for authentic communication and as a result become catalytic by evoking collective efficacy and promoting collaborative learning. Indeed, fractal patterns self-replicate in amazing ways.

We also hold another fundamental belief that pervades all of our work and has led to the organization for this book: When others are given space to think and act, they accomplish goals that exceed expectations and contribute to larger goals—both personal and collective. Over and over in conversation with others, we have been continuously surprised by the deep reservoirs of nuanced understanding and compassion that emerge when humans feel safe to think out loud. This found wisdom—that humans are their own best authors of both individual and collective destinies—can seem counterintuitive, and yet it is foundational to the concept of collective efficacy.

> This found wisdom—that humans are their own best authors of both individual and collective destinies—can seem counterintuitive, and yet it is foundational to the concept of collective efficacy.

Slowing down and taking time to engage in these Nine Conversations can appear cumbersome and time intensive. Resistance is a natural response to mandates given without first checking to learn what is known or in slowing down to build understanding and to answer the question "why." Despite all the evidence to the contrary, change leaders continuously rush to solutions for efficiency's sake. They assume compliance and do not take time to converse about the process of implementation. Indeed, when resistance is a byproduct of a change, it signals that the time has come to slow down and engage in collective reflection. The strategies in this book are best studied with the attitude of "going slow to go fast," to paraphrase a Chinese proverb. In the beginning, the conversations will take more time, but in the end, they can save time by cutting deep into what is essential.

Instead of one enlightened leader dragging others along and treating all as if they are ignorant, this process invites group members to take control of their own learning and to reflect on just what it is they need to know. This approach teaches all learners to become catalytic and to be responsible for the future they desire. As in chemistry, a catalyst facilitates a reaction without being used up in the process. For our purposes in describing human interactions, we consider catalytic actions as renewing in that they preserve and increase energy. When groups talk about what they know and do not know, everyone learns about the capacity of the group. Those that know less learn who to go to for help; those that know the most begin to take leadership roles and foster that pride in learning from peers.

A DASHBOARD OF OPTIONS

To facilitate this open-ended approach, the Nine Professional Conversations are organized on a Dashboard graphic—the Professional Conversation Arc—from reflective to prescriptive conversations. We often use graphics as a way to facilitate understanding of key concepts; what follows is a graphic that describes the organization of this book. On the left of the arc are least-directive conversations, which assume resourcefulness and are designed to open up thinking and develop communal reflective practice. On the right side of the arc, the conversations assume limitations, such as intractable conflict or a continuous disregard for the collective needs, and hence the conversations become increasingly more directive. As such, these Nine Professional Conversations are a leadership model that promotes open-ended reflection as a norm for making change. Our dream is that most conversations in schools would begin to move into this authentic realm of personal and group self-reflection. This, however, is not always possible, for when groups are dysfunctional, they require more-focused interventions. Furthermore, not all players belong in the game, and ultimately, an appointed leader has to make the tough decision about when to let go and move someone on.

Nine Professional Conversations to Change Our Schools

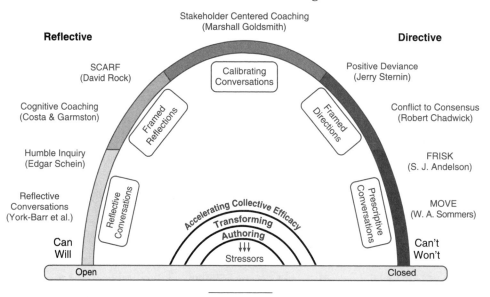

Urban Luck Design, urbanluckdesign.com

The genius of the Nine Professional Conversations is the assumption of a growth mindset by accepting that others have rich internal resources to draw from. All of the conversations on this arc focus on increasing the capacity for reflection and the opportunity to increase their effectiveness. To begin, we take a stance that all conversations should focus on the possibilities; however, over time it may become evident that a more closed and directed conversation is essential. On the Dashboard just under the colored arc are five boxes that describe this continuum from open to closed. The first two conversations on the green arc are open-ended and promote Reflective Conversations. Moving up, the blue arc represents structures that guide reflection more specifically and hence are called Framed Reflections. At the top of the arc, Calibrating Conversations in purple transition from data represented by personal viewpoints to data coming from stakeholders. The next two conversations on the downward orange arc are Framed Directions, in that the conversations assist groups in confronting behaviors that lead to less-productive results. Next, the red arc refers to Prescriptive Conversations, which direct the conversation to specifically what is not working.

As catalytic leaders, we have found that by believing that all "can and will" change, we always begin with listening and reflecting with the group. Note that it says *Can and Will* on the bottom-left side of the arc. On the opposite side, it says *Can't and Won't*. As we learn more about the group and celebrate successes, we also become aware of dysfunctional responses. Over time, we begin to discover that a few "can't or won't" thinking required changes necessary to support the collaborative learning.

These conversations are open to all and not limited to just a few in authority; even the most directive can be used and should be used to give a congruent message about how group behaviors impact thinking. For example, one brave teacher told her colleagues, "Two-thirds of the staff showed up late today for the staff meeting. I showed up five minutes early. It makes me angry when I waste time waiting for others. I need to know that as a group we are going to figure out some norms about arriving on time. What can we do?" Notice that this teacher was not only assertive, but she turned the solution back to the group. Now here is the rub: Down the line, if one group member continues to violate an established group norm the appointed leader must step in with a directive about the expectation and what corrective action will happen without compliance. This is the true test of Bill's "can't or won't" rule; when directives are clear and are not followed, something is keeping this person from reaching her or his true professional capacity. Finally, when nothing works, it is time to have a serious conversation and the development of an exit plan. And while this book is not about how to supervise an employee, we do draw from our years of supervising employees and use our stories to highlight key concepts important for supervision.

The Nine Professional Conversations listed on the outside of the Professional Conversation Arc graphic promote collective efficacy in that they ask the participants to author and transform to create a best collective future. Ultimately, it is the leaders of our systems that must step up to the plate and create cultures that set the context for these conversations to succeed. Small groups can easily adopt these conversational patterns and can influence others. Excellence promotes excellence. To transform a culture, however, the leaders must be able to initiate, participate, and model the productive behaviors. In sum, they must demonstrate "can and will."

Some will wonder why we chose these conversations and not others. With few exceptions, we have worked personally with the professionals we draw from. We worked for years with Art Costa and Bob Garmston, the founders of Cognitive Coaching. Through his work with Learning Forward, Bill also knew Ellie Drago-Severson, an expert in adult development. While looking to expand his own repertoire, Bill met Marshall Goldsmith and Frank Wagner, the developers of Stakeholder Centered Coaching.

Over ten years ago, we decided that our best learning would come from working directly with the professionals we most admired. Two of the experts we reached out to were Bob Chadwick and Edgar Schein, who are featured in this book. We invited them to work with a committed group of like-minded educators. What we have learned from almost twenty of these specialty workshops is the topic of another book. We would say, however, that there is no substitute for the gift of working directly with committed professionals who are respected as experts in the field and other learning omnivores.

These Nine Professional Conversations are not exhaustive, but they are the ones we have used most often in our work as catalytic leaders. We note that there are many other conversational patterns worthy of study. The substance of this book is focused specifically each of these Nine Professional Conversations.

Throughout this book, we use capital letters to designate the name of conversations associated to particular experts. When we refer to the skills more generally, we use lowercase letters. Likewise, for citation purposes we use full professional names, but in our writing, we refer to those experts, whom we know personally, by their first name or even their nickname. For the purposes of our work in schools, we have sometimes changed the words of the original authors. With respect, our aim is always to stay true to the intent of original authors—or to point it out to the reader if we take different stance.

In each of the next nine chapters, we offer a minimum of two learning scenarios, with the idea that stories provide important narratives that help us remember. Scenario 1 is always a story that demonstrates a dyad or small group at work; Scenario 2 will always be about how to work with a larger group. On occasion, we'll offer an additional third scenario that describes an additional process that we have used, based on this particular conversational pattern. Additional examples are also peppered throughout the book. Each one of these stories is true to the best of our memory. With that said, we have sometimes changed details and have not used names to protect confidentiality or to make a point.

THE STRUCTURE OF THE BOOK

This book is organized into five parts to aid the reader in orientation and to make it accessible as a reference for the dedicated practitioner.

Part I describes the "why" of this book and makes the assertion that conversational competence is foundational. Despite all our educators' best intentions—not to mention time, money, and energy—our schools continue to be mired in the status quo of the past. This limits inquiry and the willingness to explore, grow, and learn. Quite simply, in these schools—because teacher talk focuses on one right answer, specific results, and individuality—conversations become limited, nonproductive, and promote teacher isolation. When teachers teach in isolation, they do not develop the professional "know-how" described here as "knowledge coherence." By *knowledge coherence*, we mean the integration of complex and divergent ideas to create a coherent whole. Furthermore, these dysfunctional cultures create great stress and limit professional growth. The result is a profession without a voice.

In the center of the Dashboard graphic, the reader will see the goal of this book: Accelerating Collective Efficacy. Under this title are some smaller arcs that show that stress pulls groups away from success. We draw from the adult development literature to assert that the antidote to this is to reduce stress by creating environments that bring forth the professional voice. The purpose of these conversations is to build collective efficacy, which we believe is done when groups learn to self-author their own future and to transform their thinking in the face of discrepant information.

Part II is the centerpiece for this book. The four reflective conversations have served us well in all of our professional conversations. These two Reflective Conversations and the two Framed Reflections build knowledge coherence from the inside out and are the genesis of collective efficacy. In this spirit, we offer these conversations as a way to operationalize the growth mindset. All too often in schools, the rhetoric of "growth mindset" simply stays on the surface, with no inquiry into how to operationalize this belief.

Deep reflection requires that the participants seek feedback about the efficacy of their actions. Suffice for now to understand that once a directive has been given, humans need to process it in order to understand it and to be able to communicate intentions—I will or I won't, or I can or I can't.

> Deep reflection requires that the participants seek feedback about the efficacy of their actions.

Part III marks the transition in these conversational strategies from the "inside–out" to the "outside–in." At this point, the conversations begin to draw from external data and feedback, bringing in outside viewpoints and knowledge. Bill, in particular, has found that Stakeholder Coaching is an invaluable process in closing the "knowing–doing–learning" gap explained in Chapter 2. What this means is that external stakeholder data sets open the conversation to growing edges, providing feedback that helps one reflect and become the catalyst of his or her own learning and transformation.

Part IV begins the move into the red zone of Framed Directives and Prescriptive Conversations that are conversations designed to build knowledge from the outside–in. These kinds of conversations challenge internal perceptions and hallucinations about what is reality. For example, in Chapter 9 we describe how positive deviance breaks down limiting beliefs about "can't and won't." In Chapter 10, we tell how Chadwick broke down hallucinations that conflict is a normal state—a worst-possible outcome—and facilitated a plan for a more peaceful future—a best-possible outcome.

Prescriptive Conversations are necessary when individuals are not contributing to the greater good. It would be irresponsible for us to forgo the directive conversation entirely. An essential leadership skill is to be able to work with all and, when needed, be able to direct behaviors toward more responsible, contributory ways of working. Counterproductive behavior in any level of the organization is damaging, and failure to intervene undermines collaboration. While FRISK was created by the legal profession, it turns out the multistep process offers a template for a complete message—one that states facts, impacts, and needs. It can be used any time an open, honest statement would help set expectations for the future.

Furthermore, appointed leaders, legally, need to know when and how to create an exit strategy. And in some instances of real dysfunction, it may be the best strategy to go straight to the end of the Dashboard and engage in directive conversations around prescriptive work plans and exit strategies. These conversations are designed to set clear directions and to test Bill's rule of "can't and won't." In our experience, these conversations often get just the right attention and can change behaviors for the better. When this happens, the reflective conversations in Part II become the norm.

Part V, the conclusion, wraps up our thoughts about how to build collective efficacy and leave knowledge legacies; and we wish to leave the readers with HOPE, recommitment, and energy to make a difference.

HOW TO READ THIS BOOK

This book need not be read from start to finish, and we suggest that the busy professional might want to choose a conversation to learn about and dive in there. Over time, we are confident that you will turn back to the book as an invaluable resource and seek out additional strategies and ways of working effectively as a *catalyst*—someone who adds value to the conversational processes so important in all human interactions. We offer this book as a knowledge legacy for those who have inspired us to write about real lives in schools.

Most books are read alone, and this book is likely no exception. Our hope, however, is that you will choose to read this book in collaboration with others.

With that said, if you are a solo reader do not stop here, for this book is at its core a "how-to manual," and the first step may indeed be reading and acting alone. Accordingly, an enlightened leader or participant can gain much in the practical understanding about how different forms of conversations change both personal and group dynamics. Later, we describe how enlightened group members can become the catalysts by modeling a new way of interacting.

By following through over time, others will learn from effective modeling of these strategies. Humans are neurologically wired to imprint repeated linguistic patterns. The authors, while coaching teachers, observed this firsthand when conducting pre- and postconferences. In our experience, after only two or three cycles, teachers responded to the linguistic patterns by anticipating a question before it was asked or exclaiming proudly, "I knew you were going to ask that question." Now, years later, it is clear to us that when these linguistic patterns are made explicit, learning accelerates; hence, we recommend that the various conversations on the Dashboard are best practiced through collaborative interactions. After all, conversations are communal ventures. Even when we talk to ourselves, we are reflecting upon our relationships with the world, and reflective practitioners change the world. As Gandhi advises us, "Be the change you wish to see in the world."

Part I

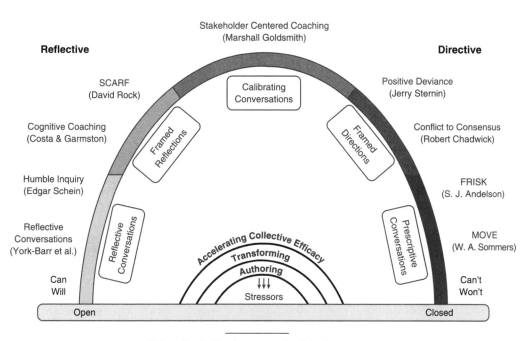

Stakeholder Centered Coaching
(Marshall Goldsmith)

Reflective

Directive

SCARF
(David Rock)

Calibrating
Conversations

Positive Deviance
(Jerry Sternin)

Cognitive Coaching
(Costa & Garmston)

Framed
Reflections

Framed
Directions

Conflict to Consensus
(Robert Chadwick)

Humble Inquiry
(Edgar Schein)

FRISK
(S. J. Andelson)

Reflective
Conversations
(York-Barr et al.)

Reflective
Conversations

Accelerating Collective Efficacy

Transforming

Authoring

↓↓↓

Stressors

Prescriptive
Conversations

MOVE
(W. A. Sommers)

Can
Will

Can't
Won't

Open

Closed

Urban Luck Design, urbanluckdesign.com

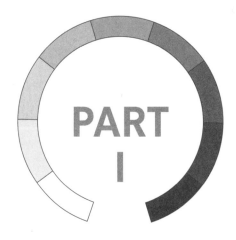

PART I

THE FOUNDATION—CONVERSATIONAL COMPETENCE

Take a few minutes and study the Professional Conversation Arc, which depicts the Nine Professional Conversations to Change Our Schools. What can you learn about this book from the diagram? Which conversations or practitioners do you already know? Which ones are new to you? For those conversations of which you are familiar, how do they relate to each other and their placement on the arc? What are you most curious to learn about?

Part I sets a context for why conversations are valuable and essential for building collective efficacy; conversations are the glue that builds cultures. While this section could be skipped in favor of going directly to the Nine Conversations, we believe it offers some important insights about why this book is so important.

Before delving more into the specifics of the graphic, we realize that we need to explain why these kinds of conversations are essential for the profession. To us, it seems obvious; to others, however, it is not so obvious. The lack of understanding about the need for professional conversations by educators, leaders, and teachers alike has been puzzling to us.

This dilemma is best told through a story. A principal new to a school offered his teachers release time to work on curricular issues. Their response was, "We do not know what we would do with the time." He was shocked. When he was a teacher, his school had used school improvement funds to buy three days of collaboration for every grade level. That time was like gold to the teachers. The agendas were teacher directed, and some even stretched the three days into six half days. They had used it to bring their curriculum into alignment, to plan together, and to learn from each other. He knew he was a much better teacher as a result of this collaboration. This principal realized he had his work cut out for him. His teachers obviously had not done much collaborative work (indeed, the school was known for its rugged individualists).

In these next three chapters, we describe why educators everywhere would be well served to add a new knowledge domain to their practices: the skill and art of the conversation for expanding professional practices. As teachers, many intuitively understand how important language is for learning but do not actively pursue ways of improving these skills in their own professional practices. Instead, they fall back on what they know, what has served them in the past, and what is needed for the situation at hand.

In Chapter 1, we argue that conversations create bridges to understanding that open up access to knowledge coherence. By *knowledge coherence*, we mean that teachers seek agreement about what is essential for teaching and learning. When they don't agree, they agree to work toward coherence and clarity about the nexus of their philosophical disagreements. Coherence does not infer agreement, but rather an understanding of the whole—the agreements, the points of divergence, and the impact of disagreements on learning.

It is only when professionals know what they stand for, can articulate how they make a difference for students, and are willing to question each other to find central truths that they can create a professional narrative of excellence.

> It is only when professionals know what they stand for, can articulate how they make a difference for students, and are willing to question each other to find central truths that they can create a professional narrative of excellence.

When teachers join together and learn to articulate about shared practices, they communicate what is important to their students and to the community. They stand tall, firm in the respect given them as professionals. When this happens, they have created a knowledge legacy, which passes this professional knowledge onto newcomers.

In Chapter 2, we explore the problems created by the knowing–doing gap often reinforced by the lack of meaningful collaboration. Quite frankly, the current preservice programs are not sufficient for a 21st century profession. For this reason, schools must step in and assure that teachers become lifelong learners. The only way that this happens is through collaborative conversations.

In Chapter 3, we focus on the problems that arise in cultures that do not work well together and describe four stress reactions that block open, honest communication. We draw from adult learning theory to demonstrate how these dysfunctional communications can impede the goals of collective efficacy—the ability to author a future and to transform our thinking in the light of new data.

Together, these three chapters address this thesis: Professional conversations are essential for professional learning by describing what, why, and how these conversations fit into the context of professional learning communities. To better understand the intention of this book, take a minute before you begin Chapter 1 to review the graphic on the opposite page one more time to get a sense of the long-term outcomes of this book.

Chapter 1

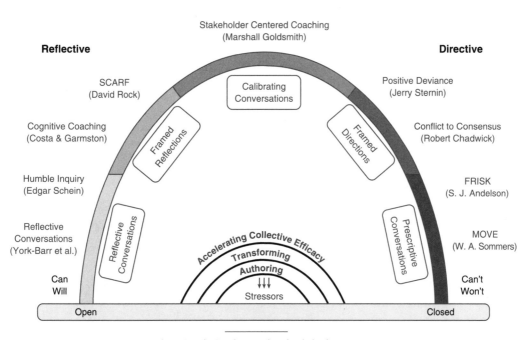

Urban Luck Design, urbanluckdesign.com

A CRISIS IN OUR MIDST—NO COHERENT KNOWLEDGE BASE

Organizations are made of conversations.

—Ernesto Gore

In our profession, a simmering crisis has been building, yet most educators do not even know what the crisis is and how dire the situation has become. The crisis is that, as a profession, education has no coherent knowledge base about standards for excellence. Paraphrasing from Hargreaves and O'Connor (2018), professional collaboration is about creating this deeper understanding, which advances our knowledge, skills, and commitment to increase learning.

Over the course of a career, teachers develop deep knowledge about how to support the learning process and student growth and development. Yet these insights are rarely shared within the larger community of professionals. Instead, educational methods cycle from one new program to the next, with little attention to how professional knowledge is developed and shaped to create a communal understanding. The end result is that educators have no control over their professional narrative or the standards used to measure excellence. There are historical reasons why other professions have not experienced the political whipsaw so prevalent in education, and educators would be well served to pay attention to this history.

KNOWLEDGE COHERENCE GROWS KNOWLEDGE LEGACIES

Over the past 100 years, other professions have amassed what have become large *knowledge legacies*—essential bodies of knowledge that were developed through coherence over time, disseminated through printed tomes, and used to ground conversations. With the advent of the digital age, this knowledge has become accessible in ways once not thought possible. Most notably, lawyers have case law and sources such as Westlaw; doctors have the National Library of Medicine now digitized as Medline; and accountants have Financial and Government Accounting Standards. Science has basic research standards and a growing body of "consensus standards" in the subspecialties. These knowledge bases are additive and adaptive as they continue to grow and change with the profession. Over time, professions that take the time to find coherent patterns, which include debated topics, can speak with an authentic voice; by doing so, they maintain a level of professional integrity that educators can only dream about. As Hargreaves and O'Connor (2017, p. 1) state, "No profession can serve people effectively if its members do not share and exchange knowledge about their expertise or about their clients, patients, or students they have in common." There is no question that knowledge builds capacity over time as it is passed from generation to generation.

> "No profession can serve people effectively if its members do not share and exchange knowledge about their expertise or about their clients, patients, or students they have in common." —Hargreaves and O'Connor

In education, the status quo has hidden behind the idea that teaching is more art than science and hence, like art, difficult to quantify. Teachers often cheer when assured, "You are the professional; do your best work." What is not stated is that this "best work" is more often done in isolation, and it is a rare school that has figured out how to capitalize on this vast storehouse of applied knowledge. A wise administrator once ruefully commented that when a teacher retires all that knowledge goes with them to the grave. There is an African proverb that sums this up: "When an old person dies, a library burns." We would add—what an unnecessary waste.

In large part, this historical failure to develop a knowledge coherence is because education is a human endeavor—learning appears to be as unique as fingerprints—making it difficult to find patterns, definitive solutions, or even agreement on basic tenants. Hence, as a profession, teaching has been controlled, even whipsawed, by outside political forces. When national debates further divide the community, as they did in the 1990s with the "curriculum wars" (and are now happening with the Common Core State Standards, or CCSS), the decisions are tossed back to local schools, which often have no understanding of the initiating beliefs or even what is being debated. These debates have a way of polarizing groups and developing contempt before investigation. These words may seem strong, yet they speak to a troubling truth. Teachers, and the parents in support of these teachers, line up to advocate for what they already know, and in the heat of the moment, all conversation is lost. In the void, governing bodies rush to simple solutions, failing to examine the underlying beliefs and assumptions.

For example, in the 1990s one school board in a university town ended conflicts by adopting two different algebra books: If you lived on the east side of town, you received one curriculum; if you lived on the west side, another. While this town was committed to democratic practices, they could not find a way through the conflict that arose around two different textbooks.

These kinds of compromises are not uncommon when communities do not have the conversational tools to open up deep understandings; as a consequence, decisions get made from a limited perspective in order to stop the conflict. This conflict avoidance serves to deepen the unspoken divides and creates crises fueled by ignorance. And most damaging of all, this glossing over of the real truths exhausts those involved in the implementation and confuses parents and students. Instead of an opportunity for professional learning, those involved tend to become even more defensive. No wonder so many teachers are leaving or plan to leave the profession as soon as possible.

An example of a better way to make policy would be to ask the educators in conflict to reconvene, possibly with someone skilled in professional conversations, to identify the similarities and differences between these two different approaches. Any one of the Nine Professional Conversations in this book could be used to open up a dialogue about these differences. The key is that agreement is not what is sought, but rather a coherence, which means that ideally the professionals will work to find overlapping understandings and to clarify points of disagreement. Just as in successful interest-based collective bargaining, when professionals can "agree to disagree" they can then move to more productive conversations. Furthermore, these debates about textbooks and programs distract from the real issues confronting educators, which is the development of a coherent understanding of teaching and learning beyond these prescriptions to what really works in the classroom.

Another example comes from the drama that has played out in the current debates about the Common Core State Standards (CCSS) that were initiated by politicians to create an internationally competitive education system. One year, teachers work hard to implement the CCSS, only to find that their state has repealed these same standards in subsequent legislative sessions. This policy whipsaw leaves teachers without direction and further undermines any desire to work toward a common understanding—the genesis of knowledge coherence. As one teacher put it, "All the public debate about standards makes me want to go back in my classroom and shut the door on the world." Meanwhile, the politicians, distracted by a polarizing debate, have ignored some of the best practices from a growing body of knowledge about what makes other countries' educational systems successful. Policy makers would be well advised to pay attention to the rest of the world. (For more information, see *Surpassing Shanghai* [Tucker, 2012]; *Finnish Lessons 2.0* [Sahlberg, 2015]; *The Flat World and Education* [Darling-Hammond, 2010]; and *Cleverlands* [Crehan, 2017].)

TEACHERS VOICE THE NEED FOR KNOWLEDGE COHERENCE

Wise teachers articulate the desire for conversation and want to become more expert, yet their voices are drowned out in all the rhetoric about failing schools. Sarah Brown Wessling, 2010 Teacher of the Year, said, "When I look at the standards, I don't see a document that tells me what to teach or gives me a curriculum; rather, I see an underlying organization that gives us collective purpose." Another teacher from a charter school, Darren Burris (2013), remarked, "To me, the Common Core represents an empowering opportunity for teachers to collaborate, exchange best practices, and share differing curricula—because a common set of standards is not the same thing as a common curriculum." There is a huge distinction between consultants telling teachers about the standards and teachers spending quality time digging deeply into the assumptions, beliefs, and strategies as part and parcel of implementation. Leaders must find creative ways to engage teachers in meaningful conversations about the changes they wish to make. Conversations matter for the implementation of any curriculum.

Well-articulated conversations open up knowledge coherence and help peers understand their differences in order to foster the development of knowledge legacies. For example, in Washoe County, Nevada, Aaron Grossman, a teacher tasked with the CCSS implementation, found himself in crippling debates about

> Well-articulated conversations open up knowledge coherence and help peers understand their differences in order to foster the development of knowledge legacies.

the purpose of the standards. The standards were not his, and he had no desire to advocate for or against the standards; but he did want the teachers to be informed consumers. So he reached out through the Internet to the knowledge base and provided the teachers with unfiltered information that began to answer some of their questions. He encouraged teachers to follow suit. This process and the conversations that ensued led to the development of agreed-upon "Core Practices."

As is so often the case, administrative leadership changes ended this committee, but the group's learnings have been memorialized on the Internet (www .coretaskproject.com). A high point for Grossman was when the team decided to reach out to the coauthors of the literary standards, David and Meredith Liben. Soon, these teachers were collaborating with these authors to develop core tasks to support the new standards. With the Libens, they created a short video that describes the high points of the project (Grossman, 2017). Through video and Internet links, these educators have created a lasting legacy that documents their knowledge.

While this book is focused on changing one school at a time, long-term changes need national support and funding to create a professional knowledge base. (The current government-sponsored What Works Clearinghouse [WWC] has not proven the test of time and is wholly inadequate; furthermore, it has been plagued by the same program debates as the school board described earlier.) We are confident that if teachers were given the power—the voice—and the national technological support to develop a coherent knowledge base, the profession would then take control over "what works." We would come to understand what really works and fulfill the mandate of a democracy—to educate its citizens to the highest level possible. We would begin to appreciate the vast storehouse of knowledge that creates excellent teaching and would begin to change the way we develop teachers from novice to expert. The problem is not the desire to have these conversations, but the ability to actually carry them out, especially on topics that may become contentious or controversial. For now, unless you are a policy maker and can impact the larger arena, we ask you, the educator, to focus on your own school and your own conversations so as to become a beacon of hope for those around you.

PROFESSIONAL CONVERSATIONS MATTER

While the long-term crisis involves a lack of knowledge coherence and limited knowledge legacies in the educational profession, the looming short-term crisis is fueled by our inability to sustain professional conversations about what matters in schools. The purpose of this book is to change that situation and to offer practitioners nine different kinds of conversational frameworks that have the potential to change the way we work in schools.

If you move conversations to a professional arena and seek all voices in the room, disagreements are certain. We offer these conversational methods as catalysts for generating meaningful, professional conversations. The goal of this book is not the conversation, but rather bringing a coherent teacher voice into

Nine Professional Conversations to Change Our Schools

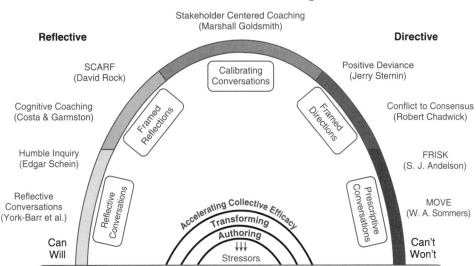

Urban Luck Design, urbanluckdesign.com

the development of a robust understanding of teaching and learning—building the profession they deserve.

By way of introduction to the Nine Professional Conversations, we organized the conversations from open to closed, as noted on the bar at the bottom of the graphic. By this, we mean that the agendas for conversations on the left ebb and flow around the interests of the group; closed agendas, those conversations on the right, require that the group focus on an identified need.

We further divided the conversations into five categories, which are listed in the boxes under the Professional Conversation Arc as follows: *Reflective Conversations*, *Framed Reflections*, *Calibration Conversations*, *Framed Directives*, and *Prescriptive Conversations*.

- The two *Reflective Conversations* open up the space for collective exploration and guide groups in finding out more about each other's professional practices.
- The *Framed Reflections* are more goal focused and assist in bringing focus to group work.
- For *Calibrating Conversations*, we chose only one conversation because it focuses more on the ways leaders can use feedback from their constituents to improve. This models what groups can do when they work together rather than simply relying on external data points such as testing.

■ As the arc swings down to the right, *Framed Directives* include approaches designed to move groups to productive workspace. These can be useful when groups need to find out more about each other's differences.

■ Finally, *Prescriptive Conversations* identify two ways to consider tough issues that need hard conversations. While prescriptive conversations may seem odd in a book mostly about open-ended, reflective conversations, the reader will be surprised to learn that the real art in tough conversations is bringing forth a reflective stance. Consider the difference between two employees: One says, "I did not know my behavior was offensive and I will change," versus another who says, "I don't agree with you, and I should be able to say what I want." One demonstrates that he or she "can and will" change, while the other says she or he "can't and won't" change.

Reflection

A Place to Pause

Consider the professional conversations that have been part of your work life:

■ What attention has been given to the quality of these conversations?
■ How have leaders modeled effective conversational practices?
■ Think of a professional conversation that made a difference.
■ What do you most remember about why this conversation was so important to you?

Conversations are an essential professional function, and skill building and practice are required for professionals to learn how to have conversations that matter. Conversational skill creates its own set of professional demands and knowledge needs. Because teachers spend most of their professional lives talking with students, they are at a disadvantage as a profession. Adult conversations in schools typically follow unexamined conventional norms, adequate for most day-to-day interactions, but inadequate for deep dialogues about teaching and learning. For the purposes of this book, we have chosen conversations that have proven the test of time and have brought us the best results. While we describe each conversation by its distinguishing characteristics, they can be interchanged and combined as the need arises. Indeed, we often pull strategies from different conversations and combine them. We might start with an open-ended, reflected conversation, only to discover that the group needs focus (so we might shift to a framed reflection) or that the group needs data (so a calibrating conversation is necessary).

Without skill and grace in the art (and now science) of the conversation as identified in this book, differences are ignored or pushed aside. These unresolved conflicts create invisible divides, limiting the capacity of any community to grow and learn together. This limited capacity shapes the quality of the conversation and defines a school culture as closed rather than open to new ideas. Art Costa often reminds us, "If the teachers are not in a mentally stimulating environment, why do you think they will create it for kids?"

> "If the teachers are not in a mentally stimulating environment, why do you think they will create it for kids?" —Art Costa

Chapter 2

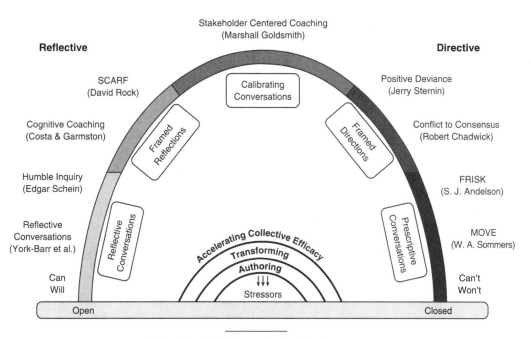

Reflective

Directive

Stakeholder Centered Coaching
(Marshall Goldsmith)

SCARF
(David Rock)

Calibrating
Conversations

Positive Deviance
(Jerry Sternin)

Cognitive Coaching
(Costa & Garmston)

Framed
Reflections

Framed
Directions

Conflict to Consensus
(Robert Chadwick)

Humble Inquiry
(Edgar Schein)

FRISK
(S. J. Andelson)

Reflective
Conversations
(York-Barr et al.)

Reflective
Conversations

Accelerating Collective Efficacy

Transforming

Authoring

↓↓↓

Stressors

Prescriptive
Conversations

MOVE
(W. A. Sommers)

Can
Will

Can't
Won't

Open

Closed

THE DISADVANTAGE OF BEING LEFT BEHIND—A KNOWING–DOING–LEARNING GAP

Wisdom is to know what you do not know.

—Socrates

Teachers begin their careers at a disadvantage. Most professions require at least three to four years of undergraduate or graduate training. Diane remembers her nursing friends who were immersed in the field as freshmen. Later when she majored in speech pathology, she had to take a year of undergraduate courses before beginning an extended-year graduate program. Most other professions require three to four years of graduate studies. In the United States, however, teaching certification requires few undergraduate education courses and only one year of graduate work to receive degrees. Teachers are also required to attend a short-term student teaching experience which is mainly focused on delivering content.

Quite simply, one year of coursework in which a practicum counts as half is not sufficient to build a knowledge base for a profession in the 21st century. Teacher development in the United States stands in stark contrast to Finland, where teachers major in education as undergraduates and follow it up with a graduate program; Finnish teachers are required to obtain a two-year master's degree. They must attend a university that is also involved in educational research. No wonder Finland is one of the best educational systems in the world; their teachers begin teaching with as much or more schooling than doctors, dentists, psychologists, and lawyers. We also recognize that Finland's educational system did not happen overnight. It took planning and commitment to increase the effectiveness of their school results. Likewise, other nations have also made great strides in elevating teacher and administrator preparation. Closely aligned with professional preparation are salaries commensurate with their training.

Noteworthy to mention here is how this subpar certification process in the United States vests teachers with a false competence. Armed with a credential, beginning teachers enter the profession believing that they have had sufficient training, only then to discover that teaching is not quite so simple, causing many to leave the profession. Others who work well with children can become overconfident, swayed by their charisma with children. Diane recalls a fairly new first-grade teacher who was popular with students and parents; her class was fun. What was not evident to the untrained eye was that she really did not understand the scope and sequence of a robust reading program and had huge gaps in the learning progression. This showed up in reading test scores; some children made no gains during the year. Even though the first-grade teachers were given some training in reading, she had not applied what was taught. This is called the "knowing–doing gap."

CLOSING THE KNOWING–DOING GAP

The knowing–doing gap, identified by Pfeffer and Sutton (2000) of Stanford, recognizes that as knowledge expands, the leadership challenge becomes one of how to turn knowledge into action. All professions require on-the-job learning, and the gap between knowledge and doing continues to be problematic in all professions. The "gap" identifies the paradox of inaction; even with knowledge, people will not act to change behaviors. In other words, exposing employees to knowledge does not produce the needed actions to operationalize knowledge. The belief that dissemination is sufficient to bring about change is a failure of leadership. Instead, the most important task of a leader is to build systems that facilitate the transfer of knowledge into action; taking time for professional conversations about practice best does this.

Pfeffer and Sutton (2000) found four problems that contribute to the knowing–doing gap that apply to schools. First, when "talk substitutes for action," schools tend to have the same conversations over and over. For example, one teacher puts "school litter" on every staff meeting agenda. Even when a plan is finally implemented, most teachers take their students out once and then forget about it. Accordingly, an abundance of trivial items on any agenda saps energy and robs time that could be spent on more substantive talk.

Second, "memory is substituted for thinking" when schools continue to plan for rituals that are no longer important, such as carnivals, spelling bees, or award assemblies based on past history. In one district, an entire school refused to adopt the new mathematics curriculum because they liked the old one better. When queried, it turned out most knew next to nothing about the new curriculum. We coined the term *contempt before investigation* to describe this attitude.

A third cause of gaps is "fear that prevents acting on knowledge." In the Introduction, we describe teachers who are afraid to speak up for fear of reprisals from peers. Yes, teachers can be our own worst critics.

A final cause of gaps is when "measurement obstructs good judgment." Nowhere is this more evident than with high-stakes testing. It shows up in small ways when teachers let kids chew gum to relax during a test or throw a pep rally to reward high test scores. It manifests in tragic ways when well-meaning educators are caught changing answers to improve scores. Another problem with end-of-process measures is that the results come too late to inform action. Receiving last year's test score as teachers return in August to begin a new year with new students has limited use for teachers.

FROM KNOWING–DOING TO KNOWING–DOING–LEARNING GAP

Closing the knowing–doing–learning gap is not an event, but rather a process of continuous learning and reflection. Learning is an adaptive act, requiring ongoing reflection about what we are coming to know, and this knowing impacts "the doing." For this reason, we prefer to use the term *knowing–doing–learning gap.* Joyce and Showers (2002), in their book *Student Achievement Through Staff Development,* studied the impact of professional development—specifically, imparting knowledge, demonstration, and coaching—and found that coaching conversations led to a 95 percent increase in learning. In other words, professional conversations have the power to close the knowing–doing–learning gap. By adding *learning* to this term, we signal our intention, which is to improve professional learning. For this reason, we have added a fifth impediment to closing the knowing–doing–learning gap, and that is the belief that "adult learning is private." Learning should be collective (see the WISE report on *Collaborative Professionalism* by Hargreaves and O'Connor, 2017).

> Learning is an adaptive act, requiring ongoing reflection about what we are coming to know, and this knowing impacts "the doing."

The lack of collective learning shows up in schools that reward competition; hence, teachers do not share or see the value of working with colleagues. These teachers view their teaching as sufficient and do not feel a need to learn from others. These schools tend to have favored teachers who get more accolades and attention from parents, students, and administrators. We have even heard teachers say, "I don't want her to steal my ideas." This attitude—that ideas are commodities that can be stolen and that popularity equals excellence—creates real barriers to the collaborative conversations described in this book. These schools in which teachers feel isolated or excluded create deep resentments that serve only to divide the staff further. It is a vicious cycle: The less we talk with our colleagues, the more we judge from limited information and the less we want to talk with them.

It is through collective conversations that groups change minds and improve practices. The conversations in this book help break down the barriers of fear. They move groups from talk to action. They challenge known assumptions and foster a willingness to explore. They help teachers learn ways to measure what they value, not what is mandated. Knowledge is important and insufficient; doing requires action; and learning is the end product and becomes collective when these processes are shared. We believe a popular aphorism about Las Vegas should be reversed in education: "What goes on here, leaves here—in fact, shout it out."

Short of a major overhaul to training requirements in the United States, it is essential for the profession to take responsibility for filling in this knowing–doing–learning gap. This capacity building cannot happen in isolation or from mandates from the outside; it does not happen from fragmented, irregular professional development. It is not uncommon that as teachers come to know more collectively about how to best meet the needs of students, they become angry—why hasn't anyone addressed this issue before? This failure that leaves teachers behind is evident throughout our school systems. As an antidote, this book offers capacity-building pathways through the morass in order to build relationships so that teachers can improve professional skills by examining capabilities, values, and beliefs.

Reflection

iStock.com/Blackjack3D

A Place to Pause

- How do schools bring new teachers into the profession?
- How do schools enrich the professional lives of veteran teachers?
- How can we learn from newer teachers with good ideas?
- How can we learn from the experienced teachers and administrators?
- How can veterans pass on their best knowledge and reevaluate what is not working? How can this knowledge be used to support new teachers?

BUILDING HIGH-CAPACITY LEARNING COMMUNITIES

Capacity, as defined here, is a developmental construct in large part influenced by personal mental models about learning. Those who demonstrate high-capacity learning are adaptive and focused, yet flexible—always inquiring and paying attention to personal assumptions and knowledge gaps. These teachers seek challenges that pique thinking and allow for adaptable, professional knowledge creation. They continue to learn and create even through retirement and often beyond. They value collaborative learning and seek it at every opportunity. They inspire others.

> Those who demonstrate high-capacity learning are adaptive and focused, yet flexible—always inquiring and paying attention to personal assumptions and knowledge gaps.

The educational community needs to find ways to open access to conversations and to create regular graduate-level conversations in which knowledge is gained, created, and practiced in context. In many systems, professional development is often taught in a manner familiar to most undergraduates—listen and get knowledge. This type of learning may be essential for foundational learning, but once the foundation has been established, learning needs to be more personalized and nuanced. The learner needs to be able to engage in intellectual dialogue and practice-based learning. This idea is not new, but it has been difficult to sustain. Bill tells how such a program was life changing.

Bill describes his first encounters with Art Costa in 1983 at an administrative workshop on the topic of thinking skills. Not only was his curiosity piqued by teaching thinking skills to students, but he also became interested in some of the research cited by Art. After the workshop, Bill read one of his first professional books since college (his humble confession). Most startling for Bill was the realization that there was a vast knowledge base about teaching and leading accessible to him through books. Anyone who knows Bill knows he reads and summarizes at least one book a week and shares these summaries widely; he even finds time in Hawaii to continue this daily ritual. An avid reader, he summarizes what he reads and shares these with hundreds of educators, building his own personal legacy (see a sample at www.learningomnivores.com and "Sommers Summaries" on Chris Coffey's website at http://christophercoffey.com/upcoming-events/).

Later, when Bill became a trainer for a summer institute, he began to appreciate even more the unique design of this program. The participants split their time between learning new knowledge and practicing this knowledge in classrooms with children. They watched each other, reflected, and learned together. Bill continues to share a professional relationship with some of these people all these years later. As Bill reflects, "This immersion in compelling ideas and then the application of this knowledge in the classroom, followed by reflection on those practices, was new to me. I was hooked." Indeed, Bill goes on:

I would never have been in a place to be a leader or to write this book if I had not taken that workshop all those years ago. It was as if a screen had been lifted as I came to a realization that continual learning is essential for professionals.

He laughs when he thinks about how one of Art Costa's questions gave him fuel for thought for the next school year. Art stated, "I am more interested in what kids do when they do *not* know the answer, rather than when they do know the answer." This question shifted both Bill's teaching and leading. Others noticed, and Bill moved into administration when his principal tapped him on the shoulder and said, "Have you ever thought about being a principal?" His first answer was no. A year later, he was an administrative intern.

THE ILLUSION OF CONTROL OVER STUDENT LEARNING

For efficiency, as schooling in the United States became compulsory, schools moved from one-room schoolhouses to clustered grade levels based on age and to larger, comprehensive high schools. This allowed teachers to specialize in the pedagogy of a particular age grouping or in the content domains. While grade-level grouping and departmentalized high schools have many advantages, they also have disadvantages; the most significant is the lack of continuity for children. All these groupings create the silo effect—the creation of artificial boundaries that serve specific needs and ignore others. This means that elementary teachers become grade-centric and secondary teachers become domain-centric, and collaboration often stays within these boundaries. The conversations in this book assume that these barriers need to be broken down.

The truth is that without professional conversations, curriculum implementation in schools will never be even. Policy makers and many administrators believe that textbooks bring alignment and fidelity. However, unless teachers are provided with quality conversations about the implementation of any program, the idea of fidelity is an illusion. Often during the first year of a textbook adoption, teachers spend time grappling with emotions tied to letting go of the "tried and true" and the mechanics of this new adoption. It is only over time that teachers get to the essential question: How is this making a difference for my students? And many schools never get to this question, leaving each teacher to answer the question and find his or her own pathway through the adoption. It is not unlike a well-manicured park: Early on, most will follow the path, but over time, some take shortcuts, making new pathways and changing the landscape. Likewise, over time, teachers even in the same grade or department can have wildly different curricula with the same textbook.

The essential question is not about fidelity but about how any curriculum makes a difference for children. By working together to explore the goals and strategies of a new curriculum, teachers begin to participate in collective reflection about practice. They begin to find points of coherence. They share successes and failures and build a robust understanding of how students learn in relation to the adopted materials. Diane used to tell her teachers, "We have paid a lot of money for this new board-adopted curriculum. Your job is to understand the new curriculum and to ask how it makes a difference. If you think you have a better way to teach something, we need to take time to understand what you are coming to know."

When curricula are developed in this way, teachers grow together rather than apart, and they speak with one voice, which is both confident and adaptive, demonstrating collective efficacy. Diane saw this firsthand when she hired eight new teachers to implement class size reduction in the primary grades. She observed a startling contrast between classrooms during the first year; some of the new classrooms were full of books and materials and looked like all the others, but some seemed empty, like her own classroom in her first year of teaching. It turned out that the first-grade team had knowledge coherence about literacy instruction and were quick to share materials, lesson plans, and support with the new teachers. The other grade levels had limited coherence, and as a result, the new teachers were left on their own. Without realizing it, one group of teachers demonstrated the importance of collective efficacy. They also had created a knowledge legacy without even realizing it; they worked collaboratively to pass down what they knew to the newcomers. In the other classrooms, the teachers were truly newcomers left to forge their own pathway.

For some, the concept of collective efficacy seems like an elusive dream because the teachers they work with do not agree. We would argue that in the face of disagreements, it is even more important for these teachers to learn how to participate in the Nine Professional Conversations outlined in this book. These teachers need to find a coherence—an understanding of what they agree about and what they are going to agree to disagree about. For us as authors, it is essential that the reader understand that speaking with one voice does not always mean agreement—it means speaking from a coherent understanding about how teaching impacts learning. We both have been successful at building productive relationships with unions, and this requires that both sides know where they agree and where they do not agree. While it is not covered in this book, interest-based bargaining sets in motion very specific types of conversations, which when done well bring this same kind of coherence.

THE CLICHÉ: CHILDREN ARE
STILL LEFT BEHIND

The real problem, however, with the lack of coherence across and between grade levels is the uneven experience offered to students. Students who struggle stop working from fatigue; those who are successful persist and puzzle through what they do not understand. When the pedagogy changes from grade level to grade level, students who lag begin to fail repeatedly. In secondary schools, this problem is compounded when failing students are siloed into remedial classes that have nothing in common with what peers at the higher levels are learning. In one local junior high, English language learners are required to take two periods of English but lose out on a year of social studies. Common sense dictates that the English and social studies teachers, with the proper support and collaboration, could create a curriculum that better serves these students. It may be cliché: School curriculums, thoughtlessly implemented, can and do leave children behind.

Diane experienced this lack of continuity firsthand as a superintendent. As she grappled with the high costs of educating special needs students, especially the cost of outside referrals, Diane began chatting with special education staff. One specialist mentioned the large numbers of students in intermediate grades being referred for occupational therapy for handwriting. The resource specialist was emphatic: "If we taught handwriting in our schools, this would not be a problem!" New to her job, this was just the opening Diane was looking for to begin a series of conversations about literacy instruction.

Diane thought (mistakenly, it turns out) that handwriting would be a low-threat conversation. She soon learned that the gaps were huge. Handwriting in many classrooms had been left to happenstance, and those classrooms that did attend to writing were using a variety of outdated methods. The resource specialist had been correct; over the years, handwriting instruction has been eroded. While handwriting to some might seem less important, it exemplifies the fragmentation that occurs when teachers are left alone, and in this case, it had economic implications for a district already strapped for funds.

SEEKING COHERENCE IN THE CURRICULUM

For schools to seek coherence in curriculum design, teachers must have quality time to codevelop a curriculum that builds one element upon another and that provides integrated, articulated learning programs. A learning consultant once told Diane that for teachers to meet the needs of all students, teachers require an understanding of five grade levels—the two before the one they teach and the two after. Likewise, at secondary levels teachers who know how thinking patterns enhance or limit student learning are able to better accommodate all students and link courses across the domains. They would never suggest that students lose an entire year of social studies in the service of learning English!

Armed with this knowledge as a superintendent, Diane began insisting that district-level collaborations include more than one grade or department. The questions were always these: What is going on here? How is what we teach the same and different across the levels? The payoffs were profound. At the elementary level, teachers found gaps in their teaching strategies. Depending upon when they had been trained, they had entirely different ideas about the difference between phonics and phonemics and even how to teach these skills. By coming together and talking about how they teach reading, they found a coherence, and it changed forever the way some teachers worked.

An example of how to do this at the secondary level would be to have one department, such as math, work to build bridges with science, economics, and even the statistics collected by PE teachers. And in the converse, other subject areas should also work to build bridges to the mathematics curriculum. When students experience these connections across a curriculum, they experience the coherence of learning—everything is connected.

There is no subject better served by these cross-pollinating discussions than the teaching of writing. When Diane brought teachers together to probe into current practices, the teachers in intermediate grades were amazed to learn that their primary counterparts were teaching basics, which were then retaught at every grade level. The question became not of what we teach, but how do we hold students accountable for what they have learned as they travel through the grades. Writing is hard work, and without an accountability system, the students had tended to slip to more immature work patterns. A special education teacher created a simple rubric that students could use to maintain expectations. This ended up being the first of many conversations about writing.

> Knowledge coherence requires that teachers talk, debate, argue, and challenge each other to find the deepest truth about teaching that they know. This in turn guides the teaching practices of a school in a coherent way.

When teachers work to find knowledge coherence for a discipline or across disciplines, they begin to speak with one voice. They find that their differences often are not as great as they thought and that many times points of divergence yield the greatest breakthrough in understandings. When they do disagree, they understand that it is nuanced and that both ways produce results for students. Confident in their knowledge, they not only help students understand how learning connects, but they also help parents—and school boards such as the one described in Chapter 1—better understand changes in curriculum. Knowledge coherence requires that teachers talk, debate, argue, and challenge each other to find the deepest truth about teaching that they know. This in turn guides the teaching practices of a school in a coherent way. When this happens, teachers create knowledge legacies that are shared, and new teachers benefit from the wisdom of the elders. Leaders focus less and less on control and more and more on how to close learning gaps and increase coherence within and across the grades.

Chapter 3

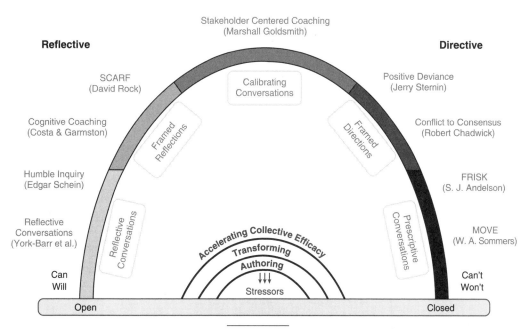

Stakeholder Centered Coaching
(Marshall Goldsmith)

Reflective

Directive

SCARF
(David Rock)

Calibrating
Conversations

Positive Deviance
(Jerry Sternin)

Cognitive Coaching
(Costa & Garmston)

Framed
Reflections

Framed
Directions

Conflict to Consensus
(Robert Chadwick)

Humble Inquiry
(Edgar Schein)

FRISK
(S. J. Andelson)

Reflective
Conversations
(York-Barr et al.)

Reflective
Conversations

Accelerating Collective Efficacy

Transforming

Authoring

↓↓↓

Stressors

Prescriptive
Conversations

MOVE
(W. A. Sommers)

Can
Will

Can't
Won't

Open

Closed

Urban Luck Design, urbanluckdesign.com

EMOTIONAL BLOCKS TO COLLECTIVE EFFICACY—HOW STRESS SHUTS DOWN COMMUNICATION

Communication is to relationships what breath is to life.

We get together on the basis of our similarities; we grow on the basis of our differences.

—Virginia Satir

When schools embark together on a mission to engage in mindful conversations, the culture shifts from isolation to collective efficacy. By this, we mean that the staff knows how to work together to solve problems and use each member's unique talents to create something beyond expectations. Over time, the staff learns to value the collective wisdom gained in community. The true test comes when newcomers are easily assimilated into the school culture—the benefit of a knowledge legacy. In schools with knowledge legacies, veterans will tell new teachers who to tap into to learn how to deal with everything from schedules to specific children or parents, science or math curricula, grading practices, and so forth.

A LEGACY WORTH FIGHTING FOR

When teachers have spent a career talking with each other about teaching and learning, they know where expertise lies within their school and how to use it to extend learning. They are aware of gaps in learning, resourceful about finding what is needed, and willing to consider multiple options. They have found excellence by adapting, perfecting, and working with others. When educators create cultures in which deep understanding about learning and teaching becomes the norm, everyone serves as a mentor. Those who join that culture are supported from Day One in ways that foster growth and development. These cultures of collective efficacy are immersive and bring out the best in all participants.

> When educators create cultures in which deep understanding about learning and teaching becomes the norm, everyone serves as a mentor. Those that join that culture are supported from Day One in ways that foster growth and development. These cultures of collective efficacy are immersive and bring out the best in all participants.

When conversational practices are mindful and focused, the energy is different—less stressful and more renewing. The difference is palpable. The challenge, we have found, is unless an educator has had the gift of working in such a culture—one of collective efficacy—it is beyond consciousness and not expected or even understood. Trying to describe collective efficacy is not unlike Bill's experience for the first time with a California artichoke. While Diane, a Californian, extolled its virtues, Bill, as an Iowan, had never eaten an artichoke. The idea of eating a thistle was puzzling to him. Likewise, the notion that teachers can and should help change school culture to build collective efficacy can seem bewildering and overwhelming.

Initially, the small bites of artichoke seemed like not quite enough, and it was a lot of work. Finally, when reaching the center, Bill understood why the luscious heart of the artichoke is worth all the work. Similarly, when starting off with one of the conversations in this book, it will be hard work, and those experimenting for the first time will wonder if it is worth it. In sum, understanding is based on context; what we do not know, we cannot act on or, for that matter, even dream about. For this reason, we have included many stories from the field to help the reader gain an understanding about how these conversations and these strategies play out in real life in schools. We have also chosen to tell stories that demonstrate the complexity of teaching and leading—it is not just about aligning teaching to standards, as so many policy makers want to believe. Excellent teachers are lifelong learners, always seeking new ways to better meet the needs of their students. Even small timesaving techniques are skills worthy of being passed on to other teachers. This cannot happen without collaborative conversations.

> Excellent teachers are lifelong learners, always seeking new ways to better meet the needs of their students.

THE CHALLENGE—DEVELOPING CULTURES OF COLLECTIVE EFFICACY

On the surface, collective efficacy seems desirable and even achievable. For practitioners, however, there are great challenges—specifically, the habits and norms that create a given school culture. Most school cultures have developed limited repertoires for conversing and overuse discussion, debate, and argument. These conversations serve daily life just fine but can stymie attempts to move beyond the surface and the desire to delve into learning. Over time, group members will tend to fall into habitual, unconscious patterns of talking too much or remaining silent, languishing in the world of unproductive meetings. Worse yet, in an attempt to change the norms, meetings have now become professional learning communities (PLCs). The problem is that giving collaboration a new name does not change the personal habits. What does change habits are experiences that allow PLCs to gain understanding and insight into their own and others' behaviors. This requires a commitment to break nonproductive habits in order to find internal and external resources that lead to solutions.

Efficacy was first labeled by Albert Bandura (1993) of Stanford University as a way of describing social learning theory. He defined *efficacy* as "the belief in an individual's ability to succeed and to follow through." Later, Goddard, Hoy, and Woolfolk (2000) of The Ohio State University expanded the theory to include group behaviors. They demonstrated a strong link between collective efficacy and student achievement. They defined *collective efficacy* as "the belief by the faculty as a whole that they will have a positive impact on students." Goddard and colleagues (2004) summarize their findings and argue that collective teacher efficacy is essential for student achievement because it transcends student socioeconomic status (SES) and prior learning. The power of collective efficacy is that teacher belief systems transcend the limitations of low-SES schools. Recently, Hattie (2015) ranked collective teacher efficacy as the number-one factor that impacts student achievement. These findings are significant because the development of collective efficacy is something that schools can control. Quite simply, a culture of collective efficacy is the result of faculty interactions. To summarize: Teacher efficacy is within our collective control, unlike poverty or other blocks to learning that are conditions outside of available spheres of influence.

> Teacher efficacy is within our collective control, unlike poverty or other blocks to learning that are conditions outside of available spheres of influence.

The real problem lies in the lack of the leadership understanding of how to create cultures that promote collective efficacy. Both of us found the best place to start was in meetings. Often when working with teachers, we use one of these Nine Conversations as a way to explore some aspect of teaching and learning. Once teachers get a taste of this new way of conversing, they want more. One teacher lamented, "I wish one of you would come and whisper in my principal's ear during staff meetings. He just doesn't get it, and as a result, our staff meetings are stressful and nonproductive."

In the center of the Dashboard is the goal of this book, Accelerating Collective Efficacy. Under this title is a smaller set of arcs that point to the corrosive effect of stress and the need for groups to learn to self-author and self-transform. This chapter describes how stress is manifest in groups and creates habit-based cultures that can become rigid and inflexible—the opposite of efficacy.

Nine Professional Conversations to Change Our Schools

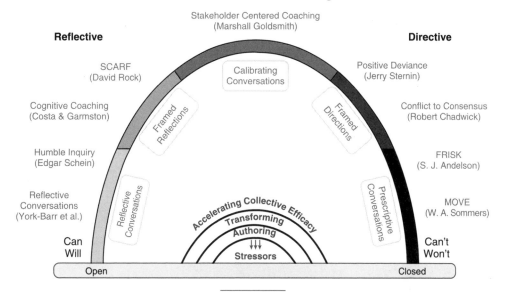

Urban Luck Design, urbanluckdesign.com

A FIRST STEP—REMOVING THE BARRIERS OF STRESS

When groups have limited conversational moves, it is no wonder that meetings become stressful. In humans, the stress response triggers protective behaviors that are self-serving and, as a result, deflect group efficacy. Years ago, renowned therapist Virginia Satir (1972) observed four stress reactions in humans that created vicious cycles of miscommunication. These emotional, protective responses limit human growth and stymie the capacity for individuals to develop. It is worth explicating these defensive behaviors here as it helps individuals and groups understand how these protective habits become embedded in cultures, making them resistant to change. Being conscious of how we respond to stress helps groups notice when trust is breaking down and when it is time to slow down and check in with group members to find out what is going on in their minds.

Satir's (1972) great gift was that she noticed four overt stress reactions in her work with clients—blaming, placating, distracting, or computing. Satir noted that these defensive habits existed below consciousness and were not obvious; by labeling them for her clients, she made them obvious. By making these habits explicit, Satir made great gains in couples counseling. We have observed all of these same responses during our collaborations with professionals. These outward manifestations are emotional responses and coping mechanisms—responses to stress—and have been observed in verbal responses during meetings. A short snippet from a staff meeting is relayed in Box 3.1 and shows how all four of these stress responses can be exhibited in one meeting. This could be any staff meeting, anywhere.

Box 3.1 Example of Staff Meeting Stress Responses

In a staff meeting, teachers are responding to this agenda item: "Pick a school-wide theme to support the Next Generation Science Standards."

- Dan is frustrated that the topic has dragged on for over thirty minutes and his colleagues continue to argue. Dan bursts out, "I am tired of these mandates from the district office that just waste our time." (Blame)
- Several teachers nod. (Placate)
- Julie, the staff joker, cracks, "Never a dull moment in Peoria! What else is new?" (Distract)

Everyone laughs, and a few shift uneasily.

- Addison chimes in with a flat voice, describing a favorite theme: "I have been thinking about this for a long time, and the rainforest is the most logical choice because it embodies all the sciences such as biology, chemistry, geology, zoology, and ecology." (Compute)

Several teachers exchange glances, silently communicating, "Not again." They have heard this before.
The end result? This group is stuck.

In sum, our lives are stressful, and these protective responses show up for all of us. We each develop our preferred style of responding. Just as in couples counseling, our verbal responses in meetings signal our stress. The goal here is to learn how to manage the context and create what psychologists call a safe "holding environment"—that safe space for growing and learning. The holding environment was first defined by Winnicott, a British pediatrician who was tasked with creating emotional safety for babies separated from their mothers during World War II. In his clinic, they literally held the babies.

When used in relation to adult psychology, a holding environment describes interactive space that promotes trust and *emotional containment*. Emotional containment is the active process of slowing down, recognizing and accepting our feelings, and finding proactive ways to use the energy generated by the emotional tensions. This literally means that leaders and groups must learn to attend to and change the surroundings to reduce the impact of the stressors. Confronting stress

> Emotional containment is the active process of slowing down, recognizing and accepting our feelings, and finding proactive ways to use the energy generated by the emotional tensions.

does not reduce stress—it increases it. It is like the classic paradox, "Don't think of blue." But what did you just think of? Blue, of course. Likewise, calling attention to stress usually just increases the stress. By changing the context, however, stress can be reduced.

In the example in Box 3.1, "wasting time at staff meetings" is the stressor. It may seem trivial, but a well-managed agenda is one of the first steps in creating emotional containment because it provides predictability and reduces stress. The conversations in this book also provide this predictive structure, allowing participants to not only manage time more efficiently but to also create space for safe explorations of ideas. Conversational processes make conversations more predictable and decrease the possibility of attacks from colleagues. Table 3.1 shows a summary of these four stressors and descriptions of the behaviors.

Table 3.1   Satir's Stress Categories

Satir Category	Protective Behavior	Verbal Behavior	Perceived As
Fighting	Criticizing others to maintain dominance	Blaming and finding faults in others, righting a wrong	Aggressive
Appeasing	Seeking others' support to protect to deflect anxiety	Placating or agreeing to avoid attack, seeking loyalties	Protective
Fleeing	Deflecting thoughts away from stress	Distracting by changing the topic, cracking a joke, or mentally leaving the meeting	Distracting
Freezing	Denying emotions	Long, analytical responses or returning to soapbox or being nonresponsive	Overintellectual

As you consider these descriptions, think of examples from meetings you attend regularly.

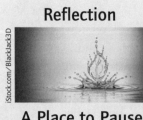

Reflection

A Place to Pause

- What kinds of habits do you notice in professional conversations?
- Think about ways to describe these behaviors as data and remove judgments.
- Be generous in your interpretation; we all experience stress and fall back on our preferred habits.
- Be mindful that when individuals exhibit these verbal responses they are responding with the emotional brain and protecting the inner self.
- What evidence can you find that signals a lack of trust and shows that others are not willing to be vulnerable?
- Consider what you observe as a signal to slow down, listen, and possibly inquire to discern the sources of the stress.

ADULT DEVELOPMENT IMPACTS THE CAPACITY FOR COLLECTIVE EFFICACY

As we reflected upon what we learned from our own work with these Nine Conversations, we realized that how schools support adult development has great impact on this work. As we thought more deeply about our stories, we realized that when adults are stressed, they respond differently. For example, a teacher turns to a colleague and says in an unpleasant voice, "Will you just shut up and let me talk?" Later, both teachers feel bad about the altercation, and their colleagues talk behind closed doors about the "blowup at the staff meeting." These kinds of interactions make colleagues less willing to even try to collaborate. Quite frankly, in this context teachers feel vulnerable to attack and start to avoid those with whom they do not see eye to eye.

When groups understand how stress causes adults to revert to more immature reactions, they can begin to take responsibility for their own thoughts and actions. For example, a more appropriate response to that situation would have been, "Hold on, I am feeling stressed, and I need to be able to complete my thoughts before others interrupt." Not only does it model a clear message, but it sets a norm for respectful behavior. In our work, we have found studies on adult development to be invaluable in our understanding of how to move from stress to collective efficacy. Drawing from the adult development terms, we define *collective efficacy* as cultures that are able to author their own futures and continuously transform their thinking to maintain a state of collective efficacy. We celebrate when we hear, "We used to . . . but now we . . . because . . ." In real life, our friend Bondo Nyembwe (Executive Director of Academia, Cesar Chavez Charter School) told Bill, "I used to think learning was about conforming to a training model, but now I believe it is about creating a culture of high expectations, which expands repertoires to engage many different students."

Once again, we draw the reader to the Dashboard. At the bottom center, we have listed stress as a key factor that brings down these conversations. Above stress, we offer the antidote to stress—creating contexts that allow professionals to author a future and transform their thinking as a result of this new learning. We draw these concepts from adult development as defined in the following section.

Nine Professional Conversations to Change Our Schools

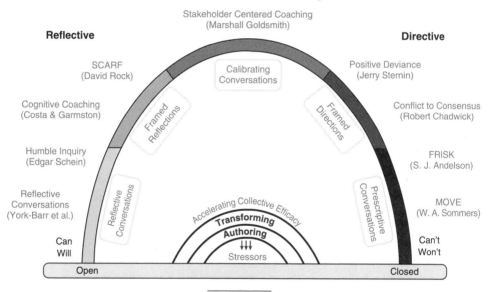

Urban Luck Design, urbanluckdesign.com

ADULT DEVELOPMENT

In the rest of this chapter, we review the thirty-five years of research by Kegan (1982), Kegan and Lahey (2009), Drago-Severson (1996, 2016), and Drago-Severson and Blum-DeStefano (2016). These thought leaders identified four distinct stages in how humans make sense of experiences, and because Drago-Severson is an educator, we use her terms here. (Note: While these terms are slightly different than Kegan's, they describe the same phenomenon.) To this end, a person's way of knowing shapes his or her understanding of roles, responsibilities, and capabilities at each level of development. These thought leaders suggest matching leadership interventions to the developmental level (Drago-Severson, 2004; Kegan & Lahey, 2009). While we have both used this strategy—and still fall back on it when seeking to understand individual behaviors—we have found that collective efficacy is best set through context. Through the conversations in this book, we invite professionals to both author and transform their thinking. The miracle of collective efficacy is that the whole pulls up the part—those who may have been more stuck in their thinking and are at lower stages of adult development. A friend told us a story of a teacher who reflected on how coaching had changed her interactions with her mother. The teacher described her mother's response: "I do not know what that school is doing to you, but I sure like the way you are showing more responsibility."

The work of Kegan, Lahey, and Drago-Severson most often focuses on individual worldviews. In contrast, our focus is on group dynamics. By drawing from this seminal work, we can articulate what we believe is a complementary view that explains how developmental mind frames limit communicative actions. We have found that when working in groups, prediagnosing individuals is not much help. In fact, our most startling discovery has been to observe how collective efficacy is value-added and becomes a virtuous cycle of improved communication for all. When groups work effectively, this behavior becomes the norm for group work and is easily adopted by newcomers. The norms do not even need to be stated, as the linguistic patterns imprint. Furthermore, working on lengthy self-help, consciousness-raising programs such as the one described by Kegan and Lahey (2009) requires excessive time and may ultimately have limited impact on group dynamics.

Understanding how these developmental stages play out in human interactions can be a great aid for working with groups and raising consciousness, which of course starts the path for change. In our experience, traditional school environments are structured to reinforce the early levels of adult development as identified by Drago-Severson (2004)—the *instrumental* and the *socializing* minds. And so we begin with a description of the status quo.

STAGES I AND II OF ADULT DEVELOPMENT

When young adults come of age and are given adult-level responsibilities, they often rely on rules or institutional norms; indeed, in the industrial–mechanical age, rules that guided workers were the norm. Drago-Severson (2004) defined this stage as an *instrumental learner.* While these early stages first emerge before adulthood, we believe that when adult participants find themselves in a vicious stress cycle, they rapidly revert to an earlier developmental stage. For the instrumental learner, they seek top-down mandates and accept that a few—the appointed leaders—know better than the whole. This is a classic bureaucratic response—to attempt to mandate what matters. A teacher stuck in this mind frame might say, "I wish someone would just tell me what to do." Schools with this top-down structure have many rugged individuals or underground guerrillas that choose to silently go their own way, creating isolated instances of excellence.

A second stage, the *socializing learner* (Drago-Severson, 2004), which most enter in early adolescence and adulthood, values social ties or loyalty to a group. Power and control evolves from intergroup relationships, with those not "in the group" being relegated to the fringes and often considered outliers. Teachers who demonstrate this mind frame stick with like-minded groups while rebuffing those that do not fit their norm. These schools are often considered cliquey, with "in" groups dominating the agenda and "out" groups feeling marginalized. In these schools, pools of excellence grow by happenstance and have little or no impact on the school as whole.

ADULT DEVELOPMENT SHAPES SCHOOL CULTURES

Lambert, Zimmerman, and Gardner (2016), in their book *Liberating Leadership Capacity,* have defined *capacity* as "the ability to grow and develop as leaders through collective efforts" (note that Diane is the second author of this book). They identified four archetypal developmental stages, which map directly onto school cultural norms. The important learning here is that school cultures have the potential to both restrict and enhance adult development.

Historically, *low-capacity* schools describe the schools many of us attended as children, where the district office and the principal were instrumental in making important decisions and in conducting all affairs of leadership. This deference to the leader is a classic hallmark of the instrumental mind. Common in these schools are the emotional language patterns described by Satir, particularly blaming others for failures and hiding behind rationales. The next level is the *fragmented* school, often found in secondary schools in which departments socialize to create "in" and "out" groups to garner power and favors accordingly. In these schools, the powerful dominate, and others learn either to placate so as to stay in favor or to flee and avoid interactions. Both low-capacity and fragmented schools demonstrate a limited capacity to grow, and like the school described in Box 3.1 are stuck in cultures that reinforce more of the same behavior—a vicious cycle.

Lambert and colleagues (2016) argue that to break from old habits, all educators need to grow the capacity to lead, and indeed, that is what most school reform movements have been about. Historically, the *limited-capacity* school emerged with the first school reform movements in which teachers joined with appointed leaders, most often the principal, to form leadership teams. As those schools found new ways to work together, they offered leadership opportunities to those who stepped up and in some cases made significant gains in their understanding of leadership development. The problem was once again with implementation. While a few were in the know, many were still outside of the leadership circle, languishing in the knowing–doing–learning gap. Once again, mandating the intended changes by an enlightened leadership team does not work.

Lambert's team (2016) argues that to liberate leadership capacity, schools need for everyone to take a leadership path to create the *high-capacity* school. This is not the traditional top-down path of directing, but rather one of cultivating knowledge, creating expertise, and passing on the gained wisdom through knowledge legacies. These schools value the time they have together as professionals and seek opportunities to meet and confer about topics of value to their own development. They are efficacious and seek challenges as a way of self-authoring a positive future.

In these schools, meetings still have a formal place; however, more often than not, teachers self-organize around different interests, and the appointed leader ends up being more like a curator of learning rather than a director. In a high-capacity school, teachers are proactive and efficacious in their belief that by working together, solutions can be authored, implemented, and articulated to create knowledge legacies.

SELF-AUTHORING—THE CRITICAL STAGE FOR MATURING ADULTS

Kegan and Lahey (2001) and Drago-Severson (2006) have written extensively about how to develop the third and fourth stages of adult development. Once again, we use educator Drago-Severson's terms: *self-authoring* and *self-transforming*. According to her, self-authoring is taking ownership of personal authority. This is

> Self-authoring is taking ownership of personal authority. This is manifest through the demonstrated capacity to generate and understand values, principles, and long-term purposes despite competing needs and pressures.

manifest through the demonstrated capacity to generate and understand values, principles, and long-term purposes despite competing needs and pressures.

Instead of looking outside for rules, or needing social relationships to validate beliefs, the self-authoring person looks both inside and outside to deal with incongruities. Probing more deeply and seeking alternative viewpoints allow the person to create an inner coherence and a more congruent identity—a person who walks her or his talk. This person is reflective and willing to modify in the face of new information or changes in the environment. At this stage, however, self-authoring individuals can still be limited by their own beliefs. And as already noted, self-authoring by an appointed leadership team can limit capacity by privileging just a few. From this worldview, these leaders are often surprised when others are not able or willing to join them and take up the authorship mantle. This points to an inner tension often seen at this stage of development. A person at this level will often wonder, "If I am willing to change my own view, why can't they" (Kegan & Lahey, 2009)?

A word of caution: Stage development carries with it an illusion of progress and can also be thought of as fixed developmental platforms or destinations. We hold a more cyclical view of the stages. While obviously groups would want to achieve higher stages, it is important to note that even sophisticated groups find bumps in the road; when this happens, the Satir stress patterns emerge, and group behavior reverts to earlier stages of development. We believe that all the stages have the potential to be present, and it is the culture that allows the better selves to emerge, allowing for competing commitments.

Drago-Severson and her colleague Blum-DeStefano, in their book *Tell Me So I Can Hear You* (2016), use these stages diagnostically as part of the leadership–supervision process. They provide a guide for structured conversations in which the coach or supervisor works with that person by matching language to the developmental levels. They identify growth edges for each stage of development and honor both the present level and the potential for growth. While we do not include those conversations in our Dashboard, we want to point out that her work is a valuable contribution for coaches and supervisors, especially as they try to diagnose that critical juncture of moving from reflecting to directing. We refer those people to the books cited earlier.

The purpose of the conversations on the Professional Conversation Arc is to assist groups in learning to author a "best future." This requires that groups interweave ideas and find common beliefs and values that support learning. This aspiration to build collective efficacy gives direction to those seeking a culture that supports self-authoring.

SELF-TRANSFORMING—FINDING
STATES OF WISDOM

The final stage of adult development is *self-transforming*. Kegan and Lahey (2009) report that the final stage of adult development, which they call *interindividual*, is only observed in 9 percent to 10 percent of the adult U.S. population. Drago-Severson says that self-transforming individuals show a high tolerance for ambiguity, are able to deal with uncertainty, and demonstrate a compassionate inner peace. They are patient, other affirming, and are mentors worth seeking. In Chapter 5, we provide a reflective conversation designed by Edgar Schein (2013). In our mind, Schein represents a person who appears to have become self-transforming. In his early eighties, he welcomed a chance to work with us and was as eager to learn from us as we were from him.

> Self-transforming individuals show a high tolerance for ambiguity, are able to deal with uncertainty, and demonstrate a compassionate inner peace.

Coming from a mental health background, Schein's (2013) mission was always about healing. Early in his work, he had insights about how feedback interferes with the ability to self-author. He found that help, given in the guise of feedback, is not what the person needs, wants, or even requires. Instead of giving help, he focused on the other's actions and would query, "So what did you do?" Listening, Schein would say, is a way to learn about the other; and while the listener learns about the other, the other gets to untangle some of the problems and solutions that suddenly emerge. Schein is unflappable in his belief that we are our own best authors of learning. Thus, in helping he does not made suggestions, but keeps probing to find out about possibilities. He contrasts this with his earlier habits, which were to cut people short—to not listen or explore differences. In these later years, he talked of his humble roots and the real life issues of losing a wife and of growing old. In the end, self-transforming is not so much as about the self as a way of being in the world, which serves as a learning model for others.

> Listening, Schein would say, is a way to learn about the other; and while the listener learns about the other, the other gets to untangle some of the problems and solutions that suddenly emerge.

Another human who has been widely sought out for his wisdom is Erich Fromm, who practiced the art of unselfish understanding—a transforming way of being. His summary of listening provides the best guide we know for seeking to be transformative. In *The Art of Listening* (1994), he offers his suggestions for achieving unselfish understanding:

- Give complete concentration.
- Free the mind of your own self-importance and personal distractions.
- Stay open to imagination.
- Practice empathy in a way that blurs the boundaries of self.
- Reach out to the other and do not fear losing the self.
- Listen for understanding, which is a gift of love to the other.

We could not have found better words to close out this first part of our book. We are where we started. Conversations that matter are within the grasp of all; we only need to personally commit to build effective habits of conversation and then use these different kinds of conversations to work collectively in order to build capacity and grow and learn as a profession. Thank you for joining us in the journey.

Part II

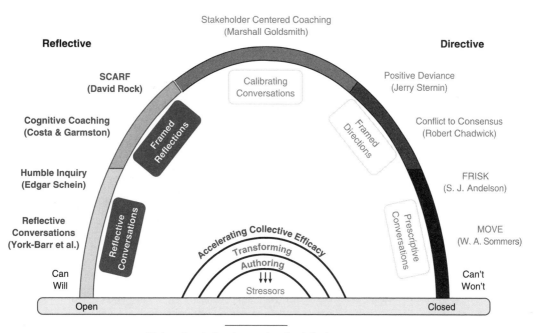

Urban Luck Design, urbanluckdesign.com

PART II

CONVERSATIONS DESIGNED TO BUILD KNOWLEDGE COHERENCE FROM THE INSIDE OUT

s a way of thinking through complex ideas, we often sketch out our thoughts. When Bill first proposed this book, Diane said, "Sketch it out, so I can see all the parts." When Bill did, Diane could immediately see what he was talking about, and a book was born. The idea of telling a leadership story focused on conversations that begin with open-ended conversations for reflection and move toward more-directed conversations seemed like an invaluable resource. Initially, we thought each conversation would stand alone; we could not have been more wrong. As we wrote, we saw relationships among all of them and came to appreciate the power of these left-arc conversations. We realized that even directive conversations require that all be active participants. Indeed, when directive conversations do not result in reflection and the desired change, they are not successful. The real difference between the left and right arcs is that on the left side of the Dashboard the professional is responsible for creating both the agenda and the criteria for success; on the right side, the external data or information drives the conversation and sets both the agenda and the criteria for success. Yet in the end, each person is responsible for making the directed changes.

Years ago, without realizing it, our thinking shifted away from needing to be the wise sages who knew it all to wanting to find ways to support others in thinking about practice. Both of us loved being principals and particularly enjoyed the intellectual partnership we formed with our staff. When we listened and paid attention, our learning accelerated. We found teachers to have a wealth of information if we only asked for their expertise.

These conversations on the left arc support our belief that setting reflective processes in action supports deeper, more contemplative thought about teaching and learning. Every one of the conversations outlined on the Professional Conversation Arc requires attention to the cycle of reflective practice. What changes as one moves across the arc is the focus, which shifts the intention and the outcome of the conversation. All too often, leaders think that the ability to reflect on practice is developmental. We do not believe this is the case, as we believe it is more often related to habits of communication learned as we grow up and grow into a profession. We have observed brand-new teachers capable of deep reflection and seasoned-veteran teachers who are quick to seek answers and initially can be resistant to slowing down to allow time to think. No matter where a conversation falls on the Dashboard, the facilitator always puts the responsibility back on the other to respond, grow, and learn from the experiences, moving the conversation back toward the left arc. It is only when someone can't or won't that we consider other options, which we address toward the end of the book.

Our experience has demonstrated that slowing down and taking quality time to reflect on practices actually speeds up learning later. When groups take the time to find knowledge coherence, they are able to communicate more clearly, learn from each other more quickly, and come to appreciate that internal resources and practices are equally important to outside expertise. In the end, these conversations build collective efficacy, and success becomes the synthesis in the process of co-creation.

> In the end, these conversations build collective efficacy, and success becomes the synthesis in the process of co-creation.

To begin our exploration of the Nine Professional Conversations, we start with the most open-ended reflective conversations. These two conversations ask the professionals to reflect on their own practices and to draw from this learning to learn from practice and from each other. When these kinds of conversations involve a group, they open up the access to learning in ways that are profound. When professionals learn from their own and peers' knowledge, it brings a coherence and accelerates learning. Bryk and Schnieder (2002) have found that relational trust has a significant effect on learning. They found that teacher-to-teacher collaboration was the most significant. Think about it: If teachers trust each other, they more readily share supplies and resources. Most importantly, they share ideas to help kids learn.

The framed reflections are two conversations that are more focused. The first one focuses on setting goals and evaluating the efficacy of those goals, and the second one demonstrates how paying attention to how and what people communicate can open up insights that expand interpersonal understandings. While the SCARF model has been used as a diagnostic tool, we find it more useful as a self-reflection tool.

Chapter 4

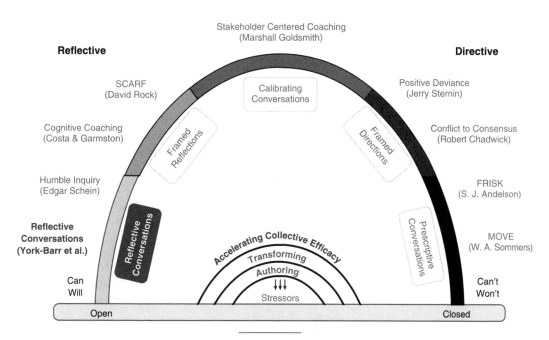

Reflective   Stakeholder Centered Coaching   Directive
(Marshall Goldsmith)

SCARF
(David Rock)

Calibrating
Conversations

Positive Deviance
(Jerry Sternin)

Cognitive Coaching
(Costa & Garmston)

Framed
Reflections

Framed
Directions

Conflict to Consensus
(Robert Chadwick)

Humble Inquiry
(Edgar Schein)

FRISK
(S. J. Andelson)

Reflective
Conversations
(York-Barr et al.)

Reflective
Conversations

Accelerating Collective Efficacy

Transforming

Authoring

↓↓↓

Stressors

Prescriptive
Conversations

MOVE
(W. A. Sommers)

Can
Will

Can't
Won't

Open   Closed

REFLECTIVE CONVERSATIONS— THE FUNDAMENTAL PROFESSIONAL ACT

Life must be understood backwards. But it must be lived forwards.

—Søren Kierkegaard, *Journals*, 1843

To be vested as a professional requires certification—proof of enough knowledge to be considered competent in a field. Certification usually means an end to formal education and the beginning of practice-based learning. This learning is not static and requires regular, personal reflections on practice. Yet all too often, reflective practices are left to happenstance. Instead, what is offered as professional development becomes an endless parade of workshops or dull collaborations organized around institutional demands.

This book is about flipping the professional development paradigm inside out and advocates for putting the professionals in charge of personal learning—not as sole practitioners, but in conversation with others. Because teachers can be lone professionals in a sea of students, they benefit from forums for reflection about practices; and those new to the profession require chances to learn from experienced professionals. Being able to reflect on actions in relationship to the outcomes is a fundamental professional practice and occurs cyclically: *before* in anticipation, *during* in response, and *afterward* to improve. Reflection in–on–for action is an essential outcome for all the conversations of this book. Our aim is to foster a school culture that has a reflective act at the center of every conversation about practice.

PERSONAL AND COLLECTIVE HONESTY
LEADS TO PROFESSIONAL GROWTH

In their core, most professionals are conscious of their own abilities and, when honest, know where they fall short. It is this deep reflection that drives improvement—knowing one can do better. Collective reflection requires deep trust and a commitment to work through differences. When honest reflection is practiced in community, teachers find that they are not alone and, more importantly, discover others with the expertise they need. The intention of *collective reflection* is about exploring, expanding, and improving repertoires of practice. Based on this broad definition, each chapter in this book is a reflective conversation framed in a variety of ways. While the reflective conversation offered in this chapter is the most open ended, others are goal focused, data focused, or more directive, but each one calls for reflective practice. For it is in reflective practice that each person takes responsibility for his or her own developmental trajectory to not only author a future, but to transform thoughts and actions in the face of challenges.

> When reflective conversations are the norm in a school, professionals learn to embrace feedback and will take the necessary steps to modify behaviors.

When reflective conversations are the norm in a school, professionals learn to embrace feedback and will take the necessary steps to modify behaviors. Indeed, we would argue that this ability to reflect on practices and make changes toward improvement is an essential professional skill. Furthermore, when teachers reflect on practices, the changes they make are interwoven with current practices and produce a higher likelihood of success. Those who are able to self-supervise in this way show the greatest potential to become expert.

In writing this book, we had many a conversation with colleagues who wanted to use these Nine Professional Conversations as a way to diagnose where to go next with a person or group. Many administrators think supervision and professional development are directive processes and that diagnosis and prescription are the important ingredients for change. In the hubris of supervisory activity, administrators get trapped in a belief that incremental learning will make a difference. By this, we mean that learning is perceived as a series of steps for improvement. While this may work for simple techniques, it is ineffective for the multifaceted changes that require a deeper examination of capacities for and assumptions about teaching. Teachers that examine their capabilities, along with core values and beliefs, learn to align their actions with their thinking—they walk their talk—and perfect their practices daily.

One of Diane's stories best describes how a principal's blindsight can play out in the classroom and impact supervision. A ten-year veteran teacher new to the district makes a rash of behavior referrals to the principal. A pattern emerges. The teacher claims that the students are at fault and seems clueless about the power struggle that now marks the student–teacher relationship. This blaming the victim is an example of protective behaviors described in Chapter 3. For whatever reason, this teacher has never learned to transcend these defensive behaviors, which blocks his ability to reflect. The principal makes recommendations to improve the student–teacher relationship, such as the teacher greeting students at the door, having lunch with students to learn more about them, and waiting for silence instead of speaking over student voices. The problem is that the teacher does not see the root of the problem as his teaching, but rather as the kids with the behavior problems. Hence, these incremental changes make no discernable difference on classroom climate.

> What evidence did the principal have that this teacher embraced problems as challenges and actively worked to reflect upon his teaching?

Later in the year, when the issue of tenure for this teacher came up, the defining question for Diane was this: What evidence did the principal have that this teacher embraced problems as challenges and actively work to reflect upon his teaching? Diane was clear; she wanted teachers who demonstrated reflective practices. The principal liked this teacher, so he lobbied hard to retain him. His rationale? "If given enough time, I know that I can fix him."

Diane, being clear on her values, said two things to this principal:

- Teachers that reflect on practice get better. This teacher not only has ten years of experience, but he has shown no ability to improve on his own.
- A ten-year veteran should be contributing to the culture of the school by modeling reflective practice, not detracting by taking up time you do not have to give.

The principal admitted that he had spent far too much time trying to fix this teacher and agreed that teachers who require this much time probably do not belong in the profession.

Quite frankly, in schools we do not have time to help those who cannot help themselves; our students deserve the best now, not later. Others also reinforce this belief that excellence grows out of reflection. For example, when Sheryl Sandberg, the CEO of Facebook, was asked what she thinks is the number-one thing to look for in an employee, she said, "Someone who takes feedback well. Because people who take feedback will learn and grow quickly" (Bariso, 2016).

Our job is to serve students with quality teaching and learning; it is not to save teachers with incremental directives. Reflective practice is a habit of mind and should begin early during preservice and then continue into the profession. It takes hard work; it requires a willingness to examine failures. When teachers practice this habit, they become contributing members of reflective school cultures. When schools develop collective reflection practices, they move toward the path of collective efficacy—they know what they do that makes important differences in the lives of all students. They are honest about what they do and do not know and always strive for the best path forward.

REFLECTIVE PRACTICE CONVERSATIONS

We begin the journey through these conversations with the more generalized Reflective Practice Conversation. Of all the conversations in this book, it is the most open ended; hence, practitioners can take this kind of conversation in any direction important to them as professionals. This work draws from Donald Schön (1983), who wrote the *Reflective Practitioner* and defined *reflection* as "an important human activity that requires an ability to step outside of the action, think about it, mull it over, and evaluate it so as to learn by doing." Schön wrote that practitioners' ability to do reflection-in-action "depends on certain relatively constant elements that he may bring to a situation otherwise in flux: an over-arching theory, an appreciative system, and a stance of reflection-in-action which can become . . . an ethic for inquiry" (1983, p. 164). The conversations described in this chapter explain how to make this process explicit so that this "ethic of inquiry" becomes a norm. We were struck by Schön's deep understanding that inquiry requires an ethic. All too often, inquiry can drift to a line of questions directed toward a known outcome. This is not inquiry, but manipulation, in which known solutions are inferred through the questions. The ethical stance is to always ask questions from a point of genuine curiosity.

In 2016, Bill completed the third edition of *Reflective Practice for Renewing Schools* with colleagues Jennifer York-Barr, Gail S. Ghere, and Jo Montie. In this updated edition, these authors changed the end of the title from *Improving Schools* to *Renewing Schools*. While much had changed, much was still the same, and their hope was that they would add to a growing body of knowledge about renewal. They state, "Reflective practice is at the root of renewed life and energy in schools. Reflective practice is the vital and largely untapped resource for significant and sustainable

> "Reflective practice is at the root of renewed life and energy in schools. Reflective practice is the vital and largely untapped resource for significant and sustainable effectiveness." — York-Barr et al.

effectiveness" (2016, p. xxii). In each edition of this book, the authors identified the attributes of a reflective school, which were demonstrated by an ability to stay focused on education's central purpose—student learning and development. These schools commit to continuous improvement of practice and assume responsibility for professional learning, which aligns with new understandings.

Furthering this line of inquiry, we also aim to create school cultures that support professionals in their reflective practices by making more time for teacher talk in collaborative learning environments. The real payoff is that when faculties can articulate how they make a positive difference in the learning of all students, they manifest collective efficacy. To review important research reasons for this emphasis, we once again remind the reader of the research of John Hattie. Hattie (2015) reviewed 1,200 meta-analyses of the effects on learning and identified *collective teacher efficacy* as the number-one factor that influences student achievement. The effect size is 1.57, meaning that collective teacher efficacy is two or three times more effective than other positive strategies. Developing collective efficacy takes time; to develop this mental discipline requires practice.

REFLECTION-ON-ACTION

Coaches celebrate when the teacher begins a reflection conversation with, "If I had it do over again I would . . ." When teachers start a conversation by knowing what to change, coaches need only to listen and reflect on the teachers' thoughts. Sometimes just pausing, paraphrasing, and asking a few discrete questions are enough. When professionals do not meet expectations, most will engage in reflection-on-action and seek ways to self-correct. Schön (1983) found that professionals often knew more than they could say, so this "thinking out loud" made it more conscious. Talking with others requires a degree of specificity in the service of clarity that is often not present in our private thoughts.

Even the writing of this book required deep reflection-on-action. As authors, we found that we had developed a kind of shorthand to describe each conversation. Because this book draws from years of practice, we had to slow down and become reflective to really understand the value of each conversation and to seek examples of these practices in action. These conversations always contributed to a deeper understanding, and the sum was always greater than the parts.

The reflective conversation can be used in any situation to simply reflect on actions and to determine what was learned from these actions. As groups or individuals ponder, they puzzle about what they are coming to understand. They discover the deeper and nuanced understandings that others have developed through personal reflective practices. Box 4.1 outlines a basic reflection-on-action conversation.

Box 4.1 Reflection-on-Action Conversation Outline

Invite others to think out loud about the actions just taken:

- What worked?
- What didn't seem to work?
- What surprises came up?
- What assumptions are informing these practices?
- How might this be done differently next time?
- What might be increased and how?
- What else is important for us to think about?

As we introduce this first set of question tools, we remind the reader that we have developed these questions with two goals in mind: first, to focus the conversation, and second, to make sure the conversation has a beginning, middle, and end. All too often, conversations are allowed to follow the free flow of thought and do not really honor the ethic of inquiry. It is essential that these conversations be considered chances for deeper inquiries into practice. If groups just answer the questions and do not converse about what they are coming to understand, they are not in conversation, but are in an obligatory, get-the-job-done stance. We remind readers that success is measured by what we learn, not what we get done. For the purposes of our work in schools, we have sometimes changed the words of the original authors. With respect, our aim is always to stay true to the intent of the original authors or to point it out to the reader when we take a different stance.

REFLECTION-IN-ACTION

To help the reader understand the real value of reflection both in and on action, we turn to the work of Gary Klein, who wrote *Sources of Power* (1998), in which he studied the in-the-moment thinking of people in high-stress jobs— firefighters, EMT workers, and operating room staff. Klein found that the top

> Klein found that the top performers in these emergency fields had an uncanny ability to not only anticipate, but in the heat of the moment, they were able to display reflection-in-action by taking decisive and lifesaving actions.

performers in these emergency fields had an uncanny ability to not only anticipate, but in the heat of the moment, they were able to display reflection-in-action by taking decisive and lifesaving actions. In the study of the thinking patterns that supported this high performance, he identified two key concepts: pattern recognition and mental simulation. Not only did these emergency responders have a high degree of knowledge about what to expect, but they were keen to notice and adapt when a pattern did not fit expectations. It turned out it was this moment—a change in noise from the fire or a breathing pattern in a patient—that triggered decisive and often lifesaving actions. Pattern recognition and mental simulation are forms of reflection-in-action that become even more powerful when made explicit. His book is full of stories about how these brave people used reflection-in-action to save lives.

> Pattern recognition and mental simulation are forms of reflection-in-action that become even more powerful when made explicit.

Pattern recognition and mental simulation are forms of reflection-in-action that become even more powerful when made explicit. As Schön (1983) noted and Klein (1998) discovered, these experts knew more than they could say. It was not uncommon for them to start out describing what happened in vague terms such as, "The patient didn't look right." When prodded, however, they often could describe in detail what it was that they had noticed, and this detailed recall could then be used to create simulations or mental maps for the future. It turned out that these emergency workers had skills that others had not learned; hence, they were positive deviants (see Chapter 9).

We have found that many teachers have deep reservoirs of unconscious thought process, which they draw from in moments of need. If this deep intuitive knowledge were shared, it would greatly enhance teacher excellence in schools, yet this intellectual capital goes untapped. It marks the distinction between teachers who year after year seem to be working too hard and those who become more conscious and make teaching seem effortless. This knowledge that lives deep in teachers' psyches goes well beyond the standards. In particular, this is where teachers could learn about the nuances of dealing with high-stress moments in the classroom. In the chapter on positive deviance (Chapter 9), we offer many examples.

For a conversation of reflection-in-action, see Box 4.2 for questions to delve into the consciousness of teaching in the moment.

Box 4.2 Reflection-in-Action Conversation Outline

Invite others to think out loud about moment-to-moment decisions made during the action:

- When teaching is not going as expected, what do you do?
- What did you notice in the moment that you did not expect?
- What else did you notice? (Repeat several times.)
- What data could you collect to expand your observational skills in the moment?
- How can you test your new knowledge?
- What assumptions may be limiting your thinking?
- How will you know when you are successful?

REFLECTION-FOR-ACTION

Schön (1983) did not discuss this type of reflection in his work, but early in the application to teaching, reflection-for-action was added. Hence, in most education-related writing, the authors start with the planning cycle. This is likely because teaching is ultimately a performance art that requires planning before action. Indeed, lesson planning has always been considered an important teacher behavior. In the business world, however, this type of thinking is often separated from reflective practice. Instead, this forward thinking is often described as scenario planning, which is a form of reflection-for-action that focuses on creating multiple stories about the future that serve as a blueprint for actions.

In the feedback about this book, we were told to put reflection-for-action first in this chapter's discussion. We discussed this and realized that to stay true to Schön's work, we needed to put it last. Schön did not address reflection-for-action directly; for him, planning for the future was part of reflecting upon the past to change behavior. In the business world, these conversations for action or planning almost always come out of a reflection-on-practice. This is that old adage "If I had it to do over, I would . . ." Essentially, reflection-on-action turns into reflection-for-action, demonstrating the cyclical nature of these conversations. For teaching, reflection-for-action, which includes planning and goal setting, has always been a natural starting place. In Chapter 6, we will return to this goal-setting pattern again when we describe Cognitive Coaching. Box 4.3 offers the basic questions for a reflection-for-action conversation.

Box 4.3 Reflection-for-Action Conversation Outline

Invite others to think out loud about what is planned:

- What are the goals or outcomes?
- What steps are necessary to accomplish this plan?
- How will you know that you are successful?
- What data might you collect to measure success?
- What learning question have you framed for yourself?

THE QUALITY OF REFLECTION IS EVIDENCED BY THE RESPONSES

Diane is a lover of art and has worked for over ten years with a community involved in Visual Thinking Strategies (Yenawine, 2013). Philip Yenawine's program instructs teachers how to engage others—adults and children alike—in reflection conversations about fine art. It uses the elements of authentic listening to encourage the viewers to talk about what they are coming to understand as they linger over a piece of art. What is amazing to watch is how even young children go from short, vague responses to long, descriptive responses. Some start to organize their thinking in paragraphs. They dig deep and go well beyond the surface, interpreting nuances and giving evidence as to why they think that way. Likewise, when given a chance, teachers will give lengthy, nuanced responses. In the dedication for this book, we describe how one teacher dealt with bullying in an elegant and nuanced approach. She described how she could read subtle changes in classroom climate and identify antecedent behaviors and intervene early. Teachers who have learned to linger and reflect on practices have great insight and will give very complex answers to questions about how they responded in the moment in the classroom.

It is a joy to converse with these reflective, thoughtful professionals. As longtime administrators, we give credit to these teachers for increasing our own professional repertoire. We have learned more from our conversations with colleagues than we ever learned sitting in our offices or classrooms with the door shut. When given the chance, educators' professional learning is accelerated through these highly refined conversations. One teacher described her two years as a writing mentor:

> We have learned more from our conversations with colleagues than we ever learned sitting in our offices or classrooms with the door shut.

Those years were so rich in learning. It was such a gift to work with other professionals who had such a high degree of understanding about writing. When the funding was cut and I no longer had this professional partnership, I got angry. I felt robbed; my grade-level partner and I do engage in deep conversations, but my school never spends time on quality conversations.

At this point, it is appropriate to ask the reader to stop and reflect upon what you are learning from this text. Bill offers his technique for learning something new—for example, he might copy the information in the Reflection Box onto an index card and then keep it in his front pocket for quick reference. Because Diane doesn't always have a front pocket, she likes to put her memory jogs on the top bar of her computer. When working on agendas, they remind her to think about these processes.

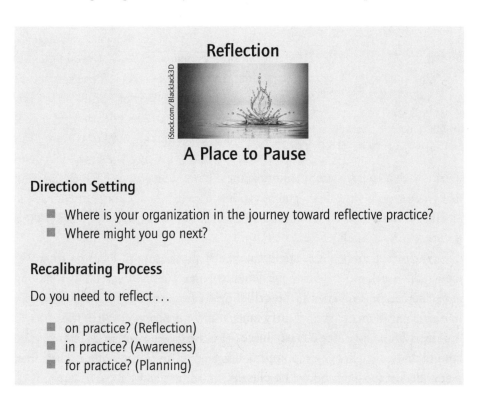

Reflection

iStock.com/BlackJack3D

A Place to Pause

Direction Setting

■ Where is your organization in the journey toward reflective practice?
■ Where might you go next?

Recalibrating Process

Do you need to reflect . . .

■ on practice? (Reflection)
■ in practice? (Awareness)
■ for practice? (Planning)

REFLECTIVE PRACTICE IN ACTION

By reflecting on practices together, teachers gain a collective understanding of each other and of their capacity as a group to effect change. They build collective knowledge—deep understandings about practice—and pass this on as knowledge legacies. We have found that when schools regularly share knowledge and expertise through reflective conversations, the learning is exponential. Excellence is spread throughout the school. The cycle of reflection can start at any point, as each step leads to the next. The point is that the context dictates the type of reflection needed. Over time, it becomes that all-important cycle of reflection.

In our bid to develop knowledge legacies, we have also begun to think in terms of building learning histories, often oral and sometimes written. The questions that focus on what has been learned from reflection almost always elicit a level of "layered complexity." By *layered complexity*, we mean a multifaceted, rich description of how this reflection fits into practice, or a provocative question that pushes at the group to seek a coherent understanding.

With the advent of professional learning communities (PLCs), we have found that asking explicitly about what has been learned during the PLC meeting is essential. We measure the success of each conversation by the value it adds to teaching practices and find that these types of questions are invaluable for calibration of the success of a conversation. Essentially, we are asking this: How will this conversation make a difference in professional work? What is important to remember, and how will it deepen practices?

> According to David Perkins, "Learning is a consequence of thinking." Here is our corollary to that: Thinking is a consequence of questions that emerge out of our own innate desire to learn.

As David Perkins said in *Smart Schools* (1992, p. 31), "Learning is a consequence of thinking." Here is our corollary to that: Thinking is a consequence of questions that emerge out of our own innate desire to learn. And we would offer that when groups slow down conversations to authentically listen and engage in an ethic of inquiry, the questions emerge out of our own innate curiosity. That is the secret of engagement.

When teachers begin to appreciate the fractal nature of learning improvements, they seek more diverse ways to challenge the knowing–doing–learning gap. They are emboldened to find their own paths and communicate a collective efficacy. In this environment, teachers self-organize and collaborate on real problems of practice. Instead of mandated grade-level meetings, they organize around mutual challenges and seek understanding from each other. They trust that collective wisdom brings clearer understanding and increased capacity to respond adaptively in the classroom. Adaptive teachers are conscious and purposeful in choosing from a repertoire. They grow in the capacity to learn, and instead of being left behind, they shine a torch toward the future.

In conclusion, the process of collaborative reflective inquiry has great potential to change professional habits. There are many definitions of *reflection*, all of which date back to Dewey's (1933) definition: "active, persistent, and careful consideration of any belief or supposed form of knowledge in the light of the grounds that support it and the further conclusion to which it tends" (p. 9).

In each of the next nine chapters, we offer a minimum of two learning scenarios, with the idea that stories provide important narratives that help us remember. Scenario 1 is always a story that demonstrates a dyad or small group at work; Scenario 2 will always be about how to work with a larger group. On occasion, we'll offer a Final Note, which will offer an additional process that we have used based on this particular conversational pattern.

SCENARIO 1

This reflection comes from a special education supervisor who was working with a teacher who was struggling with classroom management. During the reflective conversation with her supervisor, the teacher explored what *was* and *was not* working. Through the reflective inquiry, the teacher discovered an inner tension; she had assumed that her main job was to teach and not to manage behaviors, yet she was spending all her time managing behaviors. As the teacher grappled with this tension, she decided she needed to spend less time on behavior management, so she needed some new strategies. Together, the teacher and supervisor brainstormed ways to intervene. They listed intervention strategies that took fewer than thirty seconds to implement and then sequenced the list from most promising to least promising, providing a layered action plan.

One month later, the teacher beamed and reported, "That thirty-second rule helped me change my behavior in the moment, and that has made all the difference." The supervisor smiled, excited to note how the teacher was reflecting and changing behaviors based on student responses. For the observation on that day, the teacher asked the supervisor to collect specific data on her interactions with two students. Afterward, they laughed as they reviewed the data: Both students had been on task and engaged—gone were the behaviors of a month ago. The teacher said, "So can we focus on another question I have about my teaching?" She was now seeking reflective conversations as a regular part of her growth and development.

SCENARIO 2

During her second year as principal, Diane's superintendent reminded her he needed a nomination for the teacher of the year. Fortunately, the teacher Diane wanted to nominate warned Diane that this was a "hot topic" for this staff. It turns out that years ago, these teachers had agreed to never single out just one teacher—after all, they were all excellent. Realizing that there were deeper issues, Diane missed the superintendent's deadline but resolved that when she had a chance, she would engage the staff in a reflective conversation about the assumptions behind this decision to opt out of a district program.

When they had some extra time on an agenda, Diane used a reflection-on-action conversation to focus on an assumption check to get at beliefs and values. She went into the conversation with no preconceived expectations. To begin, Diane started the conversation with a simple statement of facts: The superintendent expected her to make a recommendation that spring for the teacher of the year program, and she needed to better understand how the school wanted to respond to the superintendent's request. As she explained, if she was going to say no, she needed to have some good reasons for why. (Notice that Diane was also asking these teachers to self-author a future they were willing to support.)

Diane's inquiries focused on the underlying assumptions behind their beliefs and what the other teachers thought of these assumptions. For example, early in the conversation it became evident that the award was not considered an honor and that at most schools the teachers took turns receiving the honor. These teachers believed that an honor should be given for honorable behaviors. Much to Diane's surprise, the group said they loved to be appreciated, but only when it was for specific things they had done well. For example, the superintendent at that time often sent personal notes to teachers, thanking them for things they had done, and they all treasured those notes. They had no problem with recognition if it was specific and for something that was worthy of recommendation. And if Diane would only recommend when she had a teacher worthy of that honor, they would participate. Diane laughs, "I should have known this. If this school had a fault, it was their high standards. Not only were they known for setting high standards with kids, but they had set them for themselves."

As Diane looks back, this conversation was a pivotal one in changing the school culture. What made the difference was not that Diane asked them to comply, but that she asked them to think deeply about what they believed and to develop a way of informing the superintendent about those beliefs. Even though the solution put the pressure on Diane to make a selection, Diane almost always had a teacher who had gone above and beyond, and when she checked in with the leadership team, they always agreed. What also surprised Diane was that some of her teachers who had seemed the least reflective about other topics were the most reflective and thoughtful about this conversation. It reminds us: Not all conversations are created equally, and not all conversations are of equal value. In fact, those who normally do not speak up often have the most nuanced responses.

A FINAL NOTE—A PROCESS TO ENGAGE IN REFLECTIVE PRACTICE

The School Culture Reflection tool reproduced at the end of this chapter is from Bill's book, *Reflective Practice for Renewing Schools* (York-Barr et al., 2016, p. 3). Bill quickly adapted this to use as a focus for group reflection in his staff meetings. Any one of these questions could be slightly reworded and would be worthy of a whole-school inquiry.

A Possible Staff Meeting Adaptation

Choose at least two of these questions and ask participants to complete a quick write at the end of a meeting. Between meetings, tabulate the data and bring it to the next meeting for a reflecting conversation. By having a wide variety of viewpoints, it opens the discussion quickly and breaks down barriers of distrust. At the end of the reflecting conversation, have the teachers reflect on the process with these questions:

- How were our discussions pertinent to teaching and learning?
- How do structures and processes support reflection during the meeting?
- What evidence do you have that we either listened well or not so well?
- How did we make our learning explicit and visible to the group today during the meeting?
- How are we growing in the desire to create a culture of openness and inquiry?
- Inquiry—What are the questions we want answers to? What data do we have now that is relevant? What data do we need that we do not have?
- Insight—Are there knowledge and skills that we need not found in the school? What observations from experienced staff can be useful? Where else can we gain insights?
- Action—What actions can we take that we think will answer the questions and help staff and students? What leading indicators will tell us we are on the right track?
- Results—What will be the assessment plan? If the plan is working or part of the plan is working, how do we scale it up or let people know about the results? If the plan is not working, what are some alternatives that we might try, and how will we let people know so they do not waste valuable time?

When a team takes time to answer these questions, they can then return to them later to assess how the reflective conversations are going and to determine if they are meeting expectations or need to be adjusted in some way to better serve the group or school.

School Culture Observation Tool: Casual Observation of Teaching and Learning in School

---

Walking, Watching, Listening, Learning: A Menu of Questions to Guide Casual Observations of Teaching and Learning in School

Before starting your walk, (1) clarify for yourself a particular purpose or focus for your casual observation; and (2) skim questions on this tool, highlighting items aligned with your particular areas of interest.

> Observation Focus: I want to learn more about . . .

Guiding Questions—Some Possibilities to Consider

In Classrooms

Who is doing most of the talking: adults or students?

Are all students receiving "first best instruction" in their home class?

Do students seem clear about what and how they are learning? How do you know?

To what extent are learning rituals and practices in place for student engagement?

When teachers introduce new material, do they model practices expected of students?

What do you see and hear that affirms students' race and cultures, including home languages?

In what ways do students talk with each other to make sense of their work?

Who receives high levels of attention from the teacher and for what purposes?

As students work, in what ways are effort and perseverance reinforced?

In Meetings

Are meeting purposes pertinent to teaching and learning?

Are meeting purposes clarified and additional priorities invited for considerations?

Is a guiding question used to move participants to the present and to hear each voice?

In what ways do members reflect on connections between teaching practice and student learning?

When current instructional routines and practices are not resulting in growth or success for particular students, how do team members think together about ways to improve?

Overall, how reflective and generative is the "conversational space"?

To what extent do structures and processes support reflection and deliberation?

Is it apparent that members listen well and are respectful of other perspectives?

When decisions are made, what types of follow-up actions are generated and agreed on?

In what ways do meetings conclude such that learning is made visible, collective work is affirmed, and follow-up is agreed on?

Overall, was a conversational culture of openness and inquiry about practice present and supported?

Chapter 5

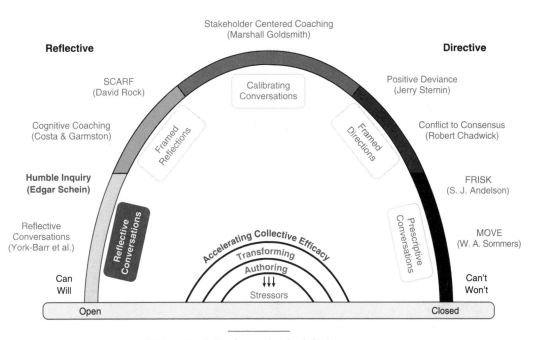

Reflective

Directive

Stakeholder Centered Coaching
(Marshall Goldsmith)

SCARF
(David Rock)

Calibrating
Conversations

Positive Deviance
(Jerry Sternin)

Cognitive Coaching
(Costa & Garmston)

Framed
Reflections

Framed
Directions

Conflict to Consensus
(Robert Chadwick)

**Humble Inquiry
(Edgar Schein)**

FRISK
(S. J. Andelson)

Reflective
Conversations
(York-Barr et al.)

Reflective
Conversations

Accelerating Collective Efficacy

Transforming

Authoring

↓↓↓

Stressors

Prescriptive
Conversations

MOVE
(W. A. Sommers)

Can
Will

Can't
Won't

Open

Closed

Urban Luck Design, urbanluckdesign.com

HUMBLE INQUIRY—
EXPLORING NEEDS
INSTEAD OF HELPING

*Be self-accountable for your own reactions and nonjudgmental
about others' reactions.*

—Carol Sanford

Edgar Schein—professor emeritus from MIT Sloan School of Management—
who in his pioneering role defined *organizations* as "cultures" and was a
great mentor to us. It seems odd today, but when we both started teaching, no one talked about school culture; now forty years later, information on
school culture pervades the leadership development literature. As Peter Block
says in the acknowledgments of his book *Flawless Consulting* (2011), "All of
us who consult today owe a debt of gratitude to the work of Ed Schein" (p.
xxii). In the rest of this book, we refer to the agent of action as the coach, the
facilitator, or the catalyst. In this chapter when describing Humble Inquiry, we
use Schein's term *consultant* because that is the word from which this wisdom emerged. Schein learned that just that word alone—*consultant*—caused
problems, as others expected him to be expert and were willing to defer to his
expertise. The problem is that other people's solutions are never as efficacious
as the ones we author ourselves.

As mentioned in the Introduction and in Chapter 3, we had the pleasure of
working directly with Edgar Schein on two occasions. In Chapter 3, we introduced Schein as a wise human who personified the self-transforming level of
development. To understand the transforming perspective, one need only to pick
up Schein's books. In *Humble Inquiry* (2013), his goal is to establish an ethic
of inquiry in order to understand underlying assumptions and beliefs, which
define the cultures we work in. He often begins his consultations with the

simple question, "What do you have in mind?" In *Humble Consulting* (2016), he emphasizes the importance of understanding the right goals before moving to solutions. As he explains, expert consultants, in their zeal to help, offer solutions that are neither needed nor wanted and are then surprised later by limited follow-through. In *Helping* (2009), Schein acknowledges the importance of setting the relationship on equal footing—hence, the term *Humble Inquiry.*

BENEFITS OF HUMBLE INQUIRY

Schein advocates for Humble Inquiry as a way to reduce stress and build the organizational capacity for cross-cultural teamwork. By engaging in Humble Inquiry, each person learns about the self and the other. Subsequently, with this dual understanding, the participants are better able to negotiate meanings and learn from diverse perspectives. Only by paying attention to personal reactions can one set them aside and become fully present; and only then can the diverse perspectives of the other be appreciated. "Humble Inquiry is the fine art of drawing someone out, of asking questions to which you do not already know the answer, of building a relationship based on curiosity and interest in the other person" (Schein, 2013, p. 2).

> "Humble Inquiry is the fine art of drawing someone out, of asking questions to which you do not already know the answer, of building a relationship based on curiosity and interest in the other person." — Schein

Schein argues that the Western world has a bias for task completion, and he challenges us to reexamine this emphasis. Take a moment to reflect on your own experiences. How often do participants rush through an agenda with the goal of getting it done? Schein would argue that this is the wrong goal and that task completion shortchanges thinking. Humble Inquiry opens up space for groups to explore the right kinds of questions, which also improves the quality and efficiency of the communication. Box 5.1 lists some questions to strengthen the ethic of inquiry.

In Cognitive Coaching, we have long valued the ethic of inquiry and understood the value of staying in inquiry for extended periods to generate thoughtful actions. To stress the power of inquiry, we often tell the story of Isidor Rabi, the 1944 winner of the Nobel Prize for Physics. After winning this prize, Rabi told audiences, "I don't think I am smarter than others; I just know how to ask good questions." He credits his mother with this

> "I don't think I am smarter than others; I just know how to ask good questions."
> —Isidor Rabi

Box 5.1 Humble Inquiry—Strengthening the Ethic of Inquiry

- How can I learn to listen instead of talk?
- How can I ask more open-ended questions?
- When can I make the time to connect with others this week?
- How can I humbly inquire about what they need, want, and think?
- How can I practice the behaviors of asking and listening to learn something new?
- How can I practice sharing and transparency before we need it (in a crisis)?
- What would they most like to tell me? What would be vital to know?

habit of mind. When he came home from school each day, she would not ask the expected question—What did you learn in school today? Instead, she would ask, "Izzy, what good questions did you ask in school today?" By living in the question, Rabi went on to develop radar, which changed the course of World War II and human communication networks.

Likewise, Schein suggests extended inquiry as the essential step for first framing the problem and then finding the best solution. Schein's conversational frameworks are best used for complex issues, in which a school may have unstated but conflicting values and beliefs. In Scenario 2 at the end of this chapter, Diane describes how she used a similar strategy to deal with a potentially contentious curriculum challenge that centered on racial prejudices.

HUMBLE INQUIRY

For the uninitiated, basic Humble Inquiry questions seem deceptively simple. Their simplicity is what makes them so powerful. To make this point, Schein (2013) tells this story. At a meeting, the participants complained that the two-hour meeting was disorganized and, as a result, was too long and substantive issues were not addressed. Schein finally asked the question, "Where did this agenda come from?" The answer? "The executive's secretary."

Schein then asked the secretary to join the meeting and asked her how she developed the agenda. She said she put down the items in the sequence they were given to her. She did not have the knowledge of how to prioritize. It turned out that the appointed chair had paid no attention to the priority or the time needed for different items; he simply followed her typed agenda. This chair now knew he needed to take time to organize the agenda. How many procedures endure because no one asks a question or challenges the process? Box 5.2 holds the inquiry process Schein followed.

Box 5.2 Basic Humble Inquiry—Simple but Elegant

- What is going on here?
- What would be the appropriate thing to do?
- On whom am I dependent in order to act?
- Who is dependent on me?
- With whom do I need to build a relationship in order to improve communication?

Schein reminds us that humility is a lifelong goal by reflecting upon his own behavior. He often shares about a time when his daughter came to his study to ask a question, and he responded by telling her she was interrupting his work. He didn't give his daughter a chance to explain what she wanted, and she left crying. His wife came to tell him that his daughter just wanted to know if he wanted a cup of coffee. We can probably relate to this story because we've have done similar things—making assumptions, not clarifying the issue, and then feeling guilty later. The moral is this: Slowing down, paying attention, and asking a simple question are such simple acts, yet they require great humbleness. On the other hand, with questions, the other responds differently. Questions are an invitation to contribute. Humble questions create a feeling that what is being discussed has not been finalized and that your contribution is useful.

Humble Inquiry is necessary if we want to build a relationship beyond rudimentary civility. The complex adaptive issues of today require a dedication to Humble Inquiry so that communication can occur across status boundaries. It is only by learning to be more humble that we can build up the mutual trust needed to work together and open up communication. These kinds of questions also begin to build knowledge coherence—an appreciation for both similarities and differences. The group gets smarter as a result of the work.

STOP TELLING, START ASKING

Another barrier to Humble Inquiry is what Schein calls the "culture of TELL." We expect our leaders to be knowledgeable, and they want to be perceived in that way. As a result, they fall back into the "telling" trap, and the culture becomes dependent on the knowledge of a few. People also quit thinking on their own because the answer will be forthcoming from the person with positional power. Knowing the answer, or certainty, is a trap that devalues the use of inquiry. Indeed, inquiry and directing behaviors are diametrically opposing concepts. As Schein reminds us, when appointed leaders are not careful, they offer help that is not desired or useful. Instead, the goal of a consultant should always be first and foremost to find out what is on the group's mind—what are the issues they are dealing with, and what support do they need to move forward to make the situation better?

> When Schein stopped telling and started asking, he discovered that most people could solve their own problems. As those he worked with gained confidence in their own skills, they were less willing to defer to the consultant.

When Schein stopped telling and started asking, he discovered that most people could solve their own problems. As those he worked with gained confidence in their own skills, they were less willing to defer to the consultant. He found that beginning with inquiry served to level the playing field; now both parties were equals in seeking out the best solutions. Schein cautions that appointed leaders must continually work to create equal, reciprocal relationships. He observes that humility comes easily for those of lower status, as they often look up to a boss. When working with peers or superiors, however, it is easy to slip and take charge, forgoing humility. Humility has a palpable quality; it is felt when another engages in the simple act of paying deep attention, listening, and asking questions from a point of curiosity. Humility contributes to the subtle form of awe that emerges when we experience the joy of learning in community.

PROBLEM-FOCUSED HUMBLE INQUIRY

Many solutions are multifaceted and not just technical. Heifetz (1994) reminds us that complex problems need more "adaptive solutions." The process of finding solutions is about multiplicity of options and long-term strategies rather than the one problem/one solution mindset displayed in the circus game "Whack-a-Mole." Box 5.3 contains another simple but elegant set of questions designed to consider a problem.

Box 5.3 Problem-Focused Humble Inquiry

- Tell me about what you have in mind.
- Why do you want to do that?
- What problem are you trying to solve?
- How is what we are doing really helping?

These questions open up groups in ways often not thought possible. When groups realize they can author their own futures, the topics are endless. The key here is to introduce this problem-focused inquiry and then let groups learn how to self-organize with these open-ended questions as starting places. When Diane first became a principal, her teachers told her, "Do not schedule grade-level meetings—they are a waste of time." Diane was puzzled, but let it go for the moment. Within the year, teachers were scheduling their own grade-level meetings; as it turned out, they were fine with grade-level meetings as long as they got to set the agenda on "what they had in mind." In the past, grade-level meetings had been mandated with no attention to content.

What If We Are the Problem?

While asking, "What is on your mind?" often opens the conversation to topics and problems that really matter, Schein found one topic was often avoided— groups rarely reflect on their own behavior. In his humble way, Schein developed a reflection-in-action strategy to go directly to the heart of the situation. His simple question, "What is going on right now?" asks the group to look at their own behaviors in the moment. Initially, groups can struggle with this question. For example, a common dysfunctional behavior for groups is when the conversation splinters and only a few—typically three or four—are doing all the talking. This is a perfect time to ask this question and then to wait for just one person to speak up. For example, when asked, a participant might say, "I think we were done with this conversation five minutes ago." Usually, this is enough to get others to also give their perceptions, and once this happens, others will weigh in. The focus and responsibility shift back to the entire group.

Just asking "What is happening here?" turns the question toward a reflective pause; see Box 5.4 for more ideas.

Box 5.4 Process-Oriented Humble Inquiry—A Reflection-in-Action

- What is happening right now?
- How is this conversation meeting, or not meeting, our mutual goals?
- Anything else we should say about this?

Additional inquiries to probe further, depending upon the situation:

- How is it that we are responding defensively?
- Have I offended you in some way? How is that?
- What should I be asking now?
- Are we OK, or do we need to talk more?

In the end, the goal is to find out: (1) what the other is worried about, (2) what are the immediate and long-term problems that need to be addressed, and (3) what do they see as the preferred future.

This conversation does require a willingness to set aside egos and enter the Humble Inquiry arena. Once again, it is a powerful tool for transcending awkward or difficult conversations. In the end, the goal is to find out: (1) what the other is worried about, (2) what are the immediate and long-term problems that need to be addressed, and (3) what do they see as the preferred future. This process can go a long way in producing better outcomes for the individual learner and the organization as a whole.

RELATIONSHIP TRAPS

Despite a leader's best intentions to engage in Humble Inquiry, "relationship traps" will interfere. Schein spent a career developing seven organizational principles and watching leaders struggle with their own needs for helping. Out of this learning, he developed the principles of Humble Inquiry, which are an antidote to relationship traps and are listed in Table 5.1.

All too often, it is easy to slip into a codependency. Professionals who need approval for even little actions are not secure in their own thinking and can also trap others in codependency. Diane reflects, "Initially, it feels good to help another person. But when they become dependent upon you and you realize how much time they take, you begin to try to avoid them." Instead of codependency, the goal of Humble Inquiry is coauthoring a future that benefits all.

Table 5.1 Schein's Principles of Humble Inquiry and Their Corresponding Relationship Traps

Principles of Humble Inquiry	Relationship Traps
Principle 1: Effective help occurs when both giver and receiver are ready.	Believing that the other person wants help; dispensing wisdom prematurely
Principle 2: Effective help occurs when the relationship is perceived to be equitable.	Creating dependence by taking on the problem
Principle 3: Effective help occurs when the helper is in the proper helping role.	Deciding to reassure rather than inquire
Principle 4: Everything you say or do determines the future of the relationship.	Stereotyping or projecting values on the other
Principle 5: Effective helping starts with pure inquiry.	Having an a priori or a fixed expectation
Principle 6: It is the learner who owns the problem.	Meeting defensiveness with more pressure
Principle 7: You never have all the answers.	Believing that some know more than others

Reflection

iStock.com/Blacklack3D

A Place to Pause

The Humble Consultant

- How has Schein's wisdom changed your own thinking?
- What move might you take to start a journey into Humble Inquiry?
- Who are role models in your life for the humble way of life?
- What can you learn from them?

HUMBLE INQUIRY IN ACTION

Humility is required for learning. Humility signals "I don't know, but am curious to find out how or what others know." Humble people are positive, productive team members. Think about it—if you already know everything, what's the point of a conversation? Schein suggests that the helper's role is to keep the process open to inquiry. Here are some other thoughts about staying in Humble Inquiry:

- Slow down and ask what is on the other's mind.
- Explore the relationship to understand assumptions and beliefs.
- Ask questions that require explanations and expand the information flow.
- Ask for examples to clarify general statements and push thinking.
- Resist the urge to jump in and provide answers.
- Listen intently and frame questions from a stance of curiosity.
- Stay open to questions—no one question is ever the right question.

To make the point about how questions communicate different intentions, Schein (2013) contrasts confrontational questions with open-ended questions, as shown in Table 5.2. We have also added the relationship traps embedded in confrontational questions.

In conclusion, Schein is a true learning pioneer. He has created an enduring knowledge legacy. Not only did he reflect deeply on his own professional work, but he transformed his thinking as a result of this deep reflection. The insight was so profound that he spent a lifetime imparting his wisdom through his teaching and writing.

Table 5.2 Schein's Humble Inquiry Responses to Confrontational Questions

Confrontational Question	Relationship Trap	Humble Inquiry	Elicits
"Did that make you angry?"	Projecting values on other	"How did that make you feel?"	Feelings and reactions
"Do you think they sat that way because they were scared?"	Having a priori or fixed expectations	"Why do you suppose they sat that way?"	Causes and motives
"Why didn't you say something to the group?"	Meeting defensiveness with more pressure	"What did you do?"	Actions
"Were the others in the room surprised?"	Projecting values on others	"How did the others react?"	Shared systems and situations

SCENARIO 1

A key element in Humble Inquiry is the setting aside of personal judgments in order to fully attend to and maintain equity in the relationship. This is because the act of judging splits the attention away from the other and toward internal thinking. Indeed, most humans notice intuitively when another's intentions are no longer mutual, and the protective mechanisms described in Chapter 3 begin to set in. So in this scenario, we offer a counterexample, as it best explains both the traps that limit Humble Inquiry and the dilemmas of "helping."

This particular example offers a key to how to use the knowledge gained within this book. All of these conversations can be mixed and matched, and Humble Inquiry is perhaps the single best strategy when we as leaders find ourselves in a relationship trap or limited by our internal judgments of the other. Any time a participant views his or her ideas as superior, it is a signal to move to Humble Inquiry.

A fourth-grade special education teacher has agreed to be coached by a team of administrators who are practicing their coaching skills. Diane had asked this teacher to volunteer, as the teacher is not only skilled but also highly reflective. As mentioned in Chapter 4, reflective practitioners are well able to talk in detail about what they know and are coming to know. They often are self-supervising. Diane thought this would be a great first immersion into coaching for these novice coaches.

The problem arose when the lead coach was not clear on his own intentions. Early on in the planning conference, it became evident he did not understand the teacher's lesson. Instead of asking more questions (the humble path to understanding), he began judging her lesson and assumed her lesson needed fixing. He completely missed the point of the lesson and instead focused on his confusion about a complex behavior management program that used checkbooks as a reward system. Instead of clarifying his own ignorance, he shifted to judgment and assumed she needed help, which she of course did not need or want. Fortunately for the teacher, the bell rang, and it was time to teach.

To the visiting coach's surprise, the students had no difficulty with the routines related to the checkbooks, and the teacher swiftly moved on to the lesson she had planned for the day. After the lesson in the reflection conference, the visiting coach complimented the teacher on how well the students performed the checkbook exercise. He then tried to coach her on the actual lesson, which had not been discussed previously and so limited his ability to stay nonjudgmental. This advice is reminiscent of Schein: Remember—as coaches, we don't know what is on the other person's mind unless we ask. We would add that as coaches—unless we engage in both planning and reflection conversations—we do not know what the teacher needs or wants in the way of help. In this example, the visiting coach's own limitations reduced the potential of the coaching opportunity. Later when Diane checked in with the teacher, the teacher responded, "I thought it would be like your coaching—you always listen." Diane sim-

> Remember—as coaches, we don't know what is on the other person's mind unless we ask.

ply apologized for the ignorance of the administrator, and the story became part of the lore about the arrogance of some administrators.

SCENARIO 2

Diane reflects on a process she put teachers through years ago, well before she could call it Humble Inquiry. An African American parent had challenged a sixth-grade anchor text in which an Afro-Caribbean man saves a shipwrecked Caucasian boy. From the Caucasian perspective, it is a story of redemption in that the boy transcends his prejudice and loves his black savior. The boy's character is the central theme of the book and is well developed. The African Caribbean man is portrayed as a grizzled, one-dimensional man who is only focused on helping the boy. The complaint from the parent centered on the lack of character development of the minority person. Not only was the character of this man devalued and narrow, but his patronizing way was a weak role model for her own daughter—the lone African American student in this predominately Caucasian school.

Diane knew that for teachers these book choices were sacred and that any challenge to these choices were often greeted by emotional, defensive behaviors. This challenge was even more problematic because of the overlay of the racial tensions and a mandate from the superintendent that the school address questions raised by the minority community directly. Diane was working on her PhD at the time and realized that this was a great opportunity to conduct a microaction research project on how literature themes impact students; however, before starting on this journey with her teachers, Diane decided to engage in the ethic of inquiry to help develop a productive path for studying the issues.

Diane started the discussion with her teachers with two open ended-questions that focused on the existing belief systems: (1) What do we know about this book? and (2) How does our Caucasian perspective shape our knowing? It turns out the teachers loved to read this book with their sixth graders because they thought it transcended racism.

Diane then asked, "What do we know about how this book shapes the African American perspective?" This question stopped the group cold. They realized the only information they had was from the student's mother, so they asked to see her letter again. This was the breakthrough. The student's teacher became particularly vocal in support of the student viewpoint after considering the mother's words: "My sixth-grade daughter is extremely shy and, as the only African American student in the classroom, does not feel comfortable speaking up about her own viewpoints." The teachers were fascinated and wanted to know more. This opened the door for the action research project that focused on the colonizing themes found in this and other books used as anchor texts.

While this example did not draw from Schein's *Humble Inquiry* (the book had not yet been written), the example describes how powerfully a humble approach can open doors for robust conversations about sensitive ideas, values, and beliefs. The interesting thing for Diane was that once the teachers had this discussion, the debate was gone. Not one teacher was in favor of using this book as an anchor text in the future. Diane says,

> As I look back on this, the words of Schein ring true. If I had taken another path, the teachers would have focused on their problem, which was who controls the curriculum, and completely missed the opportunity to learn from this parent. The problem was elegantly framed by the mother, but without taking time to thoughtfully consider her insights, we would have solved the wrong problem.

As we look back over our careers, we wonder how many other times we hid behind policies in an attempt to solve our problem and didn't listen to the stakeholders.

A FINAL NOTE—THE QUICK INTERVENTION

Here, we offer an example of how Humble Inquiry can be used in the moment to shift the work of a group toward more productive ends. Working in the district office required Bill to sit through many a meeting that spent too much time on the "killer Bs": budgets, buses, and boundaries. At an appropriate time in a meeting, Bill reflected, "What is going on here? I am wondering what is really on our minds, what really matters to us." It was as if a dam broke, and everyone started talking about the real issues of educating students, particularly students who were not thriving. Looking at the district mission posted on the wall, Bill again wondered, "What is going on here? How have we forgotten our mission that focuses on student learning?" He was met with silence. Then he asked, "What do we really want to spend time in meetings doing?" Answers were not forthcoming, and time was up. But the gift was that these questions caused the key leader to reflect on his agendas and to set aside quality time to talk about learning and teaching.

Chapter 6

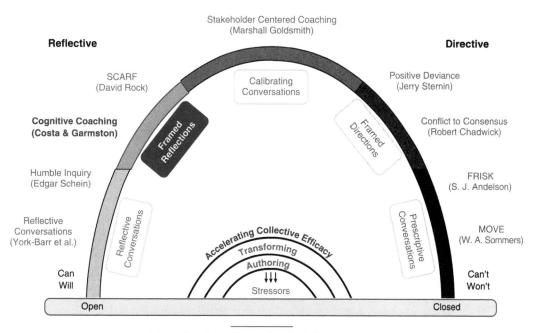

Reflective   Stakeholder Centered Coaching
(Marshall Goldsmith)   Directive

SCARF
(David Rock)

Calibrating
Conversations

Positive Deviance
(Jerry Sternin)

**Cognitive Coaching
(Costa & Garmston)**

Framed
Reflections

Framed
Directions

Conflict to Consensus
(Robert Chadwick)

Humble Inquiry
(Edgar Schein)

FRISK
(S. J. Andelson)

Reflective
Conversations
(York-Barr et al.)

Reflective
Conversations

Accelerating Collective Efficacy

Transforming

Authoring

↓↓↓

Stressors

Prescriptive
Conversations

MOVE
(W. A. Sommers)

Can
Will

Can't
Won't

Open   Closed

Urban Luck Design, urbanluckdesign.com

6

COGNITIVE COACHING— LINGERING IN CONVERSATIONS TO LEARN

Fight the temptation to "know" and instead work to become curious about what the group "knows."

—Micah Jacobson, *Open to Outcome*, 2004

Over thirty years ago during the formative years of Cognitive Coaching, we were invited, along with others, to join Art Costa and Bob Garmston to form a collective partnership to support the development of Cognitive Coaching in schools. While Cognitive Coaching was originally conceived of as a one-on-one coaching cycle, the emphasis was always on communication skills, such as building trust, listening through the paraphrase, and building a culture of inquiry. Early in our collaboration, those of us working in schools observed how powerful these communication skills were for shifting school cultures from scarcity and limitation to abundance and reflection. This work challenged us to not only perfect communication strategies but to also build communities for reflection. We talked often about how to grow schools as "homes for the mind"—how to build cultures of inquiry.

As conceived of by its founders, Cognitive Coaching was about changing thinking, not about changing behaviors. This meant that rather than giving technical advice, often a common aspect of coaching, we taught others how to inquire into the thinking processes. In this respect, this work is similar to Edgar Schein's. The goals are not to fix another person, but rather to build trust to ensure learning and to encourage autonomy and self-reflection. This requires that the coach or facilitator set aside personal agendas in order to seek possibilities generated by the others. This means that the coach needs to stay open to outcome. This ability to set aside personal solutions and to become curious about possible outcomes allows agendas to unfold. This ability to take a neutral stance and be of service to another or a group is central to our work as cognitive coaches and the thesis of this book. We are not advocating fixing others, but rather opening up pathways for others to find their own best solution. We seek schools where this open access to human thinking changes school culture.

We seek schools where this open access to human thinking changes school culture.

DEDICATED TO PROCESS—PLANNING AND REFLECTION CONVERSATIONS

Process matters and determines the outcome of conversations. Each of the conversations in this book describes how changes in process can tip the outcome ever so slightly and yet make huge differences. As cognitive coaches, we teach communication strategies for trust building and how to build inquiry cycles designed to open up deep thinking about teaching and learning. The job of the coach is to listen, paraphrase, and ask questions designed to explore intentions and expectations, as well as actions. We learned to linger in a conversation until we can discern a shift in thinking. These shifts, always accompanied by a change in posture or prosody, give powerful clues to the coach that indeed this "thinking out loud in public" brings new insights. We labeled this moment the *cognitive shift*.

The core conversations of Cognitive Coaching—planning and reflecting conversations—focus specifically on goal setting and attainment. These types of conversations are important for any type of performance art, such as teaching, facilitating meetings, or leadership actions. Planning and reflection conversations extend the reflection for–in–on practice to deeper levels. These conversations raise consciousness and invite introspection and work equally well with one-on-one coaching for group planning and evaluating.

Most teachers go through a process of planning for and reflecting on instruction; however, these practices vary widely and depend upon the teachers and their own diligence in lesson design and evaluation. No teacher can ever possibly reflect on everything he or she might do in a day, so by definition, this process is selective. As teachers become more skilled, some teaching behaviors become habitual and routinized, and reflection tends to decrease. For this reason, most teachers find the coaching cycle a refreshing reminder about the importance of this type of introspection, which might have been forgotten had they not been coached. We have found that the simple planning and reflection questions embed in the teachers' thinking and become habitual processes for thinking after only a few sessions. These questions become a resource that the enlightened professional can pull from at any time to reflect on practice.

We have worked in the world of coaching for most of our professional careers and, as a result, are discriminating about how to describe the various coaching models. Our obvious bias is to work toward thoughtful reflections about practice.

> While technical coaching can have its place in assuring that a particular way of teaching is being implemented, we find that for most teaching acts, teachers are guided by far more interesting and complex questions about their practices.

While technical coaching can have its place in assuring that a particular way of teaching is being implemented, we find that for most teaching acts, teachers are guided by far more interesting and complex questions about their practices. As mentioned earlier, the simple planning and reflecting conversations are invaluable for quick interventions; however, we find the real work occurs during the longer conversations that we have when we take the time to probe the other's deepest thoughts. There are no shortcuts to thoughtful conversations.

PLANNING CONVERSATION

As stated in Chapter 4, the ethic of inquiry requires that the listener slow down and ask questions to learn more from the other person or to probe from a deep well of curiosity about the topic of focus. A major portion of Cognitive Coaching training focuses on building this ethic of inquiry—that commitment to ask questions that neither person has a preconceived answer for.

In Box 6.1, the thinking prompts of a planning conversation are outlined. For the purposes of this book, we have used slightly different words than found in the training materials. This is partly for brevity and partly to make the questions applicable to both individuals and groups. Take moment to review the key inquiries. Remember the goal is not to get done, but to linger long enough to allow the other person to delve more deeply into his or her own thinking. The linguistic skills of pausing, paraphrasing, and probing further enhance these conversations and are reviewed in more depth later in the chapter. The ethic of inquiry is assumed in that these questions are asked in the spirit of learning more about outcomes and going deeper, not just covering the territory.

> ## Box 6.1 Planning Conversation—Organized Around Four Key Inquiries
>
> - What goals/outcomes have you set? (Goal)
> - What steps will you take to accomplish these goals? (Plan)
> - How will you measure your success? (Criteria)
> - What data might you collect? (Data)

Teachers report that these questions have helped them think specifically about what they want the students to learn and how to begin to collect data as part of the teaching process. It turns out that these questions also require that a teacher step out from behind the overly scripted teacher's manuals, which are part and parcel of the high-stakes testing environment. These simple questions help the teachers pull what is important from these manuals, while encouraging them to include their own expertise. As one teacher put it, "During the first year of our language arts adoption, I was overwhelmed with all the materials. I found that your questions helped me narrow down and focus on what I really wanted from my students."

It turns out that planning conferences have an additional benefit of increasing awareness during teaching by increasing consciousness. The planning conference serves as a mental rehearsal for the lesson, thereby increasing preparedness. Teachers often report that the conversation before the lesson made them much more attuned and observant during the lesson itself—as defined in Chapter 4 as reflection-in-action.

PLANNING AND REFLECTION ARE A CYCLE

In the 1980s when the lines between supervision and coaching were often blurred, some decided that a planning conversation, formerly referred to as the *preconference*, was not necessary. It was during these years that Madeline Hunter first started to quantify elements of effective instruction and many supervisors saw their job as inspection: Was the teacher using the five elements of a lesson plan or not? When the supervisor considered the work that of inspection, he or she considered preconferences a waste of time. The problem with this assumption was that it limited the conversation to technical discussions about how the teacher did or did not meet the expectations. The irony of this is when a teacher was competent, the supervisor often skipped the postconference as well. It was not uncommon to find a note in the mailbox that said, "Great lesson. All five elements of instruction were present. No need for a postconference."

This digression into history points to the heart of the issue still with us today. Reflective practices require conversations. Reflective practices happen when school cultures establish them as a norm for how they do their work. How refreshing it would have been all those years ago if the principal had said, "You have the elements of instruction down, so what else are you thinking about when you plan for instruction?" In the end, teachers in California turned to unions to protect them against the tyranny of such a narrow view of instruction, and in some districts, the Madeline Hunter model was specifically written out of evaluation clauses in contracts. When one person holds a tool that she or he perceives as "the solution," thinking shuts down and defensive behaviors often kick in.

To make the point, in Cognitive Coaching training, we'd tell the story of how one expert marksman gained his reputation. Instead of worrying about hitting the bullseye, he'd shoot and then draw the bullseye, creating a perfect shot every time. He never needed to become a better marksman. While the coach cannot quite hit every bullseye, deciding after the fact what to focus on has the same impact: It shuts down learning.

So we cannot stress enough that these two conversations—planning and reflecting—belong together, not apart. As previously mentioned, reflection can start at any point in the process; however, when these conversations bookend teaching, both conversations are essential. Without one, the other will lose its potency as a reflective tool.

THE REFLECTION CONVERSATION

While the planning conversation is focused on goal setting, the reflective conversation is organized around how humans compare and contrast to evaluate the efficacy of actions. Once again for brevity, the terms here are slightly different than those found in the manual, and the ethic of inquiry is assumed.

Bill found that the simple question frames in Box 6.2 were invaluable to him while working as a high school principal. While out and about campus, it was not uncommon to have to conduct business on the fly. Teachers would often reach out to him for help, and rather than offering his own solutions, he'd often ask them about outcomes and strategies. Instead of asking about lessons, he would ask, "So what happened that raised your concerns?" and then would follow up with "Based on what you observed, what might you try?" While it was not possible to linger while walking the campus, these questions would bring solutions. Even in a three-minute conversation, Bill states, "Teachers would regularly find their own solutions."

> ## Box 6.2 Reflection Conference—Organized to Elicit Reflective Thought
>
> - How did the lesson turn out? (Comparing intentions to impact)
> - What teaching actions supported your successes? (Causal actions)
> - Based on what you observed, what might you try? (Data focus)
>
> or
>
> - What got in the way of your success, and what would you change? (Causal actions)
> - What teaching practices would you change and why? (Evaluation)
> - How might we collect better data to inform your teaching? (Data focus)
> - How would you apply what you are learning to future lessons? (Applications)

LINGERING IN THE CONVERSATION

One of the most significant differences between Cognitive Coaching and other models of coaching is the focus on deep thought. Early in our work, we learned to use inquiry as a way to help others solve problems for themselves. This focus on problem resolution expanded Cognitive Coaching repertoires from a strictly supervisory focus to a model for adaptive change. Cognitive Coaching was our first experience of the power of deep, reflective conversations to change the way we think and also our practices. Teaching, being full of dilemmas, is well suited for this unique, adaptive form of reflection. When teachers come together to think deeply about practices, based on personal understandings and what is learned from others, they report renewal.

A by-product of the listening skills that are taught as part of the Cognitive Coaching process is that they slow down the conversation and open up space for deeper thinking. Important to the coaching process is pausing, paraphrasing, and probing. We find that when a coach uses paraphrasing to communicate understanding, it encourages expanded thought. Often, the response is, "Yes, and another thing I am thinking about is . . ."

Likewise, the act of paraphrasing and inquiry require that both parties slow down and respond in thoughtful ways. When questions are asked from a point of curiosity, they are engaging to both parties. While these conversations can be short, the real value comes when the teachers decide to talk in depth about what they are coming to understand. The value is both the frame and the ability to linger. This learning is so important for the success of all conversations that we explicate it in more detail here and call it *accountable listening*.

ACCOUNTABLE LISTENING EXTENDS AND EXPANDS REFLECTION

> Accountably requires acting with congruence on intentions—in other words, to match intentions to actions.

Accountably requires acting with congruence on intentions—in other words, to match intentions to actions. If we intend to listen, we need to demonstrate that intention.

Accountable listening employs three practices that make listening overt, authentic, and accountable, as summarized in Box 6.3. Because these behaviors are overt, they are also observable; hence, there is never any question about the commitment to listening. Indeed, the commitment to listen is necessary for any of the conversations in this book to be effective. Listening is the true catalyst for all conversations, creating cultures that are authentic and leave personal identities intact.

> ## Box 6.3 Accountable Listening Practices
>
> ▪ Confirming paraphrase—Confirm the commitment to listen deeply by summarizing understandings.
> ▪ Thoughtful pause—Confirm this commitment by taking time to think.
> ▪ Ethic of inquiry—Confirm this commitment by inquiring for learning.

Confirming Paraphrase

The first commitment of accountable listening is to *listen deeply*; this is demonstrated by authentic paraphrases—a restatement of what the listener is coming to understand—sprinkled throughout the conversation. To emphasize, paraphrasing is not the parroting of words, but a statement of what the listener is coming to understand. In order to paraphrase, the listener pays deep attention to the message and often comes to understand nuances that are otherwise missed. Communicating that we understand is one of the most inexpensive and authentic gifts we can ever give another person.

Effective paraphrasing requires deep focus and is a summary of what has been understood in the listener's own words. The paraphrase serves to validate that the listener understood the message. Paraphrases also allow time for clarification;

when the message is not received as intended, the speaker corrects it. Paraphrases take us deeper into the conversation. When humans feel understood, they breathe more deeply, bringing more oxygen to the brain and opening up to deeper reflections. When humans hear their thinking reflected back to them, they feel validated and, as a result, will often add more information. By design, paraphrases elicit more contemplative speech. When paraphrasing is used with regularity, the speaker comes to expect this authentic response and appreciates the way it slows down the conversation by opening up space for thought.

Yet over our thirty-plus years as trainers, we have found some who resist or even refuse to paraphrase. The reasons are varied: it does not feel comfortable, why state what is obvious to me, it seems like overkill to me, and so forth. But when we ask the speakers how they received the paraphrase, the response is overwhelmingly positive—I felt supported, I felt listened to, and so on. Notice that all the reasons for not paraphrasing are about the listener, not the speaker. Time after time, these novice paraphrasers have missed the point—this is not about the listener, but about being of service to the speaker.

Reflection

iStock.com/BlackJack3D

A Place to Pause

- How is accountable listening of service to both the speaker and the listener?
- What is your own relationship with the paraphrase?
- Based on your reflection about your own habits, what would you change?
- How might using paraphrasing change the cadence of your conversations?

What is often not known about paraphrasing is that it is a powerful way to shift conceptual focus toward a more global or detailed way of thinking about something. It turns out that this form of summarizing also helps the listener organize thoughts. For example, when a teacher gave a particularly long paraphrase that detailed student responses, the coach summarized just a few examples and then added, "Cooperative behavior is an important value for you." Adding this label was like turning on a lightbulb for the teacher, and she responded, "Yes, that is exactly what I value—cooperation."

In another example, a teacher was confused by a behavior exhibited by a student. The coach summarized the confusion and then clarified, "So you assume that the behavior was purposeful?" In this case, the teacher thought out loud, "I am not sure about that; sometimes I do and sometimes I don't, so I guess that is why my responses to this student are uneven."

Thoughtful Pause

The second commitment to accountable listening is to take time for *thoughtful pauses*. By this, we mean slowing down the conversation, taking a deep breath, and thinking about what is being learned. This pause gives time for both listener and speaker to really think about the conversation. It gives the listener time to consider when a paraphrase is warranted or perhaps when a question would be more appropriate.

Pausing and paraphrasing go hand in hand. Initially, the listener needs the pause to think about what was heard; then the speaker needs to pause to think about answers. The pause is what gives speech its cadence and shape; it slows down breathing and signals respect for the other person's thoughts. The pause allows group members to move in sync with one another by signaling turn taking or the need to stop and think.

The pause allows time for small reflections, a necessary ingredient in the continuous development of individual and organizational learning capacities. Any teacher who has used Mary Budd Rowe's (1986) strategy of "wait time" knows how important the pause is to support thinking. Rowe found that most teachers do not provide time for students to think after asking a question and that pausing even for just thirty seconds improves student responses. For teaching, coaching, and facilitating, the pause allows for the listener and the speaker to check out each other's response and communicates how to pace the conversation, by allowing time for thought and turn taking in conversations.

Ethic of Inquiry

This ethic of inquiry requires a deep commitment to be of service to the other and to ask authentic questions for which the listener is curious and has no preconceived answer. Questions, when asked from an attitude of curiosity, heighten thinking. Consider a question asked from an expert's agenda: "Why didn't you introduce the vocabulary in the beginning?" This question assumes a correct action and, as a consequence, the answer will be a justification, not an exploration. Consider this question asked out of curiosity: "I am wondering what you might do to assist students with the vocabulary to support your goals." This question invites the other to think out loud about possible solutions.

> This ethic of inquiry requires a deep commitment to be of service to the other and to ask authentic questions for which the listener is curious and has no preconceived answer.

This emphasis on "ethic" reminds us that inquiry is a moral principal—maintaining a respect for the learning of others. Questions deepen intellectual curiosity, and the most powerful questions often shift thinking and become transforming. Questions asked from an authentic point of reference model ethical ways of relating and, as a result, produce ethical behavior in others.

Accountable Listening Assists Groups in Managing Conflicts

Before moving on, we make one more important point. Just the few moves of accountable listening can solve just about any conflict, and it can be done with any group. We know, that might seem preposterous, but consider this example.

A school is just finishing up a presentation on an action research project, and two teachers get into an argument. As part of the study of student engagement in reading, the teacher had allowed small groups of sixth-grade students to select books that he had not reviewed; the librarian was incensed that he would be so lax. They began to argue loudly in front of the entire staff. The facilitator, skilled in the Chadwick model (Chapter 11), interrupted the diatribe and said, "We have a conflict here. Let us make sure we understand the viewpoints." She divided the teachers into two groups and invited each group to work in pairs to summarize one side of the debate; half the teachers paraphrased the teacher and the other half the librarian. This took about four minutes. The facilitator then focused the group on two charts and alternated between putting up the viewpoints for each position. This took another four minutes. Turning to the two in conflict, she asked if anything was missing. They both responded no and were strangely calm; the conflict had evaporated in fewer than ten minutes, and the staff now had consensus on the problem. The facilitator then assigned the task of next steps to the leadership team. They went on with the planned agenda, knowing that follow-through would happen at a later date.

Conflicts invite accountable listening, and when used respectfully, accountable listening almost always reframes a conversation toward productivity. All the conversations in this book assume a commitment to accountable listening. We will delve more deeply into this theme in Chapter 11.

THE COGNITIVE SHIFT

Over the years as coaches, we lingered in the conversations in order to provoke deep thought, and we noticed another phenomenon. When thinking deeply about an issue or problem, it is not uncommon to find a new understanding and a change in mind. The person being coached will often report a small, internal aha moment when her or his thinking shifts to something new or enlightening. For the coach, this change is observable. The person almost always shifts posture or makes an audible sound of approval, and facial features often show a change toward a look of surprise. These changes in body language can be missed, unless the coach learns how to observe and calibrate based on these behaviors. Cognitive shifts demonstrate the power of a thoughtful conversation, which goes deep and accesses our deepest unconscious resources. There is no rushing here. And not only do these conversations offer a chance for authoring, but they are also transforming.

USING THE DISPOSITIONS OF THE STATES OF MIND TO BUILD COLLECTIVE EFFICACY

In the last two chapters, reflection was used as a general way to think on– in–for practice. In Cognitive Coaching, reflection is expanded to help reframe experience from limitations to positive outcomes. Applying the work of cognitive psychologists on reframing, Costa and Garmston (2015) identified five forward filters that shift thinking toward positive outcomes. *Forward filters* are dispositions that focus thought on solutions rather than concerns. In the *National Council for Accreditation of Teacher Education Glossary* (2017), the term *professional disposition* is defined as follows: "Professional attitudes, values, and beliefs demonstrated through both verbal and nonverbal behaviors as educators interact with students, families, colleagues, and communities. These positive behaviors support student learning and development." We know of no other coaching model than Cognitive Coaching that so directly focuses on dispositions for thought and hence works to directly build teacher efficacy.

> We know of no other coaching model than Cognitive Coaching that so directly focuses on dispositions for thought and hence works to directly build teacher efficacy.

These five dispositions, which Cognitive Coaches call "States of Mind," are efficacy, consciousness, flexibility, craftsmanship, and interdependence. In coaching and facilitating, these dispositions are used as a way to expand inquiry toward positive outcomes. Box 6.4 has examples of how these dispositional frames can anchor concepts, shape the inquiry, and foster collective efficacy.

These five mind states are gifts of thinking. They invite searching for a multiplicity of outcomes and are the grist for authoring a life. Like a flashlight,

Box 6.4 Seek Collective Efficacy—Five States of Mind

- **Efficacy:** What *resources* might best assist us?
- **Consciousness:** What are we becoming more *aware* of?
- **Flexibility:** What other *options* should we consider?
- **Craftsmanship:** What *refinements* might support us?
- **Interdependence:** How can *others* support our success?

brightening some areas and leaving others dark, these five filters focus the mind in specific ways. They build positive, solution-oriented states of mind, which move us beyond distracting habits that protect our self-importance and offer ways to consider potential. All humans would benefit from this transformational framework that seeks adaptive, positive outcomes. Each one of us has internal resources we have not used. We all fail to notice signals that would increase awareness or consciousness. Most of us forget to consider options when we rush and would benefit from slowing down and perfecting our craft. And finally, professional allies open up possibilities that we had not considered. These mind states point toward positive futures in which we make choices that support our own growth and development. The true reflective practitioner sees the process of reflecting as self-authoring and delights when these processes become self-transforming.

Reflection

iStock.com/BlackJack3D

A Place to Pause

- Which state of mind might you choose to use to frame opportunities to observe yourself and others?
- Which state of mind might best serve your thinking during teaching and learning?
- How might these five states of mind help you accelerate learning?

This inquiry frame is actually quite complex, and we have found that learning how to use it skillfully takes lots of practice. One way we have accelerated learning is by creating lists of synonyms that can be used by a coach or a group to think about questions to expand thinking for each disposition. When working with groups, we often ask them to consider a problem, consider which state of mind would be the best point of reflection, and then to frame two or three questions to frame the inquiry (see Table 6.1 for more specific details).

Table 6.1 Examples of Questions and Synonyms for States of Mind Inquiry

States of Mind as Thinking Outcomes	Sample Questions	Synonyms
Think about a problem. As you think about this problem, consider the following states of mind:	Soften inquiry with invitational stems (e.g., As you consider, As you think, As you reflect) followed by root questions (e.g., what might you . . . ? or what could you . . . ?).	Other words to embed in questions in order to access a state of mind
Efficacy	What other resources might you seek?	Resources, design, construct, commit, increase capacity, be proactive, act, how can you
Consciousness	What are you becoming more aware of in your own thinking?"	Think, facts, clarify, intend, value, believe, specifically, aware, predict, define, what else
Flexibility	What options would you want to consider?	Options, other ways, in addition, choices, generate, what more
Craftsmanship	How might you tweak our solution to make it even better?	Elaborate, change, apply, explicate, precisely, distinguish, evaluate, craft, how else
Interdependence	How might you seek the support of another to solve this problem?	Relationship, allies, support, appreciate, affirm, relate, empathize, affirm, who else

THE TRANSFORMATIVE ACT OF ASKING YOUR OWN QUESTIONS

While working to train coaches, we were diligent in perfecting inquiry skills and often took groups through lengthy practice sessions. As we grew in our capacity to facilitate change, we realized that the real questions come out of the conversation, not some preconceived notion of pattern. Indeed, one of the most powerful reflective pauses can be to ask the person or group being coached to self-author their own next question by asking, "What questions are you asking yourself now?" Indeed, the cognitive shift is a signal to the coach to get out of the way of the other person's thinking and to simply linger as they explain the shift in thinking.

The questions, which are self-authored, are exactly what are needed. They are real-time questions, not questions forced from a model. Consider this example. A friend was in the middle of coaching another, and he noted that the teacher seemed stuck; the teacher kept lamenting, "These mandates are stifling my creativity." The coach kept thinking that the teacher lacked efficacy and focused his questions on "resources" with questions such as, "What resources have opened up your creativity in the past?" Then the coach finally thought to ask this teacher to self-author the next question; it made all the difference. The coach queried, "So based on what we are talking about, what question might you ask yourself?" The teacher stopped, looked into the distance for what seemed like forever, and then came back to the coach. Something had shifted inside—a cognitive shift moment. The teacher said, "At my other school, I worked on a wonderful team—we did everything together. Now I work with a team that does not like each other, so we do nothing together. The question I am asking myself is, 'Where can I find a team to work with at this school?'" The coach was stunned; he would never have figured out that "interdependence" was the state of mind most needed at this moment. Reflective conversations create reciprocal learning; the learning goes on at all levels of understanding, and conversations that matter produce cognitive shifts for all.

For the purposes of this book, we do not have time to extend this chapter into two other models for reflective practice that have drawn from Cognitive Coaching and from which we have also learned much. The first is summarized in the book *The Adaptive School: A Sourcebook for Developing Collaborative Schools* (2016), articulated by Bob Garmston and Bruce Wellman to describe how the skills of Cognitive Coaching can be applied to group work. They both draw from their rich experience with facilitation groups and offer compendiums of adaptive strategies. The second is the work of Laura Lipton and Bruce Wellman, who have developed advanced processes for conducting learning-focused conversations (miravia.com). Each of these models draws from and reinforces the Cognitive Coaching skill set while adding additional practices from their extensive experience in training others.

SCENARIO 1

This example has been chosen to demonstrate the power of reflective practices to influence all parts of our lives. The story begins with a reflection conversation about a teacher new to special education teaching. The lesson had not gone well. Later, this day would be remembered as one of the worst days of her life.

To the teacher's surprise, the supervisor began with the question, "So how did the lesson go?" Without realizing it, the teacher burst out, "The lesson did not go according to plan!" Two students in particular had been disruptive, and she had entirely left out one of the steps in the plan. In short, the lesson had been disorganized, and as a result, the students had been confused about expectations. As she talked, the teacher started to cry, and between the tears, she explained, "Last night I learned that a friend from college committed suicide. I would have stayed home, but I did not have any way to get lesson plans to the school." (Note: This was before the Internet.)

A month later, the supervisor was back for another conference cycle and observation. In the planning conference, the teacher outlined what she expected to accomplish and was glad to have another opportunity to demonstrate her skills. After the lesson, she didn't even wait for the supervisor to talk; she started out, "If I had to do it over again, I would have asked the students to review the directions before I asked them to move. Once I asked them to move, I had difficulty getting their attention back. Otherwise, I think the lesson went well."

Two months later, the teacher began the reflection conference by saying, "Can I change what I wanted you to look at? I thought that the students would still have some difficulty with my instructions, but they didn't. Now I am asking myself how I can get them more engaged in the tasks." When she was asked to reflect on the year, the teacher responded, "When I did my student teaching, I only wrote plans when I knew I was being watched. I have learned that even if I do not write them down, I need to make plans in my head, and I need to mentally rehearse. If I do not do that, I sometimes forget important steps in my plan." She went onto say that she was much more organized and that her mother had even noticed that she was planning for things in advance.

SCENARIO 2

While working as a superintendent, Diane decided to start a districtwide focus on writing. Rather than going outside to look for expertise, she started with her staff. She invited each school to pick two or three intermediate teachers that would be released to spend a day doing a writing audit. Teachers were instructed to bring anything that helped them explain what they currently used to teach writing.

Diane wanted to approach this session in an open-ended way and knew that as a newcomer to the district she would want to organize the audit as a listening opportunity for herself. She loosely structured the conversation using Cognitive Coaching as the framework. She took the group through the process, using questions to frame current goals and measures of success, stretch goals, and strategies needed. Together, they summarized their collective knowledge and identified gaps in their programs. Here are some of the questions she asked:

- What are the teachers' current goals for an intermediate writing program?
- How do the teachers measure the success of the current writing program?
- What are the stretch goals that teachers are currently working on, and what is keeping them from reaching those goals?
- What are the next action steps you want to take individually?
- What actions steps can the district take to support the teachers in achieving the next steps?

At the end of the day, the teachers had a clear set of outcomes that were needed to build a more robust writing curriculum. They agreed to inform the other teachers at their school what they had learned and to also seek ways to close the gap between existing and desired outcomes.

A few months later, Diane brought these same teachers together to learn about a writing program that one teacher had identified as meeting many of the needs listed earlier in the year. The teachers were so enthused by this opportunity, they insisted on a pretraining so that they could serve as lead teachers the following fall when the entire district would be involved. Diane reflects,

The power of the group to facilitate the change they needed was phenomenal. I could never have imagined the leap forward this group took and how quickly it impacted the entire district. Once again, it reminded me to slow down and really listen. When teachers are honest about what they know and do not know, they find the best path forward.

A FINAL NOTE—A PROCESS OF INQUIRY THAT WILL DEMONSTRATE COGNITIVE SHIFTS

For over twenty years, we have used an *Intervision* process introduced to us by someone from Denmark. Unbeknownst to us, a similar process for problem solving can be found on the Web, with most of the references coming from European sources. Our process is different in that we only ask questions; we do not generate solutions. What we have found is that by asking questions only, we open many more options. We have also found just questions without answers help all focus on how the receiver responds to the question. It is a powerful practice exercise, as those questions that are most valuable to the receiver's thinking show an obvious shift in expression.

The most powerful questions require that the other person break eye contact to think about the answer; it is in this pregnant pause that we notice the change in expressions. We now use this process regularly when working with adults on problems of practice. It demonstrates the power of some questions to make shifts and offers the gift of an unanswered question—which is a question we take away with us and ponder long after the session.

Intervision

We have used this as a warm-up for a meeting, using only one person's problem. At other times we explore up to three people's problems as a way to expand repertoire. It takes about twelve to fifteen minutes per problem. The process is as follows:

- One person sits in front of the group and describes a professional problem, giving a brief description of the problem. The description should be just long enough to frame the problem, telling who, what, when, and where.
- A short period is offered for participants to generate a few clarifying questions to make sure they understand the problem. Limit this time.
- For the Intervision stage, participants pause and write down some questions they might ask about the problem from a point of exploration or curiosity. No embedded suggestions are allowed. (The Five States of Mind questions are invaluable for this process.) The aim is to ask thoughtful questions that will mediate thinking.

■ In pairs, the participants check each other's questions to make sure they come from a point of not knowing—a point of curiosity. If a question has an embedded suggestion, the pairs rework it.

■ The person with the problem sits in a comfortable chair in front of the group, and participants take turns asking the questions. The person with the problem is instructed, "Go internal just long enough to think of the answer, then come back to the group; do not answer the question out loud."

■ One person serves as scribe by writing down the questions as they are asked. As the participants observe the person's response to each question, the scribe notes which questions have impact. This is easily discernable. Questions that do not require much thought, which do not have impact, are quickly answered, and the person returns to the center point, reestablishing eye contact. Questions that have impact, which produce a cognitive shift, require the person to stay in their mind longer and often get a discernable change in body language, maybe even a smile or head nod. When this happens, the scribe notes a star by the question and moves on.

■ Ask the person with the problem to quickly review the questions and tell why some of them had more impact and what his or her thinking is now about the problem.

What the group observes firsthand is how some questions seem to have ready responses and others cause the person to linger in thought longer. The questions are then given to the person with the problem so she or he can reflect on the important ones on her or his own time.

Chapter 7

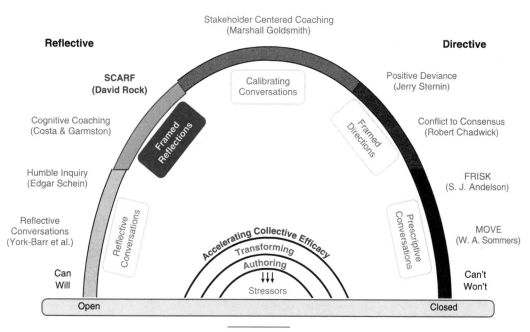

Stakeholder Centered Coaching
(Marshall Goldsmith)

Reflective

Directive

**SCARF
(David Rock)**

Calibrating
Conversations

Positive Deviance
(Jerry Sternin)

Cognitive Coaching
(Costa & Garmston)

Framed
Reflections

Framed
Directions

Conflict to Consensus
(Robert Chadwick)

Humble Inquiry
(Edgar Schein)

FRISK
(S. J. Andelson)

Reflective
Conversations
(York-Barr et al.)

Reflective
Conversations

Prescriptive
Conversations

MOVE
(W. A. Sommers)

Can
Will

Accelerating Collective Efficacy

Transforming

Authoring
↓↓↓
Stressors

Can't
Won't

Open

Closed

Urban Luck Design, urbanluckdesign.com

SCARF–OPEN TO DIVERSE VIEWPOINTS

Strive not to be a success, but rather to be of value.

—Albert Einstein

So far, for the conversations introduced in this book, it is assumed that participants are open and willing to coauthor a common future. As we have mentioned, this requires attention to building trusting relationships. When the stakes are low and of no threat, open-ended conversations appear easy; however, when the stakes are high or the work at hand carries emotional baggage, these open-ended conversations can be frustrated by responses from just one group member.

A friend tells the story about a forty-five-minute productive conversation about setting goals using a variation of the planning and reflection conversation (Chapter 6). Suddenly, one teacher raised his voice and in an angry tone said, "I am sick and tired of this. We have been down this path before; we are just wasting our time talking about how we are going to do this." The group stopped cold and turned to the principal. While it wasn't stated, they were silently asking, "What now, Boss?" Fortunately, this principal could turn to Humble Inquiry. He responded, "So this is not working for you today. What is on your mind?"

Through a few gentle questions, the principal uncovered the real issue, which was *time*. The staff had been discussing a complicated implementation plan that would require teachers to dedicate time to collaboration after school; this teacher was just getting custody of his children and did not want to commit after-school time. His real issue was about autonomy; he needed to be able to do what he had always done to stay efficient and preserve time for his family. His personal motivations were in conflict with the group's. While Humble Inquiry uncovered the motivation, the SCARF model can be invaluable in helping groups better understand each other's unstated motivations.

THE SCARF MODEL

Through coaching and work with groups, David Rock (2010) has identified personal motivations—status, certainty, autonomy, relatedness, and fairness—which he calls *SCARF*. Using results of brain research, Rock described how these five domains activate emotional response systems in the brain—either the primary reward or primary threat system. These two brain circuits reinforce with rewards (positive) or with protective behaviors (negative). In the chapter's introductory example, the negative response was provoked by the threat to this teacher's need for autonomy—control over his non–classroom time.

Interestingly, at the sample meeting there was also a grade-level partner who loved clarity and was getting profound satisfaction from the certainty of a plan, thereby activating her primary reward system—certainty. Initially, she was frustrated, as were others, by the teacher's outburst. However, when she and others learned more about his motivation through the Humble Inquiry process, the threat was reduced. When threat is reduced, groups demonstrate understanding and empathy and work to create possibilities that both acknowledge and honor others' needs.

Much to everyone's surprise, the staff found an amazing solution—this example demonstrates how the underlying motivations of SCARF can both add to and detract from a conversation. It turned out that a small group of teachers wanted to be acknowledged (status) and were willing to take the lead and make sure the after-school collaborations were on-target and focused. It just so happened that the woman who loved certainty was willing to work on implementation and then copartner with her colleague to help him focus on just the essentials. The staff agreed that for the first semester, while he was becoming reacquainted with his own children, he would not have to attend any of the after-school collaborations. They all agreed that this was a fair compromise. Our friend the principal reflects,

> The funny thing was that teacher missed the first collaboration, but once he knew the staff would support him, he did not miss any of the other collaborations. It was a win–win, and I am so glad I could find empathy for him. In the old days, I would have been angry that he had ruined my meeting.

When groups learn to work with these five social domains, they find solutions to group dilemmas that are elegant and sustaining.

This example demonstrates how expanding our conversational repertoire can be particularly useful, especially when emotional responses have the potential to break down communications. The paradox of emotional responses here was that just when one group member got what she wanted (certainty), another lost what he most needed (autonomy). When these emotional reward/threat systems kick in, the behaviors become self-protective (stress response), and if groups are not mindful, the focus on common outcomes can be lost in the power struggle over competing needs. This is often described as a *vicious cycle*, which is a habitual, nonproductive way of communicating. Variations of the vicious cycle are evidenced in most dysfunctional communication.

S–STATUS, C–CERTAINTY, A–AUTONOMY, R–RELATEDNESS, F–FAIRNESS

Each one of the SCARF motivations influences behaviors in slightly different ways and is likely best perceived as an answer to these two questions: How do individuals respond in the face of threat? What motivates individuals to make a particular response?

Status relates to a person's sense of worth based on experience, knowledge, specific skills, or life experiences. When group members don't feel validated or noticed, they seek status as a way of triggering the reward circuit. They are often called braggarts because even in everyday conversations they do not want to be perceived as any less valued than others. To reduce the threat and increase the reward

> When group members don't feel validated or noticed, they seek *status* as a way of triggering the reward circuit.

value of this motivation, groups must find ways to give more credit to each other for the learning that is taking place. School culture that values diverse input and seeks all voices allows group members to be recognized in the course of the conversation, thereby reducing the need for status seekers to assert their status through bragging.

Certainty provides a sense of security by allowing the person to operate in familiar and more certain circumstances. Closely associated with certainty is a desire to anticipate the future. On the upside of this behavior is the drive for clarity

> *Certainty* provides a sense of security by allowing the person to operate in familiar and more certain circumstances.

and perseverance in seeking to understand. On the downside is the need to control and to operate from fixed views. To reduce threat and increase reward, groups need to work toward clarity and as much certainty as possible. Process structures, such as these conversations, that remain constant also help people feel a sense of predictability. When cultures have established routines for working through differences of opinion, group members learn to trust that certain processes contribute to a sense of direction and certainty. When groups have conversational processes in place, they are more willing and able to deal with the ambiguity of not knowing. Trusting that any conversation will find a logical ending point if the participants are patient is an important thing to learn.

Autonomy creates a need for control. Directives and other efforts to control behavior are often met with resistance. Opening up choice to give some autonomy provides options and gives the responsibility for deciding back to those who will need to act on the decision. This is a powerful motivator and activates the reward circuit. It is important to note that autonomy does not mean total control, but rather some aspect of control. For this reason, boundaries (rather than strict rules) allow for more choices. For example, in our sample the teacher wanted to control his time, while

> Opening up choice to give some *autonomy* provides options and gives the responsibility for deciding back to those who will need to act on the decision.

others wanted to maintain an investment in curriculum designs. By setting parameters, the group found boundaries that worked for all.

Relatedness builds mutual trust and encourages work toward common ends. A higher sense of relatedness influences the production of oxytocin in the brain and creates the positive emotions of the

> *Relatedness* builds mutual trust and encourages work toward common ends.

reward. Building relationships becomes motivating and can be the social glue that holds organizations together; yet these alliances can also lead to dysfunction. When group members form alliances that exclude others, they create "in" and "out" groups. For the "in" group, the bond of relationship is powerful; for the "out" group, these shifting alliances can create distrust and resentment. To reduce threat and increase reward, groups need to expect to cross relationship boundaries as part of the conversational design. Opportunities for short, pithy small-group conversations provide these opportunities and then become counterpoints to the larger discussions. One quick way to manage this is to build in reflection time at set intervals. When it is time to take a reflection break, group members are instructed to find someone they do not usually talk to, someone from another department or grade, or allow those who have been in a school fewer than five years to pick a partner that has been there more than five years.

> *Fairness* communicates a sense of balance and encourages us to consider equity.

Fairness communicates a sense of balance and encourages us to consider equity. In business, issues of fairness often arise around payment and reward structures such as bonuses. In schools, where pay is based on job function or time on the job, the perceived "investment of effort or time on the job" can be seen as a violation of fairness. When one person works long hours and the other skips out early, the threat response can kick in and get in the way of productive group work. Another fairness issue is the feeling that decisions are not fair; so more transparency, especially by describing why or how a decision was made, can lead to better understanding. Bill's Minnesota friends often noted with humor when something wasn't fair—they responded with the aphorism "Fair happens the ten days before Labor Day." By this, they meant "Yes, life isn't fair, so get over it." As with most things, fair is in the eye and emotion of the beholder.

By now, it should be obvious that these five different motivations can easily promote bonding with a few and conflict with others. When a few strong people create alliances, especially if they include an appointed leader, they can make others feel decisions are not fair or that decisions are railroaded through. This can trigger any of the SCARF responses, with some experiencing reward and others perceiving negative impacts. These can be particularly toxic environments.

For those who work in organizations with cliques, the key is to find ways to open conversational doors across the relationship boundaries. Picking topics that are more neutral—less important to the group members, but still worthy of time and attention—is one way to open the door. When a friend of ours, Kim Harper, first became a principal, she found a common purpose by working on uniform spelling expectations for the school. It turns out that most teachers welcomed suggestions, as they had not given their own practices much thought and hence were not much invested in the outcome. In reflection, she describes these conversations as pivotal in building the collaborative culture, which became a hallmark for this school. She states, "The feeling we had of having found common ground was an important first step toward my long-term goal of building collaborative cultures."

> Listening for the motivations opens up understanding and makes what seemed odd or offensive understandable. When humans understand the motivations behind behaviors, they are willing to let go and engage to remove points of conflict.

To summarize, knowing about how SCARF needs drive behaviors allows the coach or group to stay more tuned in and be able to slow down to listen and engage in inquiry so as to understand these unstated motivations. Listening for the motivations opens up understanding and makes what seemed odd or offensive understandable.

Table 7.1   The Five SCARF Motivations

Status	Relative importance to others
Certainty	Concerns about predicting the future
Autonomy	Sense of control over events
Relatedness	Sense of safety with others
Fairness	Perception of a fair exchange between people

When humans understand the motivations behind behaviors, they are willing to let go and engage to remove points of conflict. Giving the teacher in the sample story control removed the protective behaviors and resulted in positive, productive team members and a team solution. To aid in recall, we offer a short review of the five SCARF motivations in Table 7.1.

Understanding how differences either limit or expand our capacity to learn together as a group is an important developmental threshold that changes cultures from ones of complaint to ones of solution. Just one person can change a vicious cycle into a virtuous cycle by deciding to act as a catalyst—by paying attention and actively listening and inquiring about underlying motivations. When a few serve as catalysts, others follow along and begin to generate solutions well beyond the normal expectation. This kind of work stimulates the reward system in the brain and creates *virtuous cycles*—the belief that a beneficial path can be found. This feeling of competence creates a feeling of renewal and the desire to have more conversations that are similar.

Once again we reinforce the theme of this book: When the coach or facilitator is seeking positive change, instead of dictating next steps the job becomes one of creating productive conversations that allow the group, and individuals within the group, to explore and produce the effective solutions. These solutions are both win–win and value added. For example, once this teacher had autonomy and trusted the group, he participated without complaint. It may seem small, but for this teacher, having choices was important.

> Understanding how differences either limit or expand our capacity to learn together as a group is an important developmental threshold that changes cultures from ones of complaint to ones of solution.

> When the coach or facilitator is seeking positive change, instead of dictating next steps the job becomes one of creating productive conversations that allow the group, and individuals within the group, to explore and produce the effective solutions.

The larger, value-added benefit was that the group had a firsthand experience in how diversity enriches group work. Issues of conflict and diversity will become stronger themes as we move to the right side of the conversation arc.

INTERACTION MODELS VERSUS DIAGNOSIS

Rock (2010) describes SCARF as an interaction model—one that minimizes threat and maximizes rewards in relation to the five identified domains. In the example, the staff did not have to label the motivation to achieve success. It turned out Humble Inquiry led to the unexpected solution. Understanding the SCARF model, however, helps peers begin to understand and appreciate diverse responses. It is important to understand at this juncture that as long as individuals are invited to explore these motivations for themselves and reflect on their work based on what they are coming to comprehend, the conversation lives on the left side of the arc. If, however, even one person imposes a diagnosis on another—makes a judgment about another—the conversation moves to the right side of the arc. When labels are applied, without realizing it the speaker directs the other's thinking in a specific way and runs the risk of shutting down creative thought. Put yourself in our teacher's shoes and consider how you would have responded if the principal or another teacher had said any of these things in response to the teacher's outburst:

> "Your comment is getting in the way of our productive work. We'll finish in 15 minutes, and then you and I can talk in my office."

> "I just went to a workshop, and I think the SCARF model would help you better deal with your need for autonomy." (Implied here is "I have been secretly diagnosing your behaviors.")

> "When you report that this 'wastes time,' I think that you are seeking autonomy. What is it that you want?"

By now, the reader can discern that none of these responses are helpful. Even the last response that begins an inquiry misses the mark. It may seem strange, but emotional responses do not come with rationale, so asking the person what he or she wants can be problematic. The heart of the matter is that when someone makes an emotional response, no amount of reasoning or rational thought will bring a solution. Emotions must be understood, accepted, and validated through the emotional mind. The simple paraphrase "So you think this meeting is wasting your time" paired with the question "What is on your mind?"

communicated an acceptance of the emotion and validated that this response was important enough to take time to understand it.

The irony of this entire story is that this curmudgeon's outburst ended up being a gift to the group. By listening and inquiring, they found elegant ways to meet his needs but also used their own talents to support the entire group. The dissenting view ended up putting creative tension into the conversation and produced a value-added response.

SCARF REFLECTIONS—CHECKING IN WITH OUR EMOTIONAL BRAINS

No matter what the topic, it is often helpful to take a reflective break to check in with group members as a way to open up the conversation and give individuals a chance to respond to concerns. One way to use this model is to teach groups to do a SCARF check-in about two-thirds of the way into the conversation. By this, we mean taking a short reflection break to ask, "What are we thinking or feeling?" At that point, the teacher described earlier would likely have voiced his concern, but it would not have been so emotionally loaded. He might have said, "Planning all these after-school meetings is problematic for me." The teacher who loved certainty might have said, "For the first time in a long time, we are all planning to do something together. This excites me!"

These check-ins should be quick and efficient, with group members rotating between giving opinions and serving as catalysts, listening and reflecting on what they are learning about differences. When initially starting a SCARF reflection, it can be important to ask all group members to respond in some way, even it is just to say they are "neutral." Once the group learns that this is a safe space for voicing different options, only those who are experiencing an emotional response—positive or negative—need to speak up. Once participants have stated problems and know they have been understood, they are more likely to negotiate to get what they need. This is the nexus of using creative tensions to come up with elegant solutions (see Box 7.1 for more details).

When these check-ins become the norm, they often do not take more than five minutes. Sometimes all someone wants is to be heard. Diane learned a valuable lesson about how even an overwhelmingly positive meeting can have silent dissenters. Indeed, the more positive a group is, the more isolated and alone dissenters will feel. At the end of a positive school site council meeting, one member quietly said, "I did not feel there was any space for disagreement today. Everyone was so excited that I did not feel comfortable voicing a concern." Because this group had worked hard to develop norms that supported open, honest conversations, they were stopped dead in their tracks. The member went on to explain that she realized she has some issues of fairness and that her opinion probably would not change the ultimate consensus, but it would have been validating had she had a chance to speak her mind. The lesson here is that dissenters can provide valuable input and should not be ignored. We will return to this when we move to the right side of the conversation arc.

Box 7.1 SCARF Reflection—A Check-In With the Emotional Self to Open Up Diversity in Thought

"At this point in the conversation, it is time to check in with the group's emotional core."

This is usually at the point when the group (1) becomes overexcited, (2) becomes overheated, or (3) begins to lull.

Prompt: "Take a moment and think about this question: As an individual, what are you gaining or losing with this change?"

- Status—Gaining or losing expertise
- Certainty—Gaining clarity or experiencing more confusion
- Autonomy—Developing or losing control
- Relatedness—Feeling more connected or more isolated
- Fairness—Gaining or losing a benefit or investment of time

Directions:

- Take a moment to reflect silently, and then turn to a partner and share insights gained from this reflection.
- Invite the group to reflect about what they are learning that builds an understanding of strengths and differences.

INQUIRY OPENS UP UNDERSTANDING

We first started using the SCARF model as a way to diagnose needs and then tried to match those needs with opportunities for contributions from the group. We now see the SCARF acronym as another way to frame inquiries. Furthermore, when groups learn to embed this type of reflection into their collaborative work, staff members become more comfortable stating needs and are able to maintain a positive contribution. Not taking these five values into account may cause missed opportunities for accelerated reflection. Indeed, Rock (2010) and those of us who have applied his model have advocated that leaders can enhance teamwork and build positive school cultures by focusing on the positive reward of each of these motivations as follows:

- Increasing perception of status with **positive feedback**
- Enhancing levels of certainty by **creating boundaries** that are the same for everyone
- Validating autonomy by **creating options** that allow for some choice
- Improving relatedness through **open communication and coaching**
- Verifying fairness by **asking for perceptions** about assumptions

These are worthy goals, yet we advocate that the solution is not in one enlightened leader but in how groups come to embody these beliefs; this only happens when groups create their own culture based on these reward systems. The old adage "You can lead a horse to water, but you can't make him drink" is true here. A leader can work hard to create a positive culture that reinforces the positive, but if the participants are not aware and hence not ready for these interventions, they will be of little avail. When leaders take responsibility for creating the culture, by diagnosing and then creating opportunities, they end up working harder than everyone else. And, as Schein reminds us, they run the risk of offering suggestions that are neither wanted or helpful. Instead, when leaders set parameters as identified by the conversations in this book, the participants create their own best futures.

As teams find coherence and alignment in their thinking, they began to develop their own knowledge legacies and take responsibility for helping newcomers understand and join the culture. This is a powerful antidote to teacher burnout that drives many from the profession. The lesson is this: When we want to drink, we drink in and nourish not just our thirst; we replenish our souls, and when this happens, the experience is renewal and the activation of a powerful reward circuit.

> As teams find coherence and alignment in their thinking, they began to develop their own knowledge legacies and take responsibility for helping newcomers understand and join the culture.

LEARNING ABOUT DIVERSITY

Learning about SCARF can open up understanding and help groups capitalize on learning about diverse skills, but it is important to note that any model of behavior that is descriptive about different viewpoints can be applied to open up understanding. It is not uncommon for facilitators to use style inventories such as Myers-Briggs (www.myersbriggs.org) or Gregorc (gregorc.com) to help groups understand personality differences.

In the early 1990s, the Federal Mediation Board introduced the Working Styles Assessment to negotiators from the Davis Joint Unified School District to help them better understand how they had almost come to a strike (see (http://partnerships .hivechicago.org/content/uploads/2016/06/01_Working-Styles-Assessment.pdf). In this case, the groups took a quick self-assessment to determine personal working style strengths: analytical, driver, amiable, or expressive. (Note: This model was originally developed by Merrill and Reid [1981]). Once the different groups were established, they took time to explore how these different styles contributed to the misunderstandings. This same process could be used with the SCARF model. The important point is that the participants were taught the model as a way for them to self-evaluate their own behaviors. No one from the outside imposed his or her assumptions about how this district almost came to a strike.

A much more complicated and nuanced way of looking at how values and beliefs influence behaviors can be found in the work of Stan Slap (2010) and his book *Bury My Heart in Conference Room B*. Slap suggests asking what is the person's most important value. Go to Slap's website (www.slapcompany.com) to find the list of fifty values he identified, and for the full directions to a group activity, go to https://tantor-site-assets.s3.amazonaws.com/bonus-content/1755_ BuryMyHeart/1755_BuryMyHeart_PDF_1.pdf. Some of the questions Slap suggests are as follows:

- If you had to pick one of these values—the one most meaningful for you—which one would it be?
- How did you get that value? (This usually elicits a story from life experiences.)
- Share your thinking and feelings with a partner.
- What are we learning about ourselves?

Bill regularly uses a shortened version of this activity with groups. He projects the fifty values at the front of the room and then takes the group through the questions Slap suggests. When we worked with Stan Slap, we found his process to be provocative and reflective. For those wanting more skill in this area, we refer you to Slap's books listed in the reference list.

VALUE-ADDED CONVERSATIONS

What is interesting to note about models that describe sets of behaviors, as the SCARF model does, the group need open only one door to begin to understand.

Through these types of discussions, group members gain insights into others' motivations and can compare and contrast these to their own motivations. For the chapter example, when the need for autonomy was understood, each person was able to respond from his or her own personal reward system. The grade-level partner who sought certainty stepped in and found ways to use her clarity to help focus on just what was important. Other members of the staff agreed that it was fair to opt the teacher out of after-school meetings for the time he needed to reestablish his after-school family time. A few gained status by agreeing to do extra organization work. Through this conversation, they all began to feel more related and empathic. In other words, the same behaviors that protect also lead to productive pathways. The trick is to get school culture to shift and seek out the diverse ways groups can support each other in the quest to create better learning for all, both students and adults. When groups learn to embrace their diversity as an opportunity to find a creative edge, they cross an important threshold and begin to seek out diverse viewpoints. This attention to diverse viewpoints builds knowledge legacies.

Reflection

A Place to Pause

How to Build Knowledge Legacies

- Create virtuous cycles of learning.
- Become a catalyst for knowledge expansion.
- Listen for understanding and amplify ideas with paraphrase.
- Use Humble Inquiry.
- Listen and inquire about underlying motivations.
- Verify assumptions by asking.
- Ask others to respond, based on this new information.

EXPANDING THE KNOWLEDGE THAT SUPPORTS SCARF CONVERSATIONS

Kim and Marbogne (2003) published an article in the *Harvard Business Review* on "fairness." We reinterpret it here as another way to think about how SCARF motivations are embedded within context. Thinking about fairness in relation to the other four motivators can add value to check-ins during or at the end of a meeting by asking from the following SCARF categories. By confirming the "SCAR" part of SCARF, fairness is more assured.

- *Engagement* (builds relatedness)—Have group members been heard? If people cannot tell their story, the process does not seem fair.
- *Explanation* (builds autonomy)—What is the thinking behind the decision? By understanding the thinking behind a decision, groups can more effectively find options and establish boundaries rather than rules for behavior.
- *Expectation* (clarity creates more certainty)—Have processes and purposes been made clear? Transparency is key, especially as groups decide on the process tools to use to shape a particular conversation.

We add a final expectation:

- *Expectation of appreciation* (builds status)—Have group members been recognized for their contributions? A genuine thank-you for something specific is always appreciated.

Together, these four ways of thinking about fairness foster successful conversations and, as a result, give the entire group status. When added to the other practices learned in this book, groups build cooperative capabilities—a belief in their own capability to take appropriate actions. To review, collective efficacy defines a *group* as one that has the skills needed to take collective actions and reflect on these actions to further improve their skills. Collective efficacy rewards with status; those schools note that they have learned to do something that was once just a dream.

Having multiple options for setting contexts for professional conversations generates positive results. What we think can divide us. What we feel unites us. Everyone knows what being mad, sad, glad, scared, or rejected means. Bring people together, and when the work is productive it creates better relationships and better responses. There is wisdom in crowds.

SCENARIO 1

Bill points out that when using SCARF as a diagnostic tool we can both hit and miss the mark. A teacher he worked with was innovative, used data as feedback about his own teaching, employed technology to expand his teaching repertoire, and was very popular with students and parents. But because of his strong personality, he was not looked upon kindly by some of the other staff members. Some thought he was a know-it-all. Thinking that elevating his status would help him connect with staff, Bill and his leadership team tried a few things, like inviting him to serve on the leadership team, putting him in charge of the school goal to raise test scores, and having him co-chair the team meetings. At the end of the year, he quit all of those positions because he did not feel colleagues respected him.

It turns out that, for this teacher, being connected to a small group of teachers and having regular visits from Bill was enough to satisfy his status issues. Furthermore, because he was such a strong teacher, Bill learned more about effective teaching, and from time to time, he would ask him to coach others. He seemed to really value the time Bill spent talking about his teaching, when he asked his opinion, or when he asked him to work one-on-one with another teacher. Honoring his status and having fruitful conversations kept his positive affect and seemed to reduce his need for public status comments in staff meetings.

SCENARIO 2

Years ago, Diane was required to give a tough message to her staff, with little time for planning or deliberation. On a Tuesday night, the superintendent told Diane that he was recommending to the school board on Thursday that they consider reconfiguring her school from an intermediate (Grades 4–6) building to an elementary (K–6) grade pattern. Housing needs of a growing dual immersion program drove his decision, and Diane's school was picked because with three grade levels it was one of the smaller schools in the district. This meant that her entire school would be disrupted and that some teachers would need to transfer.

Initially, Diane was distraught; she had worked so hard to build a culture of inquiry and an open, transparent way of working together. How could she help her teachers understand and be ready to meet with the superintendent the next afternoon? After sleeping on it, she realized that she needed to appeal to the staff's sense of fairness as a way of preparing them to meet with the superintendent that day after school.

Diane addressed fairness outright by telling the teachers how she had learned of his recommendation the night before and how she had felt that it was "unfair." She said, "Arguing with him from this position will not help. Instead, I am going to offer another path." Following an inquiry path articulated by Stephen Covey (1989), she asked her staff to "seek first to understand, and then to be understood." (Note: This is also Humble Inquiry.)

In order to do this, she reminded the staff to use the tool they used in staff meetings to Balance Inquiry With Advocacy (see p. 208). Second, she reminded them that fairness was about perceptions and that it would be helpful for them to consider the decision through lenses of Concerns-Based Adoption (2015), using a simplified modification. Diane explained that their issues would be personal and mechanical, the initial stages of concern, while the superintendent would focus on the highest level—how this decision would benefit the district (see http://www.sedl.org/cbam/stages_of_concern .html). Once again, she had a graphic they had used in a previous staff meeting (see p. 209).

The most amazing result occurred. Instead of arguing with the superintendent, the teachers began an elegant dance of listening and inquiring. Instead of advocacy, they actually coached the superintendent and helped him uncover his biases. What was even more interesting was that the sister school (K–3 configuration) joined the meeting and, after listening to the lead set by Diane's teachers, began to inquire in the same way. Neither principal said a word; together, they sat and listened to one of the most elegant group coaching sessions either had ever seen. Afterward, the other principal said, "I don't know what happened here, but I was so impressed by our teachers; they are truly amazing in their ability to listen and respectfully respond." (Note: Ultimately, this school was not reconfigured immediately, but it was reconfigured three years later. No doubt everyone in the room probably realized that eventually this action would need to happen.)

While this example did not address the entire SCARF model in its entirety, it does remind that just one of these motivations—fairness—can be put to work to look at both the negative and positive intentions of a decision. This also reinforces our belief that other participants can easily adopt models of linguistic excellence. This is an example of how the modeling of accountable listening—paraphrasing, pausing, and inquiring—had a profound effect on the entire meeting.

THE FINAL NOTE—USING SCARF
TO THINK ABOUT TEACHING

Bill has used the SCARF model as a way for teachers to reflect on their practices and also to highlight excellence. Any of these question frames would be worthy of a Reflection Conversation as described in Chapter 4.

Status

- What are some of the methods you use to get these results, and how would they contribute to the school knowledge base?
- This staff is knowledgeable and experienced. What strategies are you using that would benefit the entire school?

Certainty

- Knowing that the world keeps changing, what are the foundational instructional strategies that we believe ought to be constant?
- As you think about your experience here, what are some things you believe should be changed? How could we change those things?

Autonomy

- As veteran teachers, what are you continuing to focus on to increase your impact with students?
- How can we balance what works now with finding out what else works for these kids?

Relatedness

- Our school continues to be more and more diverse. How are we building relationships with students that come from different backgrounds?
- Student performance has gone up. What has each of you done that helped students know we care about their learning?

Fairness

- Knowing kids see fairness differently, how do you sustain the goals of learning while accommodating for such diverse needs?
- What are the things that don't change in your classroom for all students? What are things that are negotiable, depending upon the needs of the student? How do these relate to those of your peers?

Part III

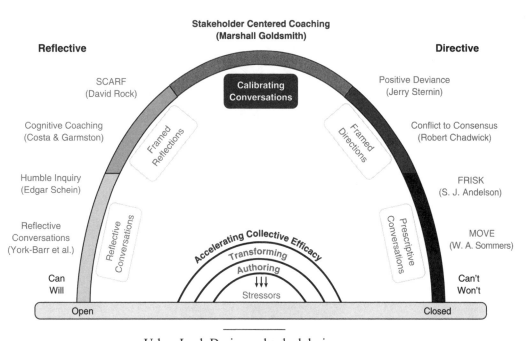

Stakeholder Centered Coaching
(Marshall Goldsmith)

Reflective

Directive

SCARF
(David Rock)

Calibrating
Conversations

Positive Deviance
(Jerry Sternin)

Cognitive Coaching
(Costa & Garmston)

Framed
Reflections

Framed
Directions

Conflict to Consensus
(Robert Chadwick)

Humble Inquiry
(Edgar Schein)

FRISK
(S. J. Andelson)

Reflective
Conversations
(York-Barr et al.)

Reflective
Conversations

Accelerating Collective Efficacy

Prescriptive
Conversations

MOVE
(W. A. Sommers)

Transforming

Authoring

↓↓↓

Can
Will

Stressors

Can't
Won't

Open

Closed

Urban Luck Design, urbanluckdesign.com

PART III

CALIBRATING CONVERSATIONS— CONVERSATIONS AT THE TIPPING POINT FROM OUTSIDE IN

As we reach the top of the Professional Conversation Arc, the foci of the conversations shift from self-directed learning toward other-directed learning. The first four conversations identified in Part II focus on bringing forth collective knowledge learned through reflection on practice. As groups open up and become more reflective and honest about what they do and don't know, they begin to seek data, feedback, and information from external sources; however, by definition, for a conversation to be on the left side of the arc, it must be self-directed. This means when external information of any kind—data, test scores, standards, rubrics, 360-degree feedback—is directed by another, the conversation runs the risk of moving to an imposed agenda. Often, these imposed agendas leave little room for flexibility because they are based on the needs of the stakeholder or the need to analyze third-party information. These imposed agendas can just as easily focus on test scores, rubrics, standards, or other such identified professional development programs.

The inherent problem noted earlier in this book about helping is also problematic here. Often, what is imposed is neither needed nor wanted.

The key distinction here is that for conversations on the left arc, the professionals decide what data to use, when it is necessary, and how it will be applied. This does not mean they ignore outside mandates, but rather they draw on this information as a way to self-diagnose to inform their own knowing–doing–learning.

Sometimes, however, the choice is beyond the practitioners and lies with the policy-making bodies that drive educational decisions. It would be foolhardy for any educator to ignore test scores or national standards; professionals have an obligation to meet the level of proficiency of a profession. With that said, however, we believe that implementation of standards-based programs could be so much better.

There is nothing inherently wrong with other imposed professional development programs; the problem lies in the failure to understand that reflective practices with others are what build knowledge and skill. A major problem for schools is that professional development time is limited; hence, teachers experience little ongoing support for implementation of the myriad of programs pushed down to them. This means that teachers rarely engage in conversations about what they are learning from practice about any new program. To find knowledge coherence that leads to knowledge legacies, learners must articulate and evaluate their own learning trajectory.

> To find knowledge coherence that leads to knowledge legacies, learners must articulate and evaluate their own learning trajectory.

Once again the key is the conversation, and as we move to the top of the arc, we advocate for *Calibrating Conversations*. A calibrating conversation is one in which both the leaders AND the stakeholders weigh in on the new information and make some determinations about what would best meet all the stakeholders' needs. The beauty of this type of conversation is that the catalyst or coach does not make the judgments; the judgments come from the stakeholders or a third-party information source. Once the data are clear, any of the conversations to the left of the arc could be used to self-analyze and act on the data. Consider the power of these questions from previously introduced conversations to help another person examine the data:

Reflective Practice: Based on this data, how are you now reflecting upon your actions (teaching)?

Humble Inquiry: How is this data informing your view about what is going on?

Cognitive Coaching: Based on the data, how are you anticipating about changing some behaviors, and how do you plan to take action?

SCARF: What do you anticipate will be most challenging for yourself and for the group when considering the changes implied in the data? (Listen for underlying SCARF behaviors.)

It is important to note here that many educators offer conversational maps for data-focused conversations. We favor the work of our colleagues Laura Lipton and Bruce Wellman at www.miravia.com. They offer training in a myriad of processes for conducting learning-focused conversations that rely on data. They draw from their deep knowledge of Cognitive Coaching and Adaptive Schools to create robust training programs, and their work supports and enhances our work. We refer the reader to them to learn more about this type of conversation.

For this book, we decided to pick a conversation that lives outside of education—Stakeholder Centered Coaching—and to introduce it as a calibrating conversation. We did this for two reasons. First, too much of the data-centered work has focused on testing and data analysis, which, while necessary, also impedes professional learning. Second, we realized that stakeholder data are powerful catalysts for change and should be a much larger part of how we bring about change in schools. While we do not address it here, getting feedback from students, as some schools are now doing, would be another powerful strategy to bring about change through stakeholder input.

Chapter 8

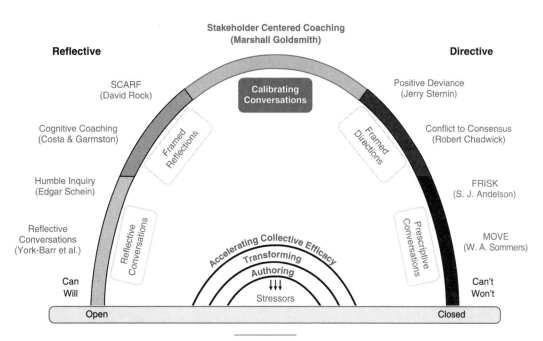

Urban Luck Design, urbanluckdesign.com

8

STAKEHOLDER CENTERED COACHING— EXPANDING CONSCIOUSNESS

The major challenge of most executives is not understanding the practice of leadership—it is practicing their understanding of leadership.

—Marshall Goldsmith

The mismatch in perceptions between stakeholders and their appointed leaders is a common problem in schools. Leaders often do not perceive their behaviors in the same way as constituents. A leader might think he or she is a good listener, only to find out that the stakeholders do not agree. Other leaders assume no news is good news, but instead, it really means the stakeholder does not know how to give constructive feedback. There is an old adage "Don't mistake silence for approval." More often than not, it is because the stakeholder does not trust that the feedback would be received in a positive way. No one wants to jeopardize a relationship with a superior. And yet as leaders, to be the best that we can be, it is important to know what others' perceptions are about how we interact.

Marshall Goldsmith (2007) has worked with businesses all over the world to build reciprocal processes to help leaders learn what their constituents think about their actions through Stakeholder Centered Coaching. Not only do leaders need honest feedback, but they need to learn how to be ready to receive this feedback as well.

> Not only do leaders need honest feedback, but they need to learn how to be ready to receive this feedback as well.

The problem with feedback, as we learned through Humble Inquiry, is that it is often not received as intended. The challenge is that feedback is not always what was wanted. Even willing receivers are not always receptive to the feedback. We have all had the experience of receiving unwanted feedback. A well-meaning friend gives us feedback, and our internal voice responds, "Well, that is not want I wanted to know." Yet external feedback is often necessary, as it exposes "blind spots" that need to be overcome in order to grow.

Initially, Bill used Stakeholder Centered Coaching to assist good leaders in becoming even better. Marshall Goldsmith's book *What Got You Here Won't Get You There* (2007) describes how to examine the discrepancy between how others view the leader and how the leader views him- or herself.

Goldsmith found that the best way to bring about change was through data collected from stakeholders. Professionals need to realize that they have blind spots, which can include habitual mindsets that keep them from understanding new information or perceptions. Stakeholder Centered Coaching breaks down the barriers by providing multiple viewpoints, making the data difficult to dismiss. Goldsmith advocates using a 360-degree feedback process, which solicits data from subordinates, superiors, and peers. Just one data point can easily be refuted; multiple data points that say the same thing cannot be ignored. When working with the data, Goldsmith suggests choosing one or two leadership behaviors and planning for regular updates on progress. Getting real feedback from those who report to the leader is critical in enhancing and sustaining long-term capacity, and these changes in key behaviors often lead to further refinements and accelerated performance.

As humans, we are faced with challenges that we "do not know what we do not know." Knowing about a problem behavior is rarely enough to change it. Doing requires, among other things, regular follow-up. Feedback to measure changes in perceptions is needed to ensure we are actually doing what we think we are doing. With an external feedback source, the coach's job is not to give feedback, but rather to help the receiver interpret and evaluate the data to make plans for improvement and then to check in to assure follow-through. It takes the coach out of the judgment role and maintains a collaborative, problem-solving framework. We call this type a calibrating conversation because external feedback is used to determine improvements. We note here that for rest of the conversations in this book, some form of eternal evaluation or judgment will be made that determines the content.

> As humans, we are faced with challenges that we "do not know what we do not know."

INCREASING SELF-AWARENESS— CONVERSATIONAL BLIND SPOTS

The major focus of the Stakeholder Centered Coaching process is to work with already-successful people to make improvements. The process is designed to help professionals shift thinking by receiving honest feedback and making the changes needed to improve performance. Einstein is credited with variations on this famous quote, "We can't solve problems by using the same kind of thinking we used when we created them." Indeed, efficacious professionals know this and seek out feedback.

The failure to model appropriate use of feedback erodes leadership capacity and trust. Leaders are vested with the job of giving feedback as part of a supervisory process. Yet when professionals allow bad habits to grow and fester and they ignore feedback, the problems expand, eroding respect. After all, supervisors often tell others to change, yet they continue ineffective behaviors and fail to model what is expected of subordinates. And sometimes, as Bill puts it, leaders need a "whack on the side of the head" to help find another way of doing business.

One goal of Stakeholder Centered Coaching is to increase self-awareness. Self-awareness is a habit of mind and must be developed and cultivated. One of the ways that Goldsmith works with leaders to help interpret the data is to uncover conversational blind spots that impede their attempts at effective communication and are judged by others in noncomplimentary terms. The list of conversational blind spots is as follows:

- Inserting opinions for every situation; others see it as arrogant.
- Interpreting with helpful suggestions; others see it as "butting in."
- Delegating to others; others see it as shirking responsibility.
- Delegating and continuing to give directions; others see it as being overcontrolling.
- Thinking they need to "hold their tongue;" others see it as being unresponsive.
- Thinking that conflicts are healthy debates; others find unresolved conflicts as emotionally damaging.
- Leaving the group to solve a collective problem; others see it as not caring.

Goldsmith views it a waste of valuable time and resources to coach someone who is unwilling to change and commit to improving their skills. As Marshall says, "I work with good people who want to get better." Marshall Goldsmith is so committed to assuring change that his firm does not take payment until a final rating scale shows improvement. It should be noted that the Goldsmith's consultant will terminate the process when the person is not responsive to the feedback or unwilling to follow through with commitments. If the leader is not going to have the discipline to follow through, there is no point investing time and energy in her or his personal and professional development. Often, this is a sign that the leader's supervisor or board needs to consider moving this person on.

LIMITATIONS OF SUCCESS

Over the years, Goldsmith was surprised to find that an additional barrier to learning was success. When successful, humans tend to bask in the good feelings of a job well done. Often, they do not reflect on their own contributions to the success, are not aware of the contributions of others, and then are surprised when the same tactics do not work in another situation. Success can shut down thinking; once an answer that works is found, many quit looking for new answers. Goldsmith writes, "The trouble with success is that it prevents us from achieving more success." An alternative is what John Carse (1986) calls an "infinite game." The goal of the infinite game is to keep getting better as opposed to finding one way that works and ending any further improvement (finite game). As De Witt Jones (1999) said, "Look for the second right answer."

> "The trouble with success is that it prevents us from achieving more success."
> —Marshall Goldsmith

While coaching others, we have observed the success trap firsthand. When people are successful, they often brag about their success during the coaching. The interesting phenomenon, however, is that when queried, they are not nearly as conscious of the specific actions that directly contributed to the success. Consider this example:

Teacher: "The kids did so well today. All the kids worked well together."

Coach: "Yes, the lesson seemed to flow, and the students were engaged. What are you learning as a teacher about how to engage these students?"

Teacher: (long pause) "I am not sure what you mean. It's just great when the class gets into the flow."

Coach: "And as a teacher, what do you do to make flow happen?"

Teacher: "That's a good question. I need to think about that."

When professionals solicit this kind of data, engage in this kind of reflection, and then change accordingly, they model open, honest appraisals of behavior.

> Learning from our successes is as important as learning from our failures. The goal is to be more conscious of how our behaviors–both positive and negative– impact others.

Learning from our successes is as important as learning from our failures. The goal is to be more conscious of how our behaviors—both positive and negative—impact others. By developing a culture that believes in continuous improvements, the conversations easily move toward the reflective posture.

Goldsmith has his own clearly delineated measures of successful coaching. To assure that the coaching is successful, he looks for three overt behaviors:

- Courage: Learners need the courage to confront issues honestly and with humility.
- Humility: Acceptance of feedback as helpful. Professionals receive feedback in the spirit in which it is given.
- Discipline to follow through: There is nothing more dangerous to reputations as a failure to follow through.

STAKEHOLDER CENTERED COACHING PROCESS

Stakeholder Centered Coaching is a cyclical process not dissimilar to the reflective cycles described earlier. The difference is that the focus of the reflection is on the data obtained from stakeholders. The first step is to obtain baseline data. In Stakeholder Centered Coaching, the 360-degree feedback process is used as a way to collect this data. Usually, the person being coached is asked to give the names of five to eight stakeholders whom they perceive would provide honest data—neither best friends nor enemies. There are many online 360-degree assessments designed for businesses, which are worth the investment for high-level administrators. For Bill's work with principals, however, he has found it more expedient and cost effective to use focused interviews of six to eight stakeholders to provide feedback to the principal, using these questions:

- What are the principal's strengths?
- What are the principal's challenges?
- If the principal could change one or two things, what would they be?
- Do you have any other observations or important data?

When using a more informal data collection system, as the coach, Bill gives stakeholders the following instructions:

- Focus on behaviors to be improved in the future (do not dwell so much on the past).
- Aim for truthfulness, not niceness, so that the feedback is helpful.
- Obtain specific examples of the behavior to be changed.
- Expect me to check in for additional feedback at set intervals.

When using easily identifiable stakeholders, Bill works with the principal to make sure that he or she understands the themes that emerge, that this is an improvement process, that no one is perfect, and that those offering feedback are providing positive support—even if the administrator does not see it that way. And it may seem excessive, but we also advise a strict rule: The principal may not engage in conversations about the data directly with those who volunteer to be of support. Any violation of this rule will terminate the process, and the termination will be communicated to a superior. For most, this would not be a problem, but Bill did have one principal who went right out and confronted a stakeholder because he did not like the message. It is noteworthy that this would be an example of counterproductive behavior, which would indicate that the person is not a good candidate for coaching and more than likely does not belong in the job. A conversation further down the Dashboard of Options would be in order.

Table 8.1 contains a greatly simplified Stakeholder Centered Coaching model and also modifications we have made to expand it into a principal coaching process.

Table 8.1   Simplified Stakeholder Centered Coaching Model and Principal Coaching Process

Steps in Process	Stakeholder Centered Coaching	Sommers's Stakeholder Centered Principal Coaching (SCPC)
Announce the program.	Explain the process and how stakeholders will be involved.	Gain commitment for SCPC and ask for humility, courage, and discipline.
Get measureable data.	Use a 360-degree feedback process.	Identify 6 to 8 teachers and communicate that they have been chosen for their honesty. Commit to use the data to make changes.
Accept the facts.	Help the person understand the data and that it is a true reflection of the other's perceptions.	Provide data around Bill's four questions: What are the principal's strengths? What are the principal's leadership challenges? If the principal could change one or two things, what would they be? Do you have any other observations or important data?

(Continued)

Table 8.1 (Continued)

Steps in Process	Stakeholder Centered Coaching	Sommers's Stakeholder Centered Principal Coaching (SCPC)
Plan for the change.	Show a process for improvement.	Use the data to create a plan for improvement and choose a reflective conversation pattern for discussing progress.
Announce the change.	Advertise efforts to get better. If needed, apologize for past transgressions.	Principal meets with stakeholders and/ or staff and confirms his commitment to change and describes his plan.
Complete routine follow-up.	Collect data again after a month or two and at the end of a set term.	Bill follows up weekly or bi-monthly, stakeholders are updated every 6 to 8 weeks, and data are again collected at the end of 6 to 9 months.

FEEDFORWARD—AN OPEN HABIT OF MIND

As Goldsmith (2007, p. 117) points out, "Getting feedback is the easy part. Dealing with it is hard." Volumes have been written about feedback, yet it continues to be one of the least understood parts of the change process. Treat every piece of advice as a gift or a compliment and simply say thank you. No one expects you to act on every piece of advice; many are satisfied to know that you listened and took the information seriously. When leaders also use this feedback to shape behaviors, stakeholders notice. Ed Koch, former mayor of New York City, became famous for riding the subways of his city and asking, "How am I doing?"

Goldsmith likes to ask his clients to take a "feedforward" stance; instead of looking back, look to how this will help in the future. Feedforward helps to facilitate a positive attitude about receiving data:

- Accept the data without judgment or prejudice.
- Listen without interrupting or giving excuses.
- Show humility and accept a possible better way.
- Show courage and acknowledge what is difficult.
- Show gratitude and say thank you.
- Show discipline and take positive steps to change.

> Feedforward focuses on what you are going to do differently. There is nothing you can do about the past; the future, however, offers an enormous opportunity to behave differently and for the better.

Feedforward focuses on what you are going to do differently. There is nothing you can do about the past; the future, however, offers an enormous opportunity to behave differently and for the better.

MAKE CHANGES PUBLIC

Another important aspect of Stakeholder Centered Coaching is to make the intended changes public. Humans get used to patterns of behavior and expect more of the same. When the pattern changes, they notice, but the disruption is not always perceived positively. Without realizing it, stakeholders can be highly critical of changes that seem out of the norm. Consider this crass statement: "Oh, boy! What workshop did he go to this week? I am not sure what he is up to, but it bugs me." When a leader announces the intention to change and why, it lets others know that they will see new behaviors and that these behaviors are not random, but goal directed. Stakeholders are much more forgiving when they perceive that the changes are for the good of the organization. Furthermore, this public disclosure offers a chance for public reflection, which models what would be wanted from the stakeholders as well. Bill has also found that a commitment to the ongoing collection of data paired with small changes over time also communicates the serious intent of the leader.

Not all leaders are ready or open to the feedback they receive, and the conversations must necessarily become more directive. On occasion, ongoing feedback will indicate that there has been no change or, in some cases, a change for the worse. When 360-degree scores are worse, it usually means that the job is beyond his or her capacity. This means it is time to move on or change jobs. Goldsmith has found that not all are coachable, and he recommends corrective action if coaching does not work. These types of conversations are further described in Chapter 11 and Chapter 12.

ROADBLOCKS TO LEARNING

Some signs that people are less willing to receive and work with feedback are as follows:

- A problem has been identified, but rather than trying to make the changes, they take a victim stance.
- They are satisfied with their level of success and think the behaviors in question are not an issue.

- They think that everyone else has the problem.
- They seem to think others should tell them what to do.

Reflection

iStock.com/BlackJack3D

A Place to Pause

- What is your relationship to feedback?
- How do you receive and act on feedback?
- In your life, when has feedback been ineffective?
- What might you now change in your reactions to feedback?
- How might you change your relationships with others based on feedback?

Goldsmith (2007) also cautions that when employees show deep blocks to learning, they may be grappling with a personal or psychological problem. This viewpoint ties directly to the stress responses described in Chapter 3. In these cases, it may be appropriate to make a referral to an employee assistance program. Now with the Internet, employers can turn to online services to get counseling for an employee. (Note: Goldsmith recommends Best Care Employee Assistance Program [www.bestcareeap.org]). Schools have not traditionally invested in these services, but we believe this is money well spent. While emotional-disturbance problems are probably not easily solved, some employees find a new lease on life by just talking through personal issues with a skilled coach.

We all face crises in our adult lives, and having support can make all the difference. As in all helping conversations, the boundary between professional coaching and psychological coaching can be blurred. We are clear: Professional coaching is not psychological coaching. When in doubt, involve a psychologist.

"Successful people love getting ideas for the future. Successful people have a high need for self-determination and will tend to accept ideas about concerns that they 'own' while rejecting ideas that feel 'forced' upon them." —Marshall Goldsmith

We conclude this chapter with the wise words of Goldsmith (2007, p. 174): "Successful people love getting ideas for the future. Successful people have a high need for self-determination and will tend to accept ideas about concerns that they 'own' while rejecting ideas that feel 'forced' upon them." We believe Stakeholder Centered Coaching provides useful processes for dealing with complex issues of change.

SCENARIO 1

Diane worked as a principal for thirteen years in a university community where the parents were highly committed and supportive of the schools; they were also assertive and critical. She used to tell new teachers that every teacher at some point would get less-than-flattering feedback from a parent. She also told them that the successful teachers learned from these complaints. Diane reflects,

> I didn't realize it then, but I developed a form of Stakeholder Centered Coaching as a way of dealing with these parent complaints. I found that when teachers just brushed off these complaints, I would almost always get a similar complaint in subsequent years. I needed the teachers to learn from the feedback.
>
> I now see working with this kind of data as a moral imperative; our job as supervisors is to help others meet the needs of all students. There is nothing like "first-person testimony" to provide notice of a problem. Parent complaints signal a failure at some level to meet a child's needs.

Diane reports that she gained more traction and improvements through this process than all other supervision methods combined. This speaks to the power of Stakeholder Centered Coaching.

What made these parent complaints challenging was that they often came at year's end and contained a multipage litany of everything they perceived the teacher had done wrong. Trying to find the real issue was sometimes difficult, and because the school year was over, the parent did not want to meet face to face with the teacher. Furthermore, these letters were always upsetting to the teacher, and teacher contract language limited the usefulness of anonymous feedback. Table 8.2 shows the process that Diane perfected to deal with these complaints.

Table 8.2   Stakeholder Centered Coaching Process to Unpack Parental Feedback

Process	Words Used by Principal	Rationale
Step 1 Set up an opportunity for reflection.	"I need to let you know that I received a letter of complaint from X parent. I need to set up a meeting later today or tomorrow to sit down with you and go over the complaint."	Try to set up the meeting so that the teacher has some reflection time between learning about the complaint and sitting down to discuss the complaint. Reflective teachers will often figure out some of the issues on their own.

(Continued)

(Continued)

Process	Words Used by Principal	Rationale
Step 2 Acknowledge the emotional content.	"We will want to discuss this letter after you have had a chance to read it, but first, I want to acknowledge that these kinds of letters can be upsetting. Were you aware of any problem with this student?"	If the teacher becomes highly emotional, she or he will not truly understand the complaint or hear what you have to say and will respond with the defensive behaviors described in Chapter 3.
Step 3 Set expectations.	"Let's review the letter together and see what we can learn about the issues."	The focus is on learning from issues and not making excuses. Communicate Goldsmith's "feedforward" model if needed.
Emotional interlude	"This is upsetting. When parents wait until the end of the year and then slam you with a list of complaints, it is frustrating." Pause and let teacher respond. "Our job is to find the germ of truth in this letter. What can you learn from this feedback that will help you in the future?"	Manage the emotions and then reframe toward positive outcomes. This cycle sometimes needs to be repeated several times. The more emotional the response, the more often the emotions need to be acknowledged and the expectation reset. This might also be a time for a pause. Sometimes, the conversation is best finished on another day.
Step 4 Feedforward the response.	"So as you think about this conversation and what the parent is saying, what are you learning?"	The focus is always on self-reflection. What is the teacher learning from this feedback (or feedforward)?
Step 5 Plan next steps.	"This has been a productive conversation. Can I check in with you at the beginning of the year to learn what you have planned in relationship to this conversation?" or "This conversation has been very emotional for you. I think you need some time to really be able to reflect on the letter and find the germ of truth. Let's meet again in a few days and talk about what you can learn from this feedback. I want you to find only one or two things to focus on. Can you do that?"	When a person is self-reflective, the emotional response is usually short. Self-reflective teachers are proactive. When the emotions are strong, sometimes the first conversation just gets them ready for a deeper conversation at a later date. The leadership message is that we all get negative feedback from time to time, and it is our job to figure out how we can learn from the feedback. And, even more importantly, when a leader persists, it communicates, "I will not let you off the hook. This is an *essential professional conversation*."

SCENARIO 2

Bill has spent years coaching administrators both in person and over the phone. In this design, he has the principal plan for a change and also seek suggestions or feedback. He has found a few pointers for success with feedforward conversations as follows:

1. He asks the administrator to pick one or two behaviors to change—ones that would be noticed by others. In other words, he wants her or him to pick changes that would make a significant, positive difference.

2. Bill has the administrator describe these objectives in detail with him. Bill's goal is to make clear the intentions to change.

3. Now Bill asks the administrator to pick a colleague and describe the changes in detail to that person—then seek feedback/suggestions from the colleague regarding the changes.

4. Bill instructs the administrator to accept the suggestions without judgment, denial, or debate and say thank you.

5. Bill has the administrator make every attempt possible to use the suggestions while practicing the new behavior.

6. If need be, Bill has the administrator seek an additional colleague to repeat Step 3.

7. Bill has the administrator report on success and challenges the next time they chat.

THE FINAL WORD—COACHING YOUR SUPERINTENDENT

Diane and colleagues used a similar process to provide feedback to a superintendent who was floundering on the job. When the school board asked for feedback, the administrators initially balked at the request. Then they realized nothing would change if they did not speak up. So a group of administrators interviewed the stakeholders and used the feedback to create a work plan based on identified leadership standards. Initially, this task was daunting—after all, the constructive feedback was going to the boss.

(Continued)

(Continued)

Diane reflects how proud she was of their work. "Not only did we provide honest, constructive feedback, but we created a document that made it clear to all what was and was not working. It reminded me that honest, constructive feedback is an ethical imperative." She goes on, "We also had to reflect on our own leadership behaviors, as they served as a basis for our comparisons. It helped us clarify our own expectations for leadership."

In the end, it turned out that the superintendent was not in the right position and moved on. Once again, the stakeholder process provided objective feedback; it was up to the superintendent to decide to make the changes.

Part IV

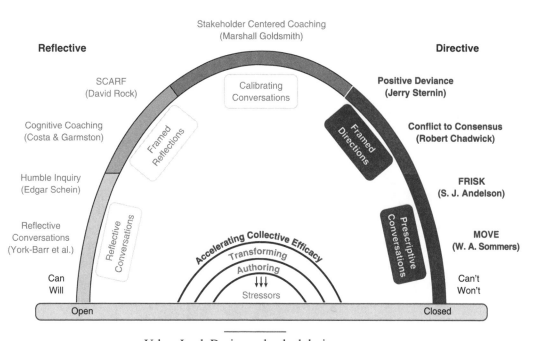

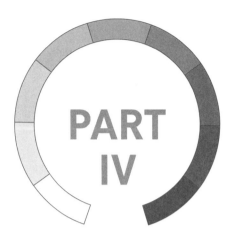

PART IV

CONVERSATIONS DESIGNED TO BUILD KNOWLEDGE FROM THE OUTSIDE IN

As authors, we write to learn. Writing in itself, particularly this kind of a book, is a reflective act. As we grappled with what we were trying to say, we had our own breakthroughs and came to a deeper understanding about our own knowledge. Early on, we agreed which types of conversations we wanted to include and the sequence for the types of conversations we would offer. What was more difficult was making explicit why we had made these choices.

We also confronted an unexpected challenge. When we showed our colleagues the Professional Conversation Arc, they were quick to want to make it a diagnostic tool. As leaders, they somehow seemed to think that it was their job to choose where to start on the Dashboard. They wanted to use it to prediagnose the other person or group and then choose where to intervene—in other words, they wanted to be directive. This puzzled us, and we struggled to figure out why we were so adamant the process be left open to choice—even though we present a continuum, it is not a diagnostic tool. The Nine Conversations are a collaborative leadership tool designed to expand repertoire for responding to real issues in real time. We hope this is clear to the reader by now.

The biggest breakthrough came when we realized that most conversations in schools really do not live on the Dashboard at all. In fact, if the arc were the top of a clock, most conversations in schools would start at about 1:00—somewhere just beyond Stakeholder Coaching. By this, we mean that most public conversations—and we include all professional development—start with someone making a determination about what others should know; hence, that is what is focused on and talked about. Even when teachers are involved in making choices, it is often a small group who decides for the larger group. The point is that most conversations are not reciprocal, but are designed to impart information and give direction so are more unilateral. While some of this type of work is necessary, these unilateral conversations should not consume all available time for collaboration. Indeed, in our view, these conversations should be organized around teachers' understanding of their own knowing–doing–learning gaps.

We also include much of the data focus of PLC work in this unilateral approach. Even though teachers are collaborating, the focus is often test scores, benchmark assessments, and other forms of data mandated by others. The problem we have learned is that these are constructed data sets that often bear no relationship to practice. Diane tells the story about how diligently she worked with teachers to analyze state-mandated assessment data. She reflects,

> To be sure, we collaborated; but in the end, we gleaned little useful information for the classroom. While it was an interesting intellectual exercise, it gave no guidance to practice. Quite frankly, the teachers told me that they already knew who struggled. They were right; after all that work, most of the time our conclusions were that we needed to improve reading comprehension or basic math concepts.

Diane finishes, "My regret is that I made this mistake at least five times— every time we had a new mandated test."

Bill tells the story of secondary teachers spending all their collaboration time designing benchmark assessments to monitor progress in algebra. One teacher later said,

> You know we did all that work and were so proud of it. The problem was that in the end we still did not really know how to reach those kids who just do not get it. We would have been better off trying to figure out how to teach those students differently.

What was startling for us was to think how long in our careers we lived by these expectations—that somehow these external directives would hold the solution. We had mistaken data study for action, but could not develop operating instructions. This is why we expanded the knowing–doing gap with *learning*.

We know, we do, and we learn, which sometimes means we modify our actions. We would have loved to know earlier in our careers the piece of Hemingway advice: "Never mistake motion for action." We have seen lots of motion in our long careers and occasionally refer to it as the "reverse butterfly effect." Remember that a *butterfly effect* means that small changes produce large results. A reverse is when huge expenditures of time and money result in small or few results. We were lucky—and persistent—and found a way out . . . hence, this book. And, we are still learning.

Part IV could be a book in and of itself, but that is not the kind of book we wanted to write. After all, most of us have become experts ourselves in planning for professional development delivered by content experts or in facilitated processes using protocols. For the purposes of this book, we have picked two specifically Framed Directive Conversations by way of example. What is important here is that in most cases, one person, or one small group, has decided that something needs to change. In the case of Positive Deviance, a failure needs to be reconciled. In the case of Conflict to Consensus (the Chadwick Process), the parties are in an intractable conflict that inhibits progress and needs to be resolved. Both are unique processes and are strategies that come from outside of education.

Finally, we finish the continuum with two Prescriptive Conversations—conversations that confront issues head on; yet they still require listening, reflective thought, conversational skill, and humane treatment. These conversations require due process, a chance for the other person to know and respond to the claims. When used appropriately, due process is invaluable in giving both sides another chance to be heard. It also helps the supervisor ascertain when the person is unable or unwilling to keep a commitment to do better. At this point, lip service or excuses are not acceptable; when responsibility for change is not forthcoming, the signal is clear that this is not the right time or place for that person. So join us in rethinking how we frame change and give directives that allow for a return to reflective thought.

So join us in rethinking how we frame change and give directives that allow for a return to reflective thought.

Chapter 9

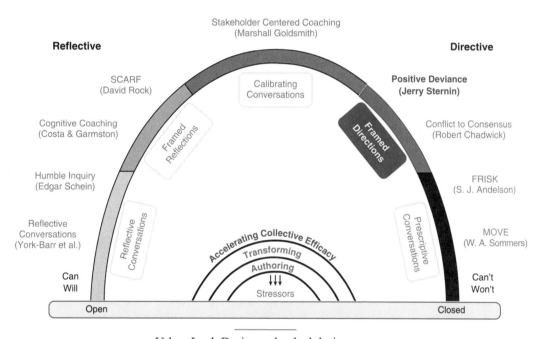

Stakeholder Centered Coaching
(Marshall Goldsmith)

Reflective

Directive

SCARF
(David Rock)

Calibrating
Conversations

**Positive Deviance
(Jerry Sternin)**

Cognitive Coaching
(Costa & Garmston)

Framed
Reflections

Framed
Directions

Conflict to Consensus
(Robert Chadwick)

Humble Inquiry
(Edgar Schein)

FRISK
(S. J. Andelson)

Reflective
Conversations
(York-Barr et al.)

Reflective
Conversations

Accelerating Collective Efficacy

Transforming

Authoring

↓↓↓

Stressors

Prescriptive
Conversations

MOVE
(W. A. Sommers)

Can
Will

Can't
Won't

Open

Closed

Urban Luck Design, urbanluckdesign.com

9

POSITIVE DEVIANCE—MINING FOR GROUP GOLD

It's easy to come up with new ideas; the hard part is letting go of what worked for you two years ago, but will soon be out-of-date.

—Roger von Oech

As we transition from Stakeholder Centered Coaching, the Positive Deviance process asks more defining questions, relies on more specific data, and includes a wider focus than just individual skills. The power of Positive Deviance (Sternin & Choo, 2000) is that through rigorous investigation it identifies pockets of success that inform new ways of solving persistent problems. This model, with its exploration into the unknown, expands the knowledge base and positively affects the learning health of organizations. When done well, it creates a virtuous cycle of success, which delves more deeply into the nuances of what works. Positive Deviance, at its core, designs intervention strategies that are scalable and efficacious. As groups learn to interrogate reality and find new solutions, they learn to use this strategy whenever they are stuck or hit an apparent dead end.

By drawing from the internal resources of the community, the changes are more acceptable and accessible, increasing the group commitment to implementing new solutions. Bill wishes he had understood this process earlier in his career. In his zeal to help, he would often send his teachers examples of outlier ideas—those ideas he thought would make a difference. He had the belief that if everyone knew current information, staff would immediately use it. As he was writing this, he laughed, "Ha! What Kool-Aid did I drink?" Diane responded, "The same one all naïve leaders drink. The one that made us believe that if we shared the right information it would bring change." In contrast, Jerry Sternin

(1991), developer of the Positive Deviance model, and his colleagues did not send out information, did not make posters and post them around the community, and did not make a report to the officials and leave. Instead, they studied the community and looked for pockets of success—or positive deviants. This enabled them to teach about the intended changes from the inside, using neighbors to teach neighbors.

Positive Deviance is asset-based rather than deficit-based and is grounded on the observation that in every community there are some who exhibit uncommon behaviors and have better solutions to problems. In a now-classic case, Sternin (1991) describes how he created a government-sponsored program to save young Vietnamese children from malnutrition. He asked the local communities to identify families that were not malnourished. These families were the "positive deviants." They were *positive* because they seemed to be doing something successful and *deviant* because their practices were outside of the norm. It turns out that some of the mothers collected tiny shrimps and crabs from the rice paddies, providing just enough protein to improve their children's diet. Others in the community believed that this food source was not good for their children, so lacking sufficient protein, their children were malnourished. Using this information about how to introduce protein into the diet, the aid workers could now build a sustainable program based on best practices right out of that community.

> They were *positive* because they seemed to be doing something successful and *deviant* because their practices were outside of the norm.

Jerry Sternin is another of those humble people that we turned to over and over to write this book. His work in Vietnam certainly gives a glimpse of Jerry as a human being and his commitment to social justice. A few of the other projects he worked to solve were female circumcision in the Middle East, getting special services for people in Appalachia, and various Peace Corps projects.

Jerry also worked with the Children's Aid Society in the Bronx in New York City to focus on the black and Latino males who were not succeeding in school. He firmly believed that increasing their success rate would lead to better citizenship, relationships, and community. They rigorously studied these adolescents' relationship with four core concepts—respect, relationships (dating and family), time management, and school activities. They searched for positive deviants in each of these core areas. In the successful students, they found high values of respect for themselves and other students—habits such as sitting toward the front of the class and family commitment to eating meals together and reviewing homework. Many of the success factors seemed basic, but they made a difference for these young men. They also found that students who were invited to do errands for the family also did better. While each one of these might not make a difference alone, it should be clear to the reader that parents whose homes have all these values raise their children in a different cultural system than those that do not.

MINING GROUP KNOWLEDGE— FINDING SUCCESS FROM WITHIN

We have found that seeking what is working, looking for what is called *positive deviance,* can be a valuable professional development activity with the possibility of adding repertoire and creating knowledge coherence. Over the years, we both noted that there were teachers who had developed little tricks of the trade that made huge differences for classroom management. A few of the things Diane learned from other teachers were so obvious, yet they saved her from hours of tedious work. As a new teacher, she spent far too much time cleaning up after her primary-aged children and making answer sheets to correct math work. She learned simple but elegant solutions from other teachers. For cleanup, she observed how a kindergarten teacher required that any toy, especially the puzzles, could only be taken apart in an aluminum tray. If the child could not put it together, which was often the case, he or she returned it to the shelf. Another child would always come along and finish it up. Another trick was instead of taking valuable time to make an answer key, she instead could compare two student papers and only work out the problems that did not match. In this way, a student paper became her answer key. Instead of having to calculate an entire sheet, she would only have to calculate one or two divergent answers. While simple, these two small changes allowed Diane to spend valuable time on learning plans instead of maintenance.

> The point is this: Schools are resource rich and steeped in tacit knowledge.

The point is this: Schools are resource rich and steeped in tacit knowledge. Yet teachers rarely share these tricks of the trade. Positive Deviance is an approach to social change that seeks out individuals, practitioners, and outliers in the school and community that model desirable behaviors. But the practice of seeking positive deviance is the act of seeking out outliers. Many times in schools, there are remarkable teachers doing great things for kids, and very few know about it. We are a humble bunch who don't want to come across as arrogant. In our experience, schools rarely look for positive deviant behavior. This means that valuable knowledge legacies are left untapped.

Teachers will often know that a teacher is successful, but rarely ever inquire as to why. Diane tells the story of a sixth-grade teacher known for teaching writing, who at retirement shared his binder full of student writing samples. Long before it became a standard practice, this teacher had figured out that well-written student samples provided attainable models for his students. It was only in retirement that the school community learned about his binder full of the best student writing. Diane laments, "If we had only looked into his success, we would have all benefited. Here we had an example of Positive Deviance in our school—a teacher who was successful—and we never thought to ask him how he did it."

This failure to notice continues to be one of Diane's regrets from her years as a principal. One cannot but wonder about all the untapped and unappreciated knowledge that accumulates in teachers' behavioral repertoire but never gets shared.

APPLYING POSITIVE DEVIANCE IN OUR SCHOOLS

Bill tells how Jerry Sternin and his wife Monique described their success to the board of directors for the National Staff Development Council (now Learning Forward). With a short time frame of six months, Jerry told us that he could not rely on preconceived questions, statements, directions, or information to find solutions. He knew he needed to immerse himself in the community in order to listen and observe very carefully and rigorously inquire about the few successes. By asking about the kids who were not starving and what their parents were doing differently, Jerry was able to identify positively deviant behaviors.

Positive Deviance is a model to find out what is working inside the system but has not been implemented systemwide. Not only do we want to find out what works for our kids, our parents, and our community, but we need to use this knowledge to build a more coherent knowledge base that can be passed on to newcomers. A leader can facilitate a mind shift from "OMG, more data, more guilt, and more time wasted!" to "We can learn from data that show deviance and better results." This shift focuses on how we know something is working and generates more interest and energy for finding new ways to improve learning for students.

> Positive Deviance is a model to find out what is working inside the system but has not been implemented systemwide.

DEFINE–DETERMINE–DISCOVER– DESIGN–DISCERN–DISSEMINATE

The Positive Deviance process (see Box 9.1), developed by Sternin and associates, is outlined with the six *D*s that are used to analyze a defined problem. Jerry's story, which follows, also helps to define the process.

Box 9.1 Positive Deviance Process *Ds*

■ Define: What are the problems? Solutions? Desired outcomes?
■ Determine: Where can we find examples of desired outcomes?
■ Discover: What are the unique practices of those who are successful?
■ Design: How can we design and implement an intervention?
■ Discern: How will we know if it is effective?
■ Disseminate: How can we make this knowledge (practice) accessible and scale up?

■ *Define*: What are the perceived causes? Solutions? Desired outcomes? Jerry asked, "Are there healthy kids in this community where many are starving?" The standard process had been to only look at the starving kids, not the healthy kids. But basically, Jerry was defining and reframing the problem.

■ *Determine*: Where can we find examples of desired outcomes? Jerry wanted to find children that were healthy who were living in the same community as starving kids. He started collecting information on the healthy kids. He also wanted to make sure that the healthy kids did not have outside resources that other kids would not have access to—for instance, an uncle who was a pharmacist in a neighboring town.

■ *Discover*: What are the unique practices of those who are successful? Once healthy children were identified, Jerry proceeded to find out what the families were doing that helped their children be healthy. He made a list of practices that parents and communities were using that produced healthier kids.

■ *Design*: How can we design and implement an intervention? Teams went out to compare and contrast the two populations. They carefully studied the practices of both groups in order to design an implementation plan.

■ *Discern*: How will we know if it is effective? In this case, the changes were observable. The successful parents fed their children four times a day instead of twice a day like the less healthy kids. The parents of healthy kids were feeding them small shrimps and crabs available in the fields; this was protein. These seemingly small differences in a couple of behaviors led to healthier kids.

■ *Disseminate*: How can we make this knowledge (practice) accessible and scale up? To introduce the new plan, Jerry and the team convened community conversations between parents of the healthy children and parents of the unhealthy children. They each shared what was working and what was not working and talked about what they noticed when their children were thriving.

Reflection

iStock.com/BlackJack3D

A Place to Pause

Think about your own experiences:

- Who could be positive deviants within the system?
- How could you find out more about them?
- How could their knowledge add to the legacy of the school?
- What insights can you gain from working with those whom you do not know well?

DATA-DRIVEN DISCUSSIONS—TAKING THE PATH OF POSITIVE DEVIANCE

In Chapter 1, we described a crisis in our midst. Of all the strategies offered in this book, we consider Positive Deviance to be the most important strategy for addressing this crisis based on current practices. Quite simply, our schools continue to look at what is wrong, not what is right, and the test scores trap practitioners in vicious counterproductive conversations. As the mandates have shifted to the need to examine data, the assumption has been that this will inform instruction. The reality is that analysis of test scores tells us nothing without looking for the behaviors that support the evidence. Actually, using the right kind of data and asking provocative questions are what is needed. We have lots of data, which alone doesn't tell us much. Frank and Magnone (2011, p. 207), in their book *Drinking From a Fire Hose*, say, "Data is a means to an end. It is the supporting character. Too often, it takes center stage." Positive Deviance conver-

> "Data is a means to an end. It is the supporting character. Too often, it takes center stage."—Frank and Magnone

sations provide ways to use the data to seek out real practices that make a difference for students.

Bill has effectively used this process to shift teachers toward solutions when analyzing test scores. He realized when he had all his teachers together, it was a prime time to seek out examples of Positive Deviance. Table 9.1 has questions that helped focus the conversation and bridge the gap of data to practice.

Table 9.1 Positive Deviance Questions to Put Data Into Practice

Question	Probing Deeper
▪ What are we not learning from our data?	Often, teachers learn generalizations from the data, such as students' need to increase reading comprehension. By asking this question in the negative, it moves the teachers away from the numbers and generalizations to real problems of practice.
▪ Where are the examples of success for this problem with this group?	This opens the door for teachers to share what they know. Have them explore this in pairs and then when it is time, report what they learned from a partner. This keeps the "know-it-all" from dominating and amplifies the voice of the humblest group members. Many times it is the quiet person who has a key to the puzzle.
▪ What are unique practices that are getting better results?	This begins the process of learning and developing knowledge coherence about what is being learned about success.
▪ How can those practices inform future interventions?	This question points to the development of a knowledge legacy. When real success is scaled and used by the entire community, it is valued and passed on to new teachers.

Bill wishes he had used these questions years ago while working with a group of high school English and reading teachers. He could see the staff was not as successful as they could be, and meetings were consumed by looking at data. When he looks back, he knows he could have shifted these conversations by using these strategies he developed later. Diane laments the years spent studying language arts data sets with elementary teachers. "More often, year after year, we concluded the same thing—that 'inference' was a critical skill." Another school spent hours working on a benchmark assessment for fractions. As one teacher put it, "We always ran out of time and never talked about how to help those students who just did not see fractions."

When we look, we find examples everywhere. High schools will often find that they have an attendance problem and yet never dig down into the data to find out what success with this same population looks like.

> Instead of developing benchmark assessments, which just generate more data, this process breaks down the abstractions and generalizations gleaned from the data and begins to map them to real teaching and learning in schools.

As we wrote this chapter, we realized that Positive Deviance is a powerful way to take teachers away from the numbers and toward seeking examples of positive behaviors that change practices. Instead of developing benchmark assessments, which just generate more data, this process breaks down the abstractions and generalizations gleaned from the data and begins to map them to real teaching and learning in schools. When humans learn to appreciate differences, they seek them out and persist in finding others that have the solution. In short, the culture begins to seek out differences and celebrate unique approaches for a myriad of challenges that teachers face daily. Furthermore, now, with the advent of the Internet, learning from deviance is much easier. Blogs, help services, and short videos are available to teach just about anything.

KNOWING HOW WE MAKE A DIFFERENCE— POSITIVE DEVIANCE IS EFFICACY IN ACTION

We consider seeking positive deviance a moral imperative for your schools. It is not acceptable to continue to ignore the years of tacit knowledge gleaned by teachers in a career working with children. It is a travesty that this knowledge is left unspoken. Even worse, the longer teachers are in a profession that does not support personal growth and development, the more likely they are to remain silent.

Wisdom comes from learning what we do not know; collective wisdom builds efficacy. When we think of positive deviants, they are highly efficacious individuals. People who believe they can have a positive influence on results, in fact, do. If they can't, they find a way to do it anyway. Finding the positive deviants, supporting them, and creating conversations that expand their influence increase collective efficacy in the system. The research by Tschannen-Moran (2004) and Hattie (2012) shows a definite correlation between collective teacher efficacy and student learning.

In addition, research on teaming by Edmondson (2012) supports that learning from each other as peers increases the exchange of ideas and promotes learning. Bryk and Schneider (2002), in their seminal work on trust, show that increasing trust among teachers has the most significant effect on student learning. When teachers learn from others, they change the way they interact and build knowledge coherence. Knowledge legacies become a way of life.

John Merrow (2015) reports that 80 percent to 90 percent of teachers go into the profession because they want to make a difference. As leaders, we want to promote learning that produces results and increases teacher efficacy. Not only is it the antidote to burnout; it also fosters high performance in students. Our belief that elevating teacher efficacy drives student achievement is important.

Bill smiles when he thinks of a conversation he had with Jerry Sternin at the board of trustees' meeting of NSDC/Learning Forward. Bill said, "Jerry, you are smart. Why didn't you just tell the officials what to do?" Jerry's answer was, "Do you think the people in Hanoi would believe two white people from Boston?" Point taken.

The fact is that we will listen to people who are working in the same school with the same kids rather than put stock in an outside expert to find THE answer. We certainly can learn from other schools/districts, which can provide possibilities, but in the end, we have to do the work in our school. Let's make sure we mine the minds of our own experts and look for group gold while we search for additional models that may help our kids.

> Let's make sure we mine the minds of our own experts and look for group gold while we search for additional models that may help our kids.

SCENARIO 1

This example would probably surprise Sternin, yet he would agree with it. Not only does Positive Deviance look to the outside, but it can also be used as a personal reflection tool. When humans get caught up in the stress of the moment, they forget what success looks like. They deviate away from practices that renewed their teaching and student learning. They start to experience burnout. In almost all cases of burnout, they have deviated from the positive.

As an antidote to burnout, teachers benefit from searching their own success stories for examples of positive deviance—something they did in the past but for some reason abandoned. This question opens doors for teachers to seek out their own deviations from the positive: "At what times in the past have you enjoyed the most success with students?" One teacher realized

> As an antidote to burnout, teachers benefit from searching their own success stories for examples of positive deviance—something they did in the past but for some reason abandoned.

that art brought joy into her classroom and decided that every week the class would complete at least one art project. Another taught Guitars in the Classroom and was thrilled with the warmth that his kids showed toward him and others during their sing-alongs. Another teacher had spent hours as a child making miniature scenes and decided that doing this same thing with his students would be a way to make some of his history units more interesting.

At another time, one teacher publicly stated her current group was the worst class she had ever taught. Later that day, her principal invited her for a check-in. As they talked about her class, the principal asked, "So tell me about your favorite class ever. What happened that year that made you enjoy teaching?"

This was a variation of the deviance question. The teacher was hesitant, but as she got deeper into the story, she realized that in the past she hadn't felt so pressured to get the textbook done (pacing guides had been mandated in the past two years). In prior years, she found time every day to do something that brought joy to her and her students, but somewhere along the way, she had abandoned this practice. Her principal gave her permission to reinstate this practice, even if the students did not finish the textbook. The teacher finished the year loving those children.

In another example, a teacher was shocked to learn that a parent had requested a transfer for her child after the first day of fourth grade. The child had come home complaining about how boring school was. Upon reflection, the teacher realized that the first day had indeed been boring; she had spent almost all their time on rules and routines. She shifted gears and pulled out a few of her favorite lessons, and by the end of the week, the student was happily settled into fourth grade. These tiny changes are like the bits of fish that the Vietnamese mothers gave their children—microscopic, tiny, seemingly unimportant details that are transformative in their power.

SCENARIO 2

Diane and her staff decided that they would take every minute they could from staff meetings to analyze student writing samples to give every teacher a chance to study writing from every grade level. Despite some grumbling from a sixth-grade teacher about looking at kindergarten writing, the staff prevailed, and he went along. They found a surprise when they hit fourth grade. Up until that time, a clear progression was noted each year as kids got better at handwriting, spelling, grammar, and their ability to put words on paper. Then they looked at the intermediate writing. Two fourth-grade classes stood apart; otherwise, there was not much distinction between Grades 4, 5, and 6. In every classroom, a few students were successful writers, but many seemed to have plateaued.

The teachers worked in grade-level teams to find answers to the question "What are the examples of success for high-performing students in each class?" The fifth- and sixth-grade teachers came to roughly the same conclusion. In each of their classrooms, about 30 percent of the students seemed to know how to write, but the rest did not. What they noted, with disappointment, was that unlike the primary writing, there was no clear developmental distinction from fourth to sixth grade. They were discouraged.

But one data set stood out—it was a positive deviant. Two fourth-grade teachers had more above-average writing samples than any of the other intermediate teachers. In the three fourth-grade classrooms, one class had a similar profile to the rest of the school—about 30 percent of the students were at grade level or above, and the rest were not. (Notable in all of the below-standard samples was a lack of complex thought.) However, the other two fourth-grade classes had 50 percent and 60 percent of the students above average.

As they talked with these two teachers about the "unique practices" that were getting the results, they discovered their answer. First, both these teachers had received advanced training in the writing process while none of the other teachers had. Second, when collecting the samples, the staff had decided that each teacher should do the setup they normally used when collecting a writing sample and assumed this would level the playing field. It turned out that this explained the deviance. These two teachers had engaged the students in their normal prewriting exercises. These teachers discussed the topic and made a visual map of what the students knew, listing words that might be difficult to spell. With the students, they generated a list of questions to get them interested in the topic. In these two fourth-grade classrooms, these teachers had learned to build in success factors before the students even started writing. Armed with the prewriting prompts, the students wrote more paragraphs with more complex thought and fewer errors in spelling. What is amazing is that Positive Deviance speaks for itself. All of the intermediate teachers wanted to receive the same advanced training as their fourth-grade peers.

Chapter 10

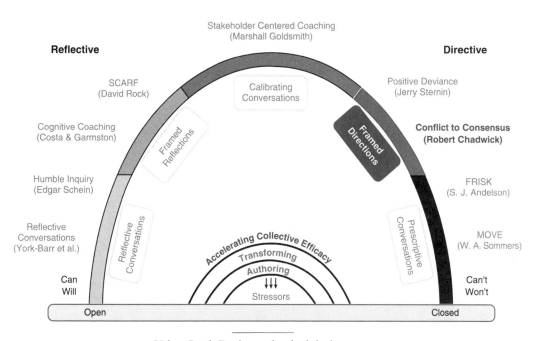

Stakeholder Centered Coaching
(Marshall Goldsmith)

Reflective

Directive

SCARF
(David Rock)

Calibrating
Conversations

Positive Deviance
(Jerry Sternin)

Cognitive Coaching
(Costa & Garmston)

Framed
Reflections

Framed
Directions

**Conflict to Consensus
(Robert Chadwick)**

Humble Inquiry
(Edgar Schein)

FRISK
(S. J. Andelson)

Reflective
Conversations
(York-Barr et al.)

Reflective
Conversations

Accelerating Collective Efficacy

Prescriptive
Conversations

MOVE
(W. A. Sommers)

Transforming

Authoring

↓↓↓

Stressors

Can
Will

Can't
Won't

Open

Closed

Urban Luck Design, urbanluckdesign.com

FROM CONFLICT TO CONSENSUS—THE CHADWICK PROCESS

What got me then, and gets me now, is your contagious insistence that we all possess huge capacity to confront conflict and find meaningful agreements with each other on public and private issues, issues that matter to most of us. You knew it was true.

—Nedra Chandler, obituary for Bob Chadwick

The Chadwick Process is the name we have given the procedures used by Bob Chadwick, who as a National Park ranger mastered the art of conflict resolution, working intractable conflicts such as preserving "old-growth forests" in Oregon. He was a master at moving from conflict to consensus. In this chapter, we use *consensus*, not *coherence*, because this is the term that Chadwick used. Indeed, he did work for consensus—an agreement to live with a "best possible outcome." While his work did bring coherence to intractable conflicts, this is not the term he used.

Bill and Diane had the privilege of working with Bob over the past twenty years. He had an unshakable belief that all possess a huge capacity to confront conflict. It took him ten years to write his book *Finding New Ground* (2013), leaving a knowledge legacy behind when he passed away in 2015. This legacy lives on through the many with whom he worked to resolve intractable conflicts over contentious environmental issues. We have benefited from his modeling and teaching in ways beyond what we describe here. We are grateful for his contribution to our world of education.

The Chadwick Process is designed to ameliorate emotional responses by facilitating deeper understandings of the conflicts. Notice that the word *conflicts* is plural; that is because most intractable conflicts are multifaceted—built layer upon layer over time. In his training, Bob made the point using a physical metaphor to demonstrate how conflicts multiply. While sitting in a circle, Bob invited the participants to throw an imaginary ball of yarn that represented the conflict. Each person continued to hold onto a section of the yarn. When the conflict first started, the yarn followed a simple trajectory. As more and more participated, the web got more and more complex. Finally, Bob said with smile, "Untangle it!" Point made.

Bob used this metaphor to foreshadow the complexity of his process; the group would spend a day or more untangling the *perceived* conflict. Early on in his work, Bob learned that conflicts were really about peoples' perceptions and that if perceptions changed, the conflict was resolved, almost like magic. This is why at the end of long days of work he could ask with confidence, "How will we know if we are making progress in dealing with our conflicts?" And, yes, everyone had an answer.

The Chadwick Process is focused on getting positive results and creating a powerful new community, made of those in conflict, organized around a new common purpose. The entire process developed by Chadwick takes considerable time. He

> The Chadwick Process is focused on getting positive results and creating a powerful new community, made of those in conflict, organized around a new common purpose.

believed it was necessary to take all the time one needed for deep questioning and listening. Bill has been able to adapt the process and shorten it in ways that work in schools. Diane has used many techniques she learned from Chadwick. No matter what a person's skill set, this process increases one's repertoire for dealing with "sticky problems." An expanded repertoire for working with conflict builds competence in facilitating group work, which leads to more confidence in the facilitator and by the group in their ability to work through any problem.

Diane remembers the first day she met Bob Chadwick. He began the workshop with twenty educators seated in a circle and asked, "What are you thinking and feeling?" With this simple act, he brought all the voices into the room and assured that everyone was listened to—an important first step in resolving any conflict. He always began his work sessions with this "grounding circle." From this first immersion, Chadwick worked to shift the focus from himself to the process and the relationship that was possible when people began to listen to each other. It was both subtle and powerful.

Later, he asked the group, "What is your relationship to conflict?" Each person reflected on his or her own personal relationship. Some of them avoided conflict, others embraced it, and a few danced with it. What was amazing was that this simple question was self-diagnosing. It was apparent why some dodged issues, while others confronted. What was interesting was the few that danced with conflict were the ones who seemed to have some sense about how to use conflict to produce creative ends; they were catalysts.

What we came to understand later was Chadwick's belief in the power of relationships. This deep understanding was not only about how we relate to each other, but how we relate based on our relationship to words that become constructs for thinking, acting, and learning. The reader will note that we have also asked relationship questions in some of our Pauses for Reflection. We ask you to once again pause.

Reflection

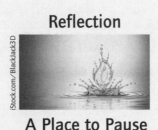

iStock.com/BlackJack3D

A Place to Pause

Powerful Questions

- What are you thinking and feeling right now?
- What is your relationship to conflict?
- What is your relationship to the conflict at hand? (Choose any conflict.)

FIVE SOURCES OF CONFLICT

Over the years, Chadwick identified five sources of conflict, which are listed in Box 10.1. We have added some examples from our experiences in the schools.

Box 10.1 Change–Power–Scarcity–Diversity–Civility

1. Change—Changing curriculum, implementing technology, new policies
2. Power—Differentials in power between students and principals, principals and central office, parents and school
3. Scarcity—Staffing, budgets, supplies, time, favoritism
4. Diversity—The Big 3 (ethnicity, race, and poverty) and also different response patterns, styles, or other ways of responding
5. Civility—Disrespect, anger, cattiness, sarcasm, criticism

When there is conflict, the challenge is how to maintain relationships while moving toward consensus. The Chadwick Process can be used with small groups, large faculties, or with two people in conflict. An individual can also use this to self-coach himself or herself through a difficult problem. Bill, who worked the most closely with Bob, has also used this process with students, staff, and parents.

SET THE EXPECTATIONS

Chadwick developed a conflict resolution process in which every action he took had purpose. He placed participants in a circle to bring balance and maintained that balance by calling on people from different sides of the circle. It was subtle, but this balancing of voices was the beginning of the goal—to learn to speak across conflicts with one voice. He had very purposeful opening activities that set the tone for the day. He would point out that even though we were all in the same room, the views of the room are different, depending upon where the focus goes. This creates different visual points of reference. From the vantage point of the circle, he'd note that some participants saw windows, while others saw doors or curtains, and only a few saw a bulletin board. All could shift their vantage point and see other things by changing their perspective. He believed if you could change your perspective in the room, you could also change it about the conflict.

Bob Chadwick had clarity of purpose, which was the unshakable belief that conflict could be turned into consensus. Balanced participation, belief in people's best intentions, and total honesty are hallmarks of this process. It is not for the faint

> Bob Chadwick had clarity of purpose, which was the unshakable belief that conflict could be turned into consensus.

of heart. But Bob would "sit in the fire" and refuse to be swayed by blame and shame; he had learned ways to persist and to break through the barriers to learning.

To slow down the process and assure that all are heard, the participants are taught how to chronicle their understandings on charts. These extended periods of writing require deep listening and slow down the process, which is why it often takes more than a day. Everyone in the circle should take turns being a facilitator, a recorder, and a contributor.

Bob's key values about this work are listed in Box 10.2.

Box 10.2 The Chadwick Process Key Values

■ Value each member by giving her or him a chance to speak.

■ Value each person by using his or her words.

■ Value collaboration by working together to draft summaries.

■ Value equal participation with roles as facilitator and recorder being changed and shared often.

■ Value honest statements about beliefs and opinions.

■ Value respect and civility.

■ Value careful design of human interactions to maximize collaboration.

■ Value shared leadership.

THE PROCESS FROM CONFLICT TO CONSENSUS

> For Chadwick, every move was purposeful and contributed to creating balance, equality of voices, collaboration, and ultimately consensus.

For Chadwick, every move was purposeful and contributed to creating balance, equality of voices, collaboration, and ultimately consensus. Chadwick designed his process so that everyone was involved and had a chance to speak and be heard. This is why he started with the "grounding circle" in which he took the time to let each person comment on what he or she was feeling or thinking. The opportunity to express one's thoughts (the cognitive) and the feelings (the emotions) created safety. Participants could also pass, but most did not. While the grounding activity could include a larger group, he often would break up large groups to between six to ten people to keep voices active and use time efficiently. We have found, however, the more intractable the conflict, the more important it is to keep the integrity of the entire group in the early stages of this work.

Chadwick was a master at bringing "balance" to everything that he did. For example, to ensure that everyone participated, he would have participants share in a clockwise order and then reverse to use counterclockwise sharing. Depending on the size of the issue, the process could take days, partly because the community groups were polar opposites.

We have shortened his process for our purposes, but those that work with conflicts regularly will want to reference his book. Box 10.3 summarizes the steps, which are explicated further later.

> ## Box 10.3 The Chadwick Process Map
>
> - Identify the issues; make sure everyone has a chance to speak. (ISSUES)
> - What is the Worst Possible Outcome of not solving this issue? (AVOID)
> - What is the Best Possible Outcome of solving this issue? (GOALS)
> - What strategies and actions are you willing to take in order to make the Best Possible Outcomes a reality? (ACTION PLAN)
> - What will be the evidence that the Best Possible Outcomes are happening or not happening? (ASSESSMENT)

1. *Identify the issues.* Whatever the problem is, what do the participants see as the most important issues at hand? Sometimes, the answers are vague and/or blame external causes (e.g., parents don't support us, kids are unruly, central office won't back us up). At the beginning, people may feel no power to change anything. But as solutions become apparent, efficacy increases, and more responsibility will appear. The goal is to get clarity on the issues from the participants' perspective and the efficacy of believing they can influence decisions or behavior. The Chadwick Process uses lots of wall charts to capture group thinking, and this sets the stage and the expectation that everyone will be both a facilitator and a recorder of ideas.

2. *Worst Possible Outcome.* The first question the groups tackle is, "What is the Worst Possible Outcome if you cannot solve this issue?" Chadwick found it was critical to get the fears and concerns out in the open. One superintendent queried, "Why start with the worst possible outcome?" The answer is that most people come into the room believing the worst will happen. If these fears are not openly expressed, people keep those issues unsaid. The Chadwick Process instructs the groups to get as specific as possible and to put their words in writing on large paper and post it so it is visible by all. Two alternative questions can sometimes bring a different perspective to this process: What is happening that they don't want to happen? What is not happening that they want to happen?

TAKE A BREAK. After discussing the negatives, Chadwick schedules a bathroom and coffee break. It gives time to shake off the downward emotion of negativity associated with the problem. If a break is not possible, pull the group back together and talk about process and the reason they are in the room. These are more neutral conversations and help to shift the mind away from the negative. The participants want to start fresh when they move to the next phase—what they really want.

3. *Best Possible Outcome.* After a break, the group is redirected to focus on the possible. Chadwick noticed that when under stress, which is the case in high-conflict situations, people talk more often about what they don't want. It is like being stuck in reverse gear. So the question is designed to shift the focus to what we do want. "What is the Best Possible Outcome by solving these issues?" Groups respond in kind. They usually pause—remember that time needed to shift into reflection? This is the time to listen most carefully, as carried in these messages are microthoughts of hope. Participants will have more energy and produce more possible actions when they are motivated by what they want, rather than having the defensive posture, avoiding what they don't want. Furthermore, hearing others with the same motivations increases the engagement, as they finally start to move toward a common understanding.

4. *Strategies and actions.* Having a goal is important and insufficient. A vision without action often goes into the "wall of binders" that most experienced educators have noted in administrative offices. When talk substitutes for action, change will not happen. So now the groups respond to the question, "What strategies and actions are you willing to take in order to make the Best Possible Outcomes a reality?" The more specific the action, the better the chance of getting the actions into the organization. Some of the actions might even focus on one person or a small group. The important part is that those who need to take the responsibility are in the workshop and agree to be responsible.

5. *What will be the evidence?* Now that goals have been set and strategies/actions outlined, it is time to develop the assessment criteria. Ask for both short-term and/or long-term evidence that we are moving toward or away from the Best Possible Outcome.

Bill has a favorite metaphor to help explain this evidence-based feedback process. When you are driving to a place like Lake Tahoe in the mountains and you see a sign that says San Francisco, which is on the coast, you know you are going the wrong way. Likewise, Bill asks groups to identify the goal posts that indicate when the group is approaching or getting farther away from the goal. This list of evidence—or the goal posts—becomes the assessment plan. Finally, finding a way through intractable conflicts is a remarkable feat, especially when at the beginning many of the people will not look at or talk to each other.

To sum up, this process is designed to shift from "What we can't get done" to "What do we want to accomplish?" Additional questions are "What are we going to do?" and "How will we know if these actions are making a difference?" The question "How will we know if these actions are making a difference?" is perhaps one of the most powerful questions of this book. This data set created by the

> The question "How will we know if these actions are making a difference?" is perhaps one of the most powerful questions of this book.

assessment plan, if done well, allows groups to follow through and reflect on their collective efficacy with any one of the various conversations in this book. Once again, the Chadwick Process opens the door; it is then up to the collective to follow through and make the commitment a reality.

An important part of this process is to feel heard, and that is validated with a verbal paraphrasing followed by the charting, which becomes a visual paraphrase by capturing each participant's words accurately. To trust the process, people need to see their own words, not words filtered through another person. By changing facilitators and recorders at every step, everyone has to take her or his turn at listening more deeply; this is a built-in, shared responsibility. To keep the groups moving and the thinking clear, only one thought is allowed per turn; however, participants can take as many turns as needed to ensure that all are heard.

No process is perfect; sometimes, a few people have not been willing to move on. The process makes it clear to the group who is willing to change and work through differences and who is not. This evidence step is critical, and in the next chapter, you will learn more about how to document these aberrant behaviors. At this point, the group or an appointed authority needs to ask this question: Who *Can* and *Will* stay on to do this work, and who *Can't* and *Won't*?

FOLLOW-THROUGH—DOCUMENTING THE KNOWLEDGE CONSENSUS

This process of writing out and merging ideas occurs four times in Chadwick's model—worst, best, strategies, and evidence. Merging the words sends the message that they are working together toward common goals. The process of working together to merge the data into summary statements is designed to help people work together. It is important for people to see their words in the document. It is

> The process of working together to merge the data into summary statements is designed to help people work together. It is important for people to see their words in the document. It is important for them to tinker with the small wording differences and the larger problems that divide. Getting small consensus on some words leads to a larger consensus later.

important for them to tinker with the small wording differences and the larger problems that divide. Getting small consensus on some words leads to a larger consensus later.

Once this process is complete, the work is not yet done. If the group is large and there are many subgroups, the ideas need to be winnowed down to the most important. Voting is best done in public before the group leaves, but it can also be done through an online voting process. Using the Best Possible Outcome chart, look for themes that emerge. During a break, combine ideas, count the final list, and ask participants to pick their top one-third. Voting for the top one-third winnows the list down to a manageable size. One voting process usually surfaces options all can live with, but the beauty of weighted voting is that if there is no clear winner, the group can vote again to pick their top one-third from a shorter list.

Initially, participants can be confused by this kind of voting process; yet over time, they come to appreciate it and even suggest it. This type of voting creates a "both/and" process instead of an "either/or" and keeps groups from repolarizing around positions. Additionally, many of the options stay alive in the participants' minds and can be operationalized without entire group input. Often, participants leave and decide to make their preferred options a reality. For example, in one meeting a participant really wanted the group to commit to a newsletter to keep them better informed. While the idea seemed good at the time, it did not get the top votes and so became a lesser goal. Realizing that she was the only one of a few that really cared about it, she had a choice: to let go or step up and be responsible to act on her desired outcome. In this case, she volunteered to do a quarterly newsletter for the group for the next year and then reevaluate. This created a win–win solution.

All of the summaries are kept for future reference and create a knowledge legacy. That act also signals the words are sacred, and the original data can be checked if necessary. Cell phone photos make collecting the data easy. And as is the nature of groups, as already noted, a few folks will stay dedicated to one of the less popular outcomes and work on it in a small group or on their own, further expanding the reach of the changes taking place in this newly formed consensus community. Well-defined positive outcomes are memes; they get into our brains and stay around until we take notice and do something about them.

Diane found that these kinds of records created by entire staffs hold a consensus that can serve as a guide for actions over the long term. When a consultant worked with her staff using a process similar to Chadwick's, the charts generated by her staff about future outcomes became an invaluable road map for Diane during her four-year tenure there as the principal. The key is to keep the record, review it, and continue to act on it. Having so many positive outcomes generated by your own staff is a gift of leadership and builds a collective consensus not often found in other group work.

Follow-up is extremely important, as is communication. We strongly recommend typing up the outcome, strategy, and evidence charts to be distributed or kept as background information. These summaries, when well done, create knowledge legacies. The summary statements should always be on top, with supporting documentation to follow. By distributing the information, you reduce the confusion of what happened in there. Transparency builds trust—no binders hidden away on shelves.

SCENARIO 1

The Chadwick Process was invaluable to Bill when he worked at high schools. Here are two examples; one was used at a staff meeting and the other to deal with departmental conflicts.

At one school, staff complained often about a wide degree of interpretation of school rules. As trivial as it seemed, hats and cell phones were hot issues. Despite school rules, some teachers let kids wear hats and use cell phones in class. By breaking the staff into groups of seven to ten people, Bill followed the process outlined earlier and brought the staff to consensus about how to implement the rules—most importantly, how to hold each other accountable. Bill reports that the process took most of the day, but they did come up with goals, actions, and ways to tell if their consensus was working. The longer-term benefit was that this was one of the first times this large high school staff (125 certified members) had ever experienced the rewards of consensus. This conversation mattered and helped to shift the culture to one based on outcomes.

Bill also used this process to work with a department that always seemed to be in conflict. Personalities clashed, and Bill realized he needed to intervene. In the end, the process did not go as planned, but it did resolve the problem. Bill worked with the department to get issues about the conflicts on the table, to determine worst possible outcomes, to come to agreement on the best possible outcomes, to identify what actions each was committed to, and what the evidence would be for a good working relationship. The meeting went well, and all left agreeing to follow through.

After two weeks, there were still issues. Another meeting was scheduled. Blaming and accusations continued. Bill made a decision to tighten the timeline for assessing the evidence. For one month, they would meet one day a week after school for a check-in. At the end of the month, it was apparent that the issues were not going to be resolved, and it was clear that one person was the problem. Using the FRISK method (see Chapter 11), Bill had a private conversation with the teacher and told her, "You will need to bid out of this department to another assignment." The teacher adamantly said, "I don't have to; you can't make me." Bill responded, "By contract, I can't move you. But I will document the lack of progress in developing professional relationships in your evaluation, and that will require, as per contract, a remedial work plan." The teacher opted out. She clearly did not want to be part of the solution.

SCENARIO 2

Bill found himself as a new principal in a very contentious athletic meeting between parents and coaches. Being new to the school, he listened and hoped for resolution. After thirty minutes, things began to escalate, and he realized he needed to intervene, or they would be there all night. Bill realized that they were not talking to each other and that no one was even dealing with the issues. Emotions were going up, not down. With all the stakeholders in the room, this was the time to manage the conflict, not later, and the chatter after the meeting would surely escalate this problem. Bill knew he needed to take control and that he needed control of the process, not the content. He stepped in and implemented a shortened version of the Chadwick Process summarized here.

Question map:

- Parents: What are the most important issues from your viewpoint?
- Coaches: What are the most important issues from your viewpoint?

To reverse the order of voice:

- Coaches: What are the worst possible outcomes if we don't resolve this issue?
- Parents: What are the worst possible outcomes if we don't resolve this issue?

To reverse the order of voice:

- Parents: What are the best possible outcomes if we resolve this issue?
- Coaches: What are the best possible outcomes if we resolve this issue?

To reverse the order of voice:

- Coaches: What strategies and actions are you willing to take to make the best possible outcomes happen?
- Parents: What strategies and actions are you willing to take to make the best possible outcomes happen?

To reverse the order of voice:

- Parents: What will be the evidence that will tell you we are moving toward the best possible outcome?
- Coaches: What will be the evidence that will tell you we are moving toward the best possible outcome?

Because Bill did not have the time to write out what was said, he used careful paraphrasing. At each step, he created a summary paraphrase and asked for agreement before moving to the next one. In the end, the group had consensus about what they wanted. Both sides had specific actions they were going to take. They planned a meeting in one month to assess their progress. Bill was exhausted; this particular meeting took almost three hours, but it was well worth the time.

The gift of this type of work is the power of the positive change that emerges when groups collaborate on their outcomes. Even agreement on the worst outcome by both sides—that the coach would lose his job—was a move toward consensus. Realizing that neither side wanted to see the coach go, they now had a common goal and created outcomes that included the coach talking with kids about changes in lineup and that the parents would go back to having spaghetti feeds before the games to help fundraise for more time on the ice. Another conversation that mattered!

Chapter 11

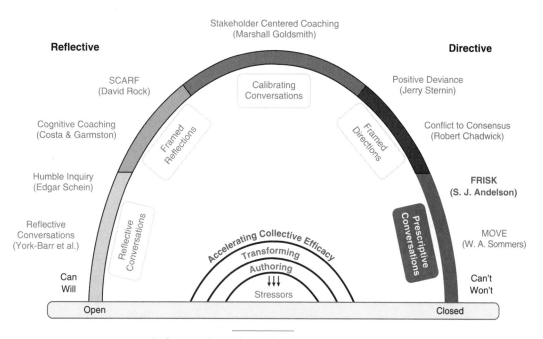

Urban Luck Design, urbanluckdesign.com

FRISK—MAKING EXPECTATIONS CLEAR

Incredible change happens in your life when you decide to take control of what you do have power over instead of craving control over what you don't.

—Steve Maraboli

The originators of the FRISK model would likely be surprised to find their documentation guide in a book about conversations, and yet as we worked on the Dashboard, it became obvious that the tools provided by FRISK belonged on the arc as an invaluable tool for providing direct, candid feedback. Leaders must attend to employees who do not meet expectations; it is especially important for the success of conversations that appointed leaders manage problems that interfere with effective group work. When appointed leaders ignore bad behaviors, they lose respect from their constituents and also run the risk of having others join in the bad behavior. At some point, it is the appointed leader's responsibility to step in and define expectations and then to hold participants accountable. This is where the FRISK model comes in.

The FRISK™ Documentation Model was developed as a communication tool to help promote positive change and correct misconduct. Developed by lawyers, its original purpose was to document the primary elements of *just cause*—the necessary information needed for termination in a progressive discipline system. The acronym reminds administrators of all the parts that need to be in a letter of warning or of reprimand.

> The FRISK model is assertive, yet considerate in that it is both instructive and corrective.

The FRISK model is assertive, yet considerate in that it is both instructive and corrective. The facts are paired with a statement of rules that make the employee accountable. So while the supervisor takes responsibility for "telling" the employee what is wrong, the clear message then places the burden of improvement squarely on the employee's shoulder.

Diane often found herself teaching this model to the administrators when it was time to document an employee's problem behaviors. Over time, she also realized it was an effective way to provide verbal feedback—an early warning signal—to an employee that he or she was not meeting expectations.

There is no substitute for clear communication. This FRISK model provides a template for providing clear messages (see Box 11.1).

Box 11.1 FRISK: Acronym for Universal Components Needed for Just Cause

- F—Facts that provide evidence of the conduct
- R—Rule that establishes the authority
- I—Impact of the behavior on the work environment
- S—Suggestions for improvement and statement of expectations
- K—Knowledge of the employee's right to respond and provide corrective information

Diane has personally used this process both informally and formally and also has coached supervisors in how to use it with their employees. Here is an informal example from Diane's work that explains the steps.

INFORMAL APPLICATIONS OF FRISK

A ubiquitous problem on elementary playgrounds is teachers who do not show up for yard duty, despite repeated reminders. When it was brought to Diane's attention that she had a repeat offender, she decided she could not ignore it. She asked to meet with the teacher after school about the duty schedule. Knowing that this teacher would have lots of excuses, she wanted to have his undivided attention when they talked. And she wanted him to know the topic in advance to provide him a chance to be reflective, if he chose.

When he arrived, he tried to act as if nothing was wrong. Diane asked him to sit down and then asked him to listen to all she had to say and that then he would be able to respond. Her speech went like this:

Today, you did not show up for yard duty at the 10:30 a.m. recess. *(Fact)* The schedule is published, and teachers are expected to show up or find another to cover. *(Rule)* When you don't show up, you put the other teacher at a disadvantage; you are also negligent, and if some-one was hurt, you would be liable and make the school liable as well. *(Impact)* I need you to tell me how you plan to make sure you do not forget this responsibility and that you will show up on time. *(Suggestion for improvement)* I consider the safety of our children so important that failure to comply will mean that I will put a formal reprimand in your personnel file. *(Knowledge)*

She finished with, "Now it is your chance to respond."

The teacher started with an excuse—he had gone to the bathroom and then had run into another teacher and forgot to go to the yard. This required Diane to circle back and make a new rule that she expected him to follow. Diane explained that if both teachers had done this, the students would have been unsupervised. The rule she expected him to follow was to let his kids out a min-ute or two before the appointed time and to report to the playground. As soon as the other teacher arrived, he could excuse himself; but he needed to come right back. She then asked him what he needed to do so he would not forget the duty schedule. He decided that he should write his duty schedule on the chalkboard and ask his kids to help him remember.

> Being nice did not work with this teacher, but being firm and clear did. I never had another problem.

Diane reflects on what really worked in this instance: Being nice did not work with this teacher, but being firm and clear did. She never had another problem.

Observable Facts—First-Person Data

One of the hardest parts of this process is getting firsthand facts. Legal advisors never want secondhand knowledge and so advise against hearsay. A principal friend of Diane's once had two teachers report that they had witnessed a teacher roughly shaking a student outside the classroom door. The principal explained that she would need them to provide firsthand testimony and asked these teach-ers to go back to the teacher at fault. She coached them how to give an honest statement of facts to that teacher. She said, "Tell her the facts of your observa-tion, then tell her the rule, which is that as professionals we cannot ignore abu-sive behaviors toward children, and then tell her that you have reported it to the principal." In this case, the principal decided that a reprimand was in order, and because she had firsthand testimony to document the letter, her FRISK letter was well done and would have held up in a hearing. Fortunately, it never went to a hearing; the teacher shared that she was having personal problems and needed some time off to sort things out. She asked that this be shared with her team-mates, and all were grateful that she would take care of her own mental health first. She came back later and retired two years after that.

Likewise, in order to solve the problem with the yard duty schedule, Diane needed her staff members to report on their peers. She used FRISK to help the teachers understand why being nice and covering for another teacher was negligent. As you read along in Diane's example that follows, label the parts of FRISK. At a staff meeting, Diane laid out her expectations:

> We have a problem. It has been reported to me more than three times in the last month that teachers have failed to show up for yard duty. It is a contractual obligation that teachers complete "other duties as assigned." Failure to report another teacher is negligent. I want to make the impact of being nice to a colleague clear. When you stand out there alone and fail to act, you are negligent, and you also make the school negligent. This is not about being nice; this is about being responsible. If a teacher is not on the yard soon after the recess starts, please send a student runner to the office to report the absence. Someone will cover until the teacher is located.

What she did not tell the teachers, she told her office staff. When a student came to report a "failure to show," they needed to contact Diane immediately so that she could go the yard and cover. This also gave Diane that valuable firsthand information. Diane laughs, "For 90 percent of the teachers, this was enough. For that one teacher, he needed to be FRISKed in order to get the message."

Having open, candid conversations with staff about these kinds of problems and helping them understand that it is once again everyone's responsibility to be accountable contributes to the overall cultural value for open, honest communication. Learning how to give difficult messages is a necessary skill. Administrators need it, teachers need it, and Diane has even taught parents to use it. The French have a proverb: "Children need models more than critics." The students need models for how to deal with difficult situations.

> Having open, candid conversations with staff about these kinds of problems and helping them understand that it is once again everyone's responsibility to be accountable contributes to the overall cultural value for open, honest communication.

A Fair Shot at Improvement

While this meets the legal requirement for documentation should the supervisor need to terminate the employee, it also gives the employee a fair shot at improvement. It is positive in that it makes clear what the expectations are and lists corrective action that gives the employee a chance to commit to change. Indeed, we have found that when an employee understands and accepts the expectations there is usually improvement; however, if the employee does not seem to hear the message and argues to defend behaviors, changes usually do not occur. This is a pivotal point in the relationship, as when no change is forthcoming, it may mean that it is time for the employee to move on, which is the topic of the next chapter.

Typically, following a progressive discipline procedure, this type of a conversation may be held several times in an attempt to help the employee improve. The supervisor has to decide if the effort to improve the behavior is worth the time invested. In some organizations, such as public employee unions, the discipline needs to be progressive, in that the first time might be a verbal warning.

Reflection

iStock.com/BlackJack3D

A Place to Pause

As professionals, we often state that we want to have open, honest, and candid conversations with peers, and yet, we avoid them.

- How might you apply FRISK to communicate a concern with a colleague?
- Which parts of the FRISK conversation are most difficult, and what does that tell you about your relationship with candor?
- How might you apply FRISK in a future conversation? Jot down some reminders or mentally rehearse so you are ready when need be. These conversations work best when they occur soon after the offending behavior.

FORMAL APPLICATION OF FRISK—
DOCUMENTING THE PROBLEM

F—Facts

At this point in the communication, the message needs to be explicit and observable with appropriate examples. It should tell what, when, where, and how the facts were gathered. To illustrate the steps, here is an example of the application. This needs to be a first-person report and not anonymous. It should not include belief statements or other justifications. It should state just the facts, as this example shows:

> On April 1, 2017, you came into the office at X school and told the secretary, XX, that you had looked her up on a dating website. You then asked if she had met anyone "hot." The phone rang, and then you left. The next day you came back in the office and said that you had told a friend that she was "hot" and that he should look her up. XX was embarrassed by your comments and told you her dating life was private. For the next week, you continued to pester her each afternoon, asking her if she had any "hot prospects." XX says she tried to ignore you. She was finally fed up and complained to me.

R—Rule

Stating the rule is easy if there is a clear violation of a written guide, such as a board or administrative policy, an employee contract, professional standards, or other such document. If this is not the case, a rule can be established that then becomes a standard by which all future behaviors will be measured. In the previous example, the behavior had become harassing in that it was unwelcome and repeated. Most workplaces have rules about harassment. While the sexual innuendo seems clear here on paper, the employee later pled that he was "just trying to be friendly." He also thought because she was on a dating site, that made it public. To avoid any future confusion, it is time to make a clear rule that will become the new standard of behavior.

> The behavior described here has occurred over time and has sexual overtones. If it continues, you will be violating the Board and Administrative Policies (list numbers for harassment and sexual harassment). Furthermore, online dating sites are designed for adults to meet other like-minded adults; they are not to be thought of as a way to delve into another's private life during work time. We expect employees to be professional and to give other employees the respect they would want for themselves. This means that what you learn about others on the Internet on your own time should not be brought into the workplace. You would not want others talking about your dating life, and you need to show others the same respect.

I—Impact

This is the first time the supervisors can weigh in with their own feelings and beliefs. At this point, they should start with the larger impact statement for the organization, but they can also include their own values and beliefs.

This is the kind of behavior that eventually leads to a hostile work environment as addressed in Board and Administrative Policies (list numbers for policies on hostile work environment). XX was very upset about your insinuations about her dating life and does not think she can work with you. As a custodian, you need to be able to work with the secretary, and she needs to be assured that you will not bring up personal topics of conversation. As a woman, I am also offended by your behavior in that describing a woman as "hot" treats her as a sexual object, not with the respect she deserves.

S—Suggestions

This is best considered as a "needs" statement in that it describes what you need them to do. It should also be thought of as a chance to teach about policies or other written documents used to guide behaviors. By taking time to teach, you are verifying that this person now understands the rules.

> I am providing you with the written policies so that you are well informed about the implications should you continue or repeat this behavior. In addition to improving the working relationship, she needs to be assured that you will not harass her further. From now on, you will need to clean the office after the staff has gone home, and when you come to the office, it will need to be for business purposes only.

K—Knowledge`

This is the part that provides the due process protections. Not only have you informed them of the problem, but you are now telling them the consequences of their action. You are also telling them that this is their chance if they want to clarify or rectify anything with you. This is an important conversation, and often, there are contractual or policy procedures in place. For example, in some districts the employees need to sign to indicate that they have been informed of their rights.

> The fact that we have written policies about sexual harassment means that we take this misconduct seriously. For this reason, I will be placing a written summary of these statements in your personal file, and as per (list policies or contractual requirements), you have a right to respond in writing as outlined in that document.

> The FRISK model makes what would normally be a difficult conversation manageable.

The FRISK model makes what would normally be a difficult conversation manageable. In most cases, it provides a civil way for the employer and an employee to meet and confer about a problem. Sometimes, employees can be less than grateful and begin to verbally attack or blame the supervisor. Once again the FRISK process assists the leader in staying on topic. When the employee attacks, the administrator can respond, "I know you are upset about this meeting, but attacking me does not solve the problem. If you think there is something we could have done differently, you can put it in writing as part of your response." This allows the supervisor to stay out of an argument with the employee.

SCENARIO 1

Interventions done early are always better than ones that occur after a longer period of the behavior. If the principal had become aware of the custodian's behavior when it first happened, she could have had the female employee use a modified FRISK message. It would have been a direct message and would have gone something like this.

> Yesterday, you came in here and started talking about my dating life and the website I use. I need to set a rule about our conversations at work. I do not talk about my dating life at work. It embarrasses me when you talk about me being "hot." I also do not like you meddling in my dating life. I need to know that you will stop telling friends about me and also stop talking about this with me at work. Will you do this?

This intervention likely would have stopped the behavior, and if it didn't, it would give the supervisor more information about how inappropriate this custodian was, despite warnings. It would have also saved this female employee from the distress she suffered as a result of his harassment. She had a great deal of emotional distress about this episode, and it took a lot of work to help her understand that this was a first warning and that they would have to have conversations from time to time, as that was the nature of the job.

SCENARIO 2

Diane used this process to facilitate a conversation that came up at a staff meeting about the norms. It turns out that one of the more senior teachers was upset that so many teachers brought other work to the staff meetings. She wanted to make a rule that staff could not bring other work to the meeting. This created quite a debate. Just looking around the room gave the facts. One teacher had a stack of papers to grade, another was knitting a shawl, another brought stationery and wrote notes to her kids, and so forth. Here is how the FRISK process worked in this meeting.

The facts were obvious; staff members did bring other things to do. The problem was there was no consensus about the rule. Some thought it was fine to not allow outside work; some were offended that others wanted to control their behavior. (Note: The SCARF themes of status and autonomy are playing out here as well.)

The valuable part of this model came with the honest discussion of impact. It turns out that the teacher with the concern felt that it was disrespectful to Diane for staff members to do other work. It did not demonstrate listening. Those that did other work pointed out that their work, such as the knitting or grading of math papers, allowed them to listen and work. Others indicated that not all agenda items were of equal value and that they should be allowed to do other things as long as they did not distract others. Diane finally had to admit that she was one of those who brought work to the meetings she attended.

As they talked, it became clear that there were times in staff meetings that Diane didn't need every teacher's attention; but they often used staff meetings for important conversations. Indeed, this conversation was one of them—everyone was engaged. They agreed on a rule. Staff members could bring other work to meetings, and when Diane needed all the staff to be engaged, she would tell staff it was time to put away their projects and to focus. They would check in to see how the rule was working at future meetings.

Diane said the rule worked like a charm. It was a win–win. The solution respected autonomy and also showed respect when needed.

Chapter 12

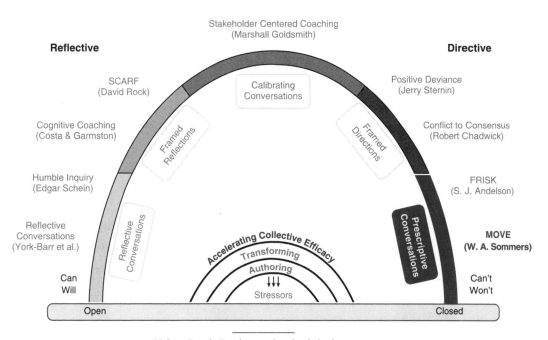

Reflective

Directive

Stakeholder Centered Coaching
(Marshall Goldsmith)

SCARF
(David Rock)

Calibrating
Conversations

Positive Deviance
(Jerry Sternin)

Cognitive Coaching
(Costa & Garmston)

Framed
Reflections

Framed
Directions

Conflict to Consensus
(Robert Chadwick)

Humble Inquiry
(Edgar Schein)

FRISK
(S. J. Andelson)

Reflective
Conversations
(York-Barr et al.)

Reflective
Conversations

Accelerating Collective Efficacy

Transforming

Prescriptive
Conversations

MOVE
(W. A. Sommers)

Can
Will

Authoring

↓↓↓

Stressors

Can't
Won't

Open

Closed

Urban Luck Design, urbanluckdesign.com

12

MOVE—TIME TO
MOVE ON

I would have preferred to carry through to the finish, whatever the personal agony. . . . But the interest of the nation must always come before my personal considerations.

—President Richard Nixon's resignation speech

What do you do when nothing seems to work? This is the question that most leaders worry about. The fact is that every strategy we have proposed will work. The truth is that every strategy we have discussed won't work. Remember, there are *NO* silver bullets.

Having said that, truth telling is challenging. Having the courage to confront teaching and leading that is less than effective is difficult. Leaders are constantly balancing expectations and actions in the belief that we can figure out the puzzle of learning and leading and supervising for improvement. When adults fall back on the tried and true, assumptions are not examined, and learning is most certainly not happening in a way that makes students successful. Progress becomes elusive and schools languish, attempting to make course adjustments that ultimately fail their students. The leader's responsibility is to kids, but ultimately, leaders must deal with the adults.

> Having the courage to confront teaching and leading that is less than effective is difficult. Leaders are constantly balancing expectations and actions in the belief that we can figure out the puzzle of learning and leading and supervising for improvement.

Having progressed to this point in the book, as a leader you now have many ways to engage individuals and groups. You have been introduced to a multitude of approaches for creating meaningful conversations. You also know that your job is to engage constituents in deep conversations about practice. This lens expects that professional collaboration can be used to measure success. When communities engage in deep collaboration, those that do not engage are easy to pick out. When you notice that it is not happening, a tough decision lies ahead.

As always, the first question to ask is "What evidence do I have that this person truly wants to learn and change?" Obviously, when employees admit to their failings, then the discussion can turn to what is getting in the way. This opens the door for counseling or other support services that might help get mental health support or even point them toward a new career. It also allows the administrator to start the process of making sure that the employees know how serious this is and that their job is in jeopardy. We have both seen employees improve when faced with this dire consequence.

Unfortunately, changes at the last minute are often too late. Diane tells the story of a special education teacher who had terrible relationships with children. Together, she worked with Diane on some strategies to improve her rapport. It was slow going and took much of Diane's time. By law, Diane had to give her notice of termination seventy days before the end of the school year. After that notice, the teacher completely changed the way she worked with the children. The change was really quite remarkable in how the fear of losing her job made her pay more attention and make changes. As Diane thought back on this experience, she realized that perhaps this teacher had a future, but it would not be in that district. Once the school board had taken action, she needed to follow through. Bill also adds, "When you have to whack employees over the head, they probably need to move on."

Let's face it: The work of leadership in schools is tough work, and despite our best efforts, we can alienate people when we tell them they do not have a job. These same people can make our lives miserable, and the worst part is they take far too much of the leader's time. Sometimes in schools, we live with problem employees because their failings are elusive. Despite our best efforts, the changes made are minimal, yet there does not seem to be sufficient grounds for termination. This is a problem of mediocrity. We admire a principal friend who chose to transfer, knowing that another leader could accomplish some of the things she had not. She stated,

> I decided to ask for a transfer after nine years. I am proud of the changes we made early on, but there are some folks who didn't come along. At this point, I am not going to change them, and it is time for someone else to try.

Let's face it: The work of leadership in schools is tough work, and despite our best efforts, we can alienate people when we tell them they do not have a job. These same people can make our lives miserable, and the worst part is they take far too much of the leader's time.

When—despite your best attempts to be increasingly clear about expectations—there are still missteps and when you have provided data to document the failings, it is essential to move to the next step. In the face of evidence that the feedback is not being received in a constructive way, the leader must assume that person is not capable or willing to make the necessary changes. As Einstein and others have said, "If you always do what you've always done, you will always get what you've always got." Without the courage to confront adult failings in the name of students, not much will change. Before giving up or shutting the door, here are some options.

MOVE

Bill loves acronyms and developed MOVE as a way to think about the next steps in a tough process. It allowed him to take a few humanitarian steps before finally saying good-bye. The first step is to decide if any kind of a move, such as a transfer or other option, is viable. As an intermediate step, the administrator should work with the personnel director to consider options requiring district support. Sometimes a leave of absence can give an employee a chance to make changes in his or her personal life or seek medication or counseling. When all else fails, it is time to confront the problem directly through termination and say, "You are done." Before finally saying good-bye, though, there are steps that Bill takes in considering other options (see Box 12.1).

Box 12.1 The MOVE Process

M—Move to another assignment.

O—Outplacement; consider other job options, including career counseling.

V—Voluntary or involuntary leave: Will this help?

E—Exit the problem by moving for termination.

The first option is the candid conversation in which you as a supervisor return to previous conversations such as FRISK and revisit the lack of progress being made. The humane next step is to inform the person that her or his job is at risk and then ask, "What is keeping you from accomplishing . . . ?" Then listen. At this point, the person might become defensive, creating less-than-pleasant circumstances. When the person only attacks the supervisor and blames him or her for the failure and is unwilling to take any responsibility, the path is clear: It is time to move on. A less obvious but also equally damaging response is an attempt at sabotage, which manifests as ignoring the supervisor and going out to try to divide and conquer by getting support from friends. This is also a signal that no changes are intended. Before final termination, consider the following intermediate steps.

Move to Another Assignment

The leader with positional authority has the right of assignment in most districts. Sometimes, a staff member is not doing well in one situation, and moving to a new area might be better. Change in venues can help a person regroup for success. We have seen this work in moving a teacher to a different grade level in elementary school, to another department in middle school, or by changing the teaching assignment in a high school setting, all assuming proper certification. This is predicated on the belief that you want to keep the staff member in the organization, and she or he has qualities worth keeping. This should not, however, contribute to the system failure sometimes called "shifting the burden" or, more crassly, "the dance of the lemons," in which failing employees are just moved around an organization.

For example, it became evident to Bill that an experienced (over thirty-five years) social studies teacher was not keeping up with the new curriculum approved by the board. He was very good person, a stellar community member, and was well liked by other teachers. The problem was further complicated by frequent complaints from students that his classes were boring, and the numbers of kids taking his advanced class were dropping each year. He always had a complaint or an excuse about why he could not address the issues. Bill was able to move him to an in-school suspension position (no loss of pay) using right of assignment—not an easy decision, but it needed to be done. This was done with the cooperation of the HR department and the superintendent. It gave this teacher the extra years he needed to maximize his retirement earnings—certainly a humane thing to do.

Being nice is not a leadership act; being thoughtful and fair in the service of students is. Bill knew it was the right decision when he was able to bring in an experienced replacement and the requests to take the AP class went up 30 percent. Within two years, they needed to add another teacher to handle the increased requests.

Offer Outplacement Services

There are times when a leader consistently is aware that staff members are unhappy with their own performance. They would like to change careers or go back to school, but taking that step is scary for many reasons. Districts are well served to offer some recompense to help this person move on. Offering outplacement services can be a positive step for the person as well as the school and has a positive, humane effect on the culture. We also have negotiated this process when there have been budget cuts resulting in staff reductions.

Here is an example to consider. Diane had a teacher involuntarily moved to her school; it was to purportedly to give her a second chance and allow her to receive some extra coaching from a vice principal. Early in the year, it became evident that something was not quite right. While her teaching seemed satisfactory, she rarely got through a week without an angry outburst from one of her students. Finally, the vice principal got a chance to see the problem in action—actually, the problem for this teacher was inaction. When a few students would start to act up, she was passive and used a voice that lacked command. Then other kids would jump in and try to control their peers' behavior; soon, the class was riled up. Even with coaching, this teacher seemed to be unable to change. Finally, Diane asked, "What is keeping you from being firm?" She began to cry. It turned out that her father had been abusive, so she never wanted to raise her voice with kids. In her case, she belonged to a church that had a preschool position open. The vice principal knew of this position and suggested that perhaps she consider taking an assignment with younger children. She applied, was hired, and actually did quite well with a more open, less structured environment with younger children.

While we have not seen it happen often, from time to time our districts have also offered employee support programs, and these have helped teachers decide to retire early or take a leave of absence to get more training. The Minneapolis Federation of Teachers, under the leadership of Louise Sundin, had a program in which the union would assign a mentor teacher to work with staff that were having difficulty in the classroom. In California, the Peer Assistance and Review Program became part of contract language and offered similar support. In some cases, these programs made a huge difference for an employee; in other cases, there was no difference at all. They did provide constructive ways to offer assistance before termination was considered.

Voluntary or Involuntary Leave

Although rare, occasionally staff members will leave the organization, either temporarily or permanently. In most cases, if they are honest with themselves, they report that they are not feeling productive, know they chose the wrong career, or personal issues are causing a decline in effectiveness. When not motivated by a job, it is better to find a new career that generates some passion, energy, or commitment.

Our example here comes from a friend who describes how a principal was handled in a district. The principal had served for many years, but over time, the mistakes he made had built up enough that he had no respect from his teachers. It is important to note that he was a nice man and that the teachers liked him and enjoyed his humor. They just did not respect him as a leader. When the board tried to terminate him, the teachers rose up in alarm—they correctly perceived a lack of ongoing support for improvement from the board. The board backed down, and the principal went back to the school—nothing changed. Fortunately, a new superintendent came in with many years of experience in personnel and found an elegant solution. The teacher had skills with technology, so he was asked to take a partial leave from the principalship and work part-time to build the technology capacity of the district. As part of this plan, he would job-share with a retired principal, who would also provide him with some coaching. Unfortunately, while the technology job was a good match, the district did not have funds for a full-time positon, and he did not make much progress in improving his relationships with the teachers, despite the coaching. It was time to move on. Once again, the principal thought he might be able to get the teachers to back him up; they refused. He had been given a more-than-fair chance to improve, and he had not changed his behaviors. He finally agreed to resign instead of being terminated. As one teacher put it, "Fair is fair, and he did not take advantage of the help."

In another example, a very dynamic, popular teacher showed up after summer break sporting a new, countercultural haircut. To make matters worse, his behavior seemed erratic. One week into the school year, he suddenly panicked, turned his class over to another teacher, and left campus without checking out through the office. By that time, parents and teachers had started complaining about bizarre behaviors. Some students reported that the teacher frightened them because of his loud, erratic outbursts. The personnel director chose to put him on immediate paid leave and forbade him to come to campus during the leave. As part of the process, a FRISK notice was given, both verbally and in writing. The principal was perplexed. How had this dynamic, creative teacher become so irrational? The teacher insisted that there was nothing wrong and was belligerent in the meeting. The following week, he showed up a block from the school, handing out copies of the letter from the personnel director on one side of the paper and his statement of dismay about his treatment on the other. Needless to say, the parents were relieved that he had been "locked out of the school," to use his words. Finally, the teacher's wife showed up in person and told the real story. She had married an amazing man, and until that summer, he had been a loving husband and father. She was aware that he took medication, but she did not fully appreciate how important this medication was for his mental health—he had been diagnosed as bipolar. Together with the wife, the personnel director confronted this teacher; he needed medical help, and if he did not get control of his life, he could possibly lose his job. This entire episode ended happily, but it took this teacher most of the school year to get his life under control. He went back into the classroom later that year and has been successful to this day. Not only did the leave give him time to rebalance his life with medication, but it also saved him from sabotaging his career. Parents were aware of the problem, but because it was handled quickly and effectively, his behavior did not become the lore of gossip. When a reputation is ruined, teachers need to change schools, grade levels, or districts to get a fresh start.

Exit the Problem by Moving for Termination

When students aren't learning at the level they should be and there has been little cooperation in trying to improve, parting company is the best alternative. After reading this, you might be thinking, "Yikes, this is the hardest conversation." Remember, you are dealing with a very small number of people. In over forty years of administration, Bill has removed only four teachers before the end of the year; Diane has been a bit tougher because of the short tenure period in California. However, only once did she remove someone before the end of the year. Caution: You must have district support before you take this step. And at this point, there should have been multiple conversations, so it should be no surprise to the staff member.

A Word on Termination

There is another *E* that will need to be addressed—*Evaluate*. Without a proper progressive evaluation process, the removal process will not seem humane. There was a time in California when teachers in the first two years could be let go for "no cause." The lawyers often advised administrators to give no input—to just say, "Things have not worked out." Diane remembers how crazy this made some teachers; they could not understand why the district was letting a good person go. Instead, in Diane's district they decided to pick the one area that stood out and use that as humane explanation for termination. It was amazing that a clear statement such as what follows calmed them down: "We have worked hard on student discipline this year, but you still have too many problems with students." Think about it; don't we owe it to others to at least leave some door open for improvement? After all, they will go on to seek other employment. We do no favors by denying information that is evident.

There are times that the four steps of MOVE do not work, and formal termination is required. Personnel directors and legal advisors will often tell administrators they have not done enough evaluation. As leaders, we do not get to make a decision based on "no data" or limited documentation. Yes, paperwork is cumbersome. Yes, evaluation takes time. Yes, we would rather not have to go to these lengths, but we must. This is a leadership responsibility and obligation to students, staff members, and society as a whole. As a colleague of ours, Skip Olsen, former business agent for Minneapolis Federation of Teachers, said, "We don't want bad teachers in the schools either. We want to ensure the process is correct. Make the case for removal. Don't expect to make an arbitrary decision." Good advice, and it is part of our job description.

In our experience, working the process using FRISK and MOVE in an unemotional way is perceived as a humane way to do business. We all are compassionate and don't want to hurt anyone; this allows for both compassion and a steadfast commitment to serve in the best interest of students. Bill once had a union representative say, "I hate to lose a teacher, but I also know how much time you have spent trying to help and change teaching behaviors. It is the right decision."

> In our experience, working the process using FRISK and MOVE in an unemotional way is perceived as a humane way to do business. We all are compassionate and don't want to hurt anyone; this allows for both compassion and a steadfast commitment to serve in the best interest of students.

We know that at some point nothing is going to work. There may not be support in the administrative levels above, or there may be political situations that make removal impossible. At that point, we recommend going back to FRISK and MOVE strategies. Continue to hold this person accountable, and do everything you can to make the situation better or build the support needed to move her or him on. On a positive note, your best teachers know that protecting inefficiency or incompetence does not help them in the school or the community. The willingness to confront hard issues turns out to be a positive cultural intervention; it sets a benchmark for high standards. Use these strategies wisely.

Reflection

iStock.com/Blacklack3D

A Place to Pause

While personnel issues are confidential, most school staffs are aware of problems with peers and almost always know something about the interventions being made by an administrator. When you are aware of administrative action

(Continued)

194 • CONVERSATIONS DESIGNED TO BUILD KNOWLEDGE

(Continued)

that may result in MOVE, how do you work with the affected peer? Do you sympathize? Do you avoid? Or do you "bear witness" (support the colleague without rescuing)?

Think about it: If you were in that situation, you would want to know that your peers cared. Here is a way to engage in a reflective, professional, and supportive conversation.

If you engage in this kind of conversation, do not sympathize; simply listen, paraphrase, and let the person know you care about him or her as a person.

- ▪ "I sense that you could use a listening ear right now, would it be helpful to talk confidentially with me about what is going on?"

Then, if appropriate, try probing further with questions that keep the person focused on what she or he might do.

- ▪ "Wise counsel once told me we learn most from our missteps. What are you learning during this tough time?"
- ▪ "What might you learn from this experience that would help you in the future?"
- ▪ "At times like this, it can help to focus on what we do well. What is it that you'd most like to focus on in these next few weeks with your students?"

It is helpful to separate the issues by stating what you can and cannot do. (This is especially necessary if you have been a mentor or a coach for this teacher.)

- ▪ "I can't really help you with this problem, but I can be here to allow you to reflect out loud with me about what you are experiencing."

If any of these probes are rebuffed, stop. The intent is to be there for the person, not to fix him or her.

Final reflection: How might these kinds of interactions make a difference for a school culture?

Part V

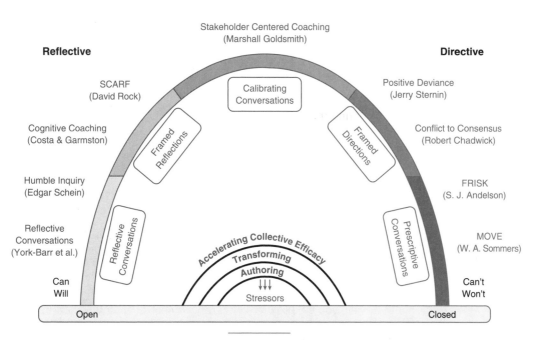

Reflective   Directive

Stakeholder Centered Coaching
(Marshall Goldsmith)

SCARF
(David Rock)

Calibrating
Conversations

Positive Deviance
(Jerry Sternin)

Cognitive Coaching
(Costa & Garmston)

Framed
Reflections

Framed
Directions

Conflict to Consensus
(Robert Chadwick)

Humble Inquiry
(Edgar Schein)

FRISK
(S. J. Andelson)

Reflective
Conversations
(York-Barr et al.)

Reflective
Conversations

Accelerating Collective Efficacy

Transforming

Authoring

↓↓↓

Stressors

Prescriptive
Conversations

MOVE
(W. A. Sommers)

Can
Will

Can't
Won't

Open   Closed

Urban Luck Design, urbanluckdesign.com

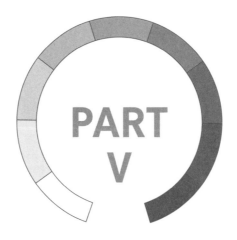

PART V

FINAL MUSINGS—
MAKING UNREALIZED
DREAMS COME TRUE

In many ways, Bill and Diane still have unrealized dreams. We no longer work daily in schools, yet we care passionately about learning. We wonder what it would have been like if we had known what we know now. Almost every day, we think of recommitting and returning to the daily work of schools—we miss it.

We think about how if we had it to do over again, we would sit down sooner, spend more time listening than talking, and seek out the tacit knowledge of teachers as a way of building knowledge legacies. We now invite you to join us in surveying the landscape of schooling; how might you apply what you have learned within these pages to accelerate collective efficacy?

This journey is not for the faint of heart, and each of you will surly stumble as we did. Know that you are not alone, and if you just reach out, you will find others who willingly will join the journey. When humans struggle together and learn to solve the most difficult challenges, they develop a sense of collective capability that anything is possible. They find satisfaction and renewal in their work and are less swayed by the passing fads, enjoying more control over their professional destinies.

The moral imperative weighs on all of us; how long can we wait? Not long— our students deserve the future we are capable of producing, not something that someone long ago thought was tried and true. The key is to understand that we are ultimately responsible for our own personal learning trajectory. Leaders must seek more and more ways to turn the responsibility for learning back to the participants and to hold them accountable to produce actionable learning. Likewise, teachers can apply what they are learning about their *own* learning to the classroom. Students can tell when adults care deeply about their craft in the ways they pass on that wisdom.

As part of this process, teachers not only question each other, but they learn to question the experts and to seek ever-greater understanding about what makes a difference in the learning of students. When professionals know what they stand for, can articulate how they make a difference for students, and are willing to question each other to find central truths, they create a professional narrative of excellence. When schools make it a priority to make time for quality conversations that matter, teachers engage in more contemplative thoughts about teaching and learning. Each one of the Nine Conversations outlined in this book opens a different door for deep reflection about what really matters for teachers. Furthermore, each one of these Nine Conversations can also be used in classrooms to invite students to reflect on their own learning trajectories.

The old model of an enlightened professional leading the way is no longer sufficient. Teaching and learning have become way too complex to depend on just a few in charge; all must engage and become contributing experts in their own way. Over time, part of the professional repertoire should be about how to engage in these types of quality conversations. Only then can teachers take control of their own professional development and insist that the implementation of mandates from outside be considered carefully and embedded in practice through a process of reflecting in–on–for action. It is this reciprocal process that will make the difference and give the profession back its voice. Not only will educators be rewarded with better working relationships, but they will find that all of these reflective practices can also be used with students.

Chapter 13

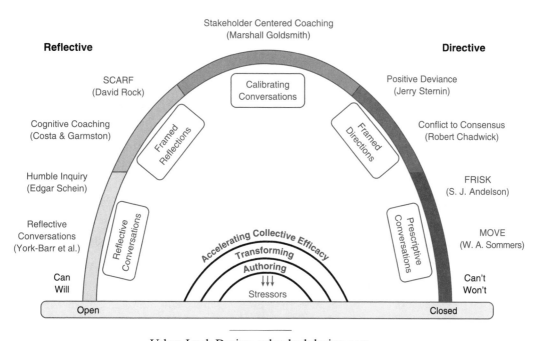

Stakeholder Centered Coaching
(Marshall Goldsmith)

Reflective

Directive

SCARF
(David Rock)

Calibrating
Conversations

Positive Deviance
(Jerry Sternin)

Cognitive Coaching
(Costa & Garmston)

Framed
Reflections

Framed
Directions

Conflict to Consensus
(Robert Chadwick)

Humble Inquiry
(Edgar Schein)

FRISK
(S. J. Andelson)

Reflective
Conversations
(York-Barr et al.)

Reflective
Conversations

Accelerating Collective Efficacy
Transforming
Authoring
↓↓↓
Stressors

Prescriptive
Conversations

MOVE
(W. A. Sommers)

Can
Will

Can't
Won't

Open

Closed

Urban Luck Design, urbanluckdesign.com

LEAVING KNOWLEDGE LEGACIES

We can, whenever and wherever we choose, successfully teach all children whose schooling is of interest to us. We already know more than we need to do that. Whether or not we do it must finally depend on how we feel about the fact that we haven't so far.

—Ron Edmonds

Unrealized dreams come back to haunt us. Ron Edmonds wrote the opening quote in 1979, almost forty years ago, and it is still germane. We use this quote to challenge the reader. The question is no longer "Can we?" but rather "Will we?" Our answer is, unequivocally, "Yes, we will. Let's get started."

First and foremost, quality conversations matter, and this book is your launching pad to start authentic, practice-based learning conversations. The hard work is left to you, the dedicated educators who will make a difference in how our teachers develop the knowledge for teaching and learning, which will be passed on as knowledge legacies.

This book is about *learning*—it is both that simple and that difficult. Learning is a dynamic process with continual cycles of reengagement at deeper and deeper levels. The job of all—leaders and participants alike—is to serve as catalysts to provoke this profound way of learning. Purposeful attention to how we learn is even more important, as the knowledge bases of our world both explode and implode.

> The job of all—leaders and participants alike—is to serve as catalysts to provoke this profound way of learning. Purposeful attention to how we learn is even more important, as the knowledge bases of our world both explode and implode.

This way of being, which seeks collective transformation, is the gold standard of learning and establishes important role models for our students. Ask any student over ten years of age, and she or he can usually articulate examples of excellence and how it made a difference in the classroom. One fifth grader described how her teacher never let the students off the hook—she'd keep nudging their thinking until they had an answer that made sense. As this wise fifth grader put it, "Now that's good teaching!" A high school student described how his history teacher differentiated on so many levels. Not only was he culturally sensitive, always including role models from diverse historical perspectives, but he also had a way of making the history come alive so that students wanted to read the textbook and other supporting material. The tests were all open book, but students needed to have studied it to do well. He remarked, "I do not think anyone ever got a failing grade—he just wouldn't let you fail." Learning legacies leave lasting impacts on students.

THE UNREALIZED DREAM— KNOWLEDGE LEGACIES

Our Professional Conversation Arc reminds the dedicated professional to seek options and to expand possibilities for building knowledge coherence. Your challenge now is to step up and respond to new ways. Trying these new strategies to change the context of learning will determine the quality of your leadership experiences. Will they be renewing? Or will they continue to sap energy and create burnout?

Kegan and Lahey (2016) state, "The single biggest cause of work burnout is not work overload, but working too long without experiencing your own personal development." In their book *An Everyone Culture* (2016), they chronicle how three businesses sustained the cultural focus on learning and progress. They argue for a

> "The single biggest cause of work burnout is not work overload, but working too long without experiencing your own personal development." —Kegan and Lahey

radical idea—that the culture that stakeholders create is the strategy. This is so important that we yell it out here: THE CULTURE WE CREATE IS THE STRATEGY. Drucker (1990) also reminds us, "Culture eats strategy for breakfast." How the culture embraces the need for transformation makes all the difference.

To this end, all of us must find our own personal truths—those honest and deep understandings about teaching and learning. And together, we must forge professional partnerships to establish knowledge coherence—knowing how we agree and disagree. No one new to the profession ought to start from scratch;

instead, those new to the profession should be assured of inheriting robust knowledge legacies—the best of all that the previous teachers gleaned through experience. Indigenous cultures have always privileged learning from a wise elder. Let's learn from our elders and our experiences to contribute to our legacy. The African proverb we quoted in an earlier chapter reminds us: "When an old person dies, a library burns." Let's not let the library burn. Let's keep adding to our learning and repertoire to reach more and more students.

Reflection

iStock.com/Blackjack3D

A Place to Pause

- As you reflect on this book, what has most convinced you that it is time to change the conversational paradigm?
- How could these conversations presented in this book have served you in the past?
- Reflect on past conversations and then mentally rehearse new patterns.
- What are some of the models that you might try in future collaborations?
- How might you introduce changing conversational patterns, and how will you take action to change the culture?

CREATE LEADERSHIP TEAMS— BRICOLEUR BUDDIES

This book, *Nine Professional Conversations to Change Our Schools*, offers a mental map for acting in "real time." Do not delay—jump in and try a few different ways of conversing—and as confidence grows, try more. Ask others to join you and support you in changing the conversational dynamics and professional interactions. When practitioners respond effectively and authentically, they model learning and grow in confidence and competence. In writing this book, an aha moment came when we realized that we often intermixed the various conversations, pulling in what was needed at any given point in time. When we work with educators, we are always tinkering, trying to stretch and learn more. Bill christened us "Bricoleur Buddies." *Bricoleur* was a term used by Marsha Sinetar years ago that means "someone who tinkers with ideas." We are

Bricoleur Buddies who are constantly trying, talking, and taking note of how our learning bridges to action in classrooms, schools, and districts.

Practice-based knowledge draws information from both outside experts and personal, internal resources. This melding of the internal and external ways of knowing bridges the knowing–doing–learning gap and allows educators to speak up for the profession about what matters and makes a difference. This agency is what will give the profession an authentic voice and the professional efficacy to stand for what matters.

This proactive stance creates a coherent voice and builds collective efficacy, creating school cultures that embrace any dilemma as a problem to be solved. When groups embrace learning in this way, it is a gift to behold. It can be a single teacher telling a student, "In my class, students do not fail; it's my job to help you figure out how to learn. And I will need your help to figure it out." Soon, a noncommittal student is talking with his teacher—another conversation that matters. Or an intake team that tells a parent, "We know you may have had bad experiences at other schools, but we do not intend to let that happen here. The minute you perceive a problem, we want you on the phone to one of us." Starting an invitation to converse on any level opens doors that have typically been shut.

Paraphrasing from a poem by William Stafford, there is a thread we follow toward collective efficacy as we learn that anything is possible. Indeed, the possibilities often exceed expectations, and others wonder how we did it. Collective efficacy to the uninitiated is difficult to see or even understand. Our strength is in knowing that when we hold that thread, we will never lose our path; despite it all, we always come back to our own capacity to adapt and learn. In the end, strategies that do not change culture become fixed and nonadaptive. Adaptive strategies always expand. Look around at your own situation. Who are the "learning omnivores" at your site? Who do you hang with—people who sap your energy or people who zap and energize you? Where you place your attention sends major signals about what you find important.

As always, we wish the wisdom imparted through this book had come to us sooner. We learned much of what we share through the school of hard knocks— trial and error. This means we made many mistakes; yet each one pushed us to learn more. Years ago, Art Costa asked, "What do you do when you don't know what to do?" Let's choose adaptive learning rather than acquiesce.

As school administrators, we dealt with teachers at their best and also at their worst; teaching is not an easy job, and the stresses of the classroom are challenging. Early in our careers, when we observed these stress responses, we felt helpless and often did not know what to do about it. Bill laughs, "When I heard teachers blame the students, I used to privately say to myself 'Bullfeathers, there has to be a better way!'" This frustration certainly propelled us to both spend our careers figuring out better ways to meet the needs of students. It is one thing to try to reduce the stress by making organizations work more efficiently; it is yet another to engage all stakeholders in becoming responsible for the solutions and creating cultures of collective efficacy that renew.

> When school cultures evolve and focus on positive futures, they value the power of the conversation to puzzle through problems. They begin to appreciate differences and to seek out those different viewpoints to both support and challenge belief systems. They report that their school culture transports them beyond personal biases and assumptions that inhibit capacity and toward understandings that open up possibilities.

When school cultures evolve and focus on positive futures, they value the power of the conversation to puzzle through problems. They begin to appreciate differences and to seek out those different viewpoints to both support and challenge belief systems. They report that their school culture transports them beyond personal biases and assumptions that inhibit capacity and toward understandings that open up possibilities. Through these experiences, staffs demonstrate a collective empathy gleaned from the capacity for deep listening. They stand tall for the profession and speak with the voice of coherence: "Yes, we do know how we make a difference." These schools appreciate the value of knowledge coherence and use this as a way to introduce newcomers to knowledge legacies. This is a tall order; yet it is not optional. Our schools depend on the collective mission to survive, thrive, and renew the spirit—knowing that we are collectively strong.

To change cultures takes courage. Dr. Dennis Peterson, superintendent of Minnetonka (Minnesota) Public Schools, told us what he looks for in principals: "They have to be willing to have the hard conversations if they want to work for me." Dr. Peterson holds his leaders to the same high standard he holds himself. That is why there is a directive side to our Dashboard of Options to use when needed. When schools are failing, leadership has the responsibility to find out what is going on and take necessary action.

COLLECTIVE EFFICACY IS OF SERVICE TO STUDENTS

An even larger issue is at stake here. Now, as we write this book, more than ever, students need adult role models that demonstrate the value of collective empathy, efficacy, and legacy. Kids watch every move we make and notice how we respond. Bill again hits the nail on the head: "Yikes, I really am responsible for my behavior."

An example comes from one young man who reminded his mother of these values and turned a tough conversation around. Early in a school year, a new teacher lost his cool and swore at this student. Knowing he had done wrong, the teacher immediately contacted the principal, and together, they sat down at the end of the day with the student and the parent. Initially, the parent was angry and unforgiving—that is, until the student said, "Mom, in my last school the teacher would have lied. My teacher didn't lie; he apologized." This turned the conversation around. This mother became one of this teacher's biggest fans, and the student worked hard to manage his impulsive behaviors. Kids intuitively know when school cultures support their growth and development; they also know when schools care more about protecting turf and live in a "culture of complaint." Paraphrasing St. Francis of Assisi, if your walking isn't your preaching, there is no sense in walking anywhere to preach.

Effective schools understand that the conversations must ultimately return to three questions:

1. What impact does our work together have on student learning?

2. What impact does our work together have on adult learning?

3. More importantly, how can we make this impact visible to students, parents, and the community?

When we ask educators about successful leaders and their schools, they repeatedly report a focus on continual learning and human growth and development. They also report that these schools and the leaders in them challenge them beyond expectations; and despite the hard work, they feel renewed. Excellence builds renewal; failure creates burnout.

Early in Bill's career, Art Costa challenged him with a question. We repeat it again here: "How are you creating a mentally stimulating environment for this staff?" Bill still says, "I have to do that, too?" This question continues to drive our thoughts and actions. Now, we ask you as the reader, how would you answer that question? In what ways do you support this goal of creating a mentally stimulating environment in schools? How do you work to expand the conversations so that those engaged want to linger and go even deeper into the collective understandings?

While slowing down to have more meaningful conversations can seem time-consuming, in the end the efficiencies brought by healthy communication far outweigh the alternative. Our goal is to reduce the amount of time spent on managing drama and direct our time and energy to individual and organizational learning as a system. This book was written to add repertoire to your

> Culture affects the leaders. Leaders affect the culture. Everyone is responsible.

skill set, to help you be more efficient and effective in the day-to-day interactions, and to help you sustain a long-term focus on learning through meaningful conversations. Culture affects the leaders. Leaders affect the culture. Everyone is responsible.

Finally, we are optimistic because we were able to experience the great gift of being part of many diverse, learning-centered communities. Through these experiences, we learned new ways to think and act to find alignment and coherence; when this happened, we experienced joy—the joy of working with those who care and who make all the difference. Who are your most treasured learning omnivores that increase your learning and are catalysts for the learning of others? When was the last time you thanked them? Thank them TODAY.

We leave you with a message of hope. As difficult as it seems, we are hopeful for a better future for kids, colleagues, and community. We have seen, at close range, how cultures can be shifted. It is NOT easy, and it is IMPORTANT. Box 13.1 holds one last gift, another of Bill's favorite acronyms, which he published earlier in 2006 in the *Journal of Staff Development*.

Box 13.1 HOPE for the Future

H = Honesty & Humility

O = Openness & Options

P = Persistence & Patience

E = Enthusiasm & Empathy

So let's add to our repertoire to create leadership efficacy and to become the catalysts that create the positive fractal that ripples out by changing the culture and the world. Educators deserve it, the kids deserve it, and most importantly, you deserve it.

We close with a quote from Angeles Arrien, a dear friend who passed away several years ago. She is literally calling us forth from the grave. "If your job is to wake up the dead, GET UP—TODAY IS A WORK DAY."

Namasté.

APPENDIX

CREATING KNOWLEDGE LEGACIES WITH MICRO-TEACHING AND VISUAL ANCHORS

Diane often solves problems of group dynamics by teaching her staff a micro-skill she has picked up from her readings. By creating a visual anchor as a reference, complex concepts are broken down and visually represented so that this micro-skill can be applied in staff meetings. She describes the context in which she taught her staff two micro-skills here.

The power of these useful reminders was brought home when she used them to frame the conversation with the superintendent as described in Scenario 2 in Chapter 7. Her instructions based on the two graphics were clear to her staff. She told them to first seek to understand, and then to think about these two things as they related to the charts:

1. Balance paraphrasing and inquiry with advocacy. (Chart 1)

2. Remember that your responses will be at the initial levels of concern. (Chart 2)

When it came time for the appointed meeting with the superintendent, several of the teachers brought these graphics to the multipurpose room and posted them behind the superintendent. Diane laughs, "I do not think the superintendent ever noticed them, but he did notice that the staff were unusually sophisticated in their approach to the conversation."

BALANCING INQUIRY WITH ADVOCACY (CHART 1)

As a young principal, Diane inherited a more senior, strong-willed, and fiercely independent staff. They set high standards for themselves and expected everyone to rise to these expectations. At staff meetings, a few tended to dominate. In order to help them learn to listen more to each other, she took about fifteen minutes to introduce them to a concept she had learned from Peter Senge (1990). As a way of teaching, she first drew the diagram the way Senge drew it in his book (no paraphrasing), and then she added paraphrasing (from her

Cognitive Coaching work) to the mix and showed how it further tips the scales toward understanding and increases the power of the conversation. She then had the staff practice this new skill with an issue already on the agenda. The new graphic stayed up in the staff room, and from time to time, she would recommend on an agenda that the conversation about that item would use the tool Balancing Inquiry With Advocacy.

Balancing Inquiry and Advocacy

Source: Diane Zimmerman. Adapted from research in Senge, P. (1990). *The Fifth Discipline: The Art and Practice of the Learning Organization.* New York, NY: Currency. *Image source*: iStock.com/iarti

CONCERNS-BASED ADOPTION MODEL (CHART 2)

When Diane first assumed the role of principal, she noted that her staff struggled with many mechanical problems that impacted their ability to teach. Teachers did not use the new computer lab because they did not understand how to use it. Several teachers spent precious instructional time cleaning acetates for a now-antiquated piece of equipment, the overhead projector. They often complained that there was not enough of a new set of math manipulative to go around and so forth.

Even more insidious was their "culture of complaint" about anything coming from the district office. Each time Diane put one of these items on the agenda, she would expect emotional outbursts from some of the staff.

As a way of helping teachers better understand the process of adoption and innovation, Diane taught them about the Stages of Concern (1990). As she told her teachers, the most important question we each need to ask is about impact: "How does what I am teaching impact my students?" She explained that when teachers get bogged down in the early stages of an adoption, they forget this aim. Diane challenged them by saying, "If we pay attention to these early levels, we can accelerate our adoption and are then in a better position to evaluate the efficacy of our work."

Diane's initial reason for introducing this concept of change was to help them self-diagnose the mechanical problems that were keeping them from excellent teaching. She used the example of the acetates and offered to work with teachers who were using the overheads to come up with a solution. "Ironically," Diane states, "it turned out the entire staff was interested. Many had not chosen to use this tool in their teaching for just these mechanical reasons. Overnight, I needed more projectors for my teachers." Once the teachers understood how important it was to manage the mechanical, they came up with all kinds of ways of solving problems. It was the first time the staff had worked together on their own to solve a systemwide problem.

Diane reflects,

What I did not realize until later is that it also gave me a tool to manage the emotional outbursts about the district office. I realized that these outbursts were often at the lowest stage of innovation and that I could use this model to frame a conversation by asking, "What is it about this district office that creates such an emotional response?" Being new to the district, I learned more from my teachers about the district history and also that they were hanging onto now-ancient memories. Most of the key players who created the angst were long gone. Just talking through the issues changed the dynamic; at future staff meetings, these outbursts disappeared.

Stages of Concern About the Innovation

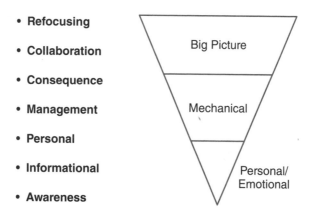

- **Refocusing**
- **Collaboration**
- **Consequence**
- **Management**
- **Personal**
- **Informational**
- **Awareness**

Source: Diane Zimmerman. Adapted from research in Hord, S. M., Rutherford, W. L., Huling-Austin, L., & Hall, G. E. (1987). *Taking Charge of Change*. Alexandria, VA: ASCD.

REFERENCES

Andelson, S. J. (1998). *FRISK™ Documentation Model.* Available at https://blogs
.svvsd.org/admininduction/2014/09/14/using-the-frisk-documentation-model/

Arrien, A. (1993). *The four-fold way: Walking paths of the warrior, teacher, healer, and visionary.* New York, NY: HarperCollins.

Bandura, A. (1993). Perceived self-efficacy in cognitive development and functioning. *Educational Psychologist, 28,* 117–148.

Bariso, J. (2016, October). *Inc.: Rising stars.* Retrieved from https://www.inc.com/ justin-bariso/it-took-sheryl-sandberg-exactly-2-sentences-to-give-the-best-career-advice-youll.html

Block, P. (2011). *Flawless consulting* (3rd ed.). San Francisco, CA: Jossey-Bass.

Bryk, A., & Schneider, B. (2002). *Trust in schools.* New York, NY: Russell Sage Foundation.

Burris, D. (2013, Aug. 21). Supportive Common Core State Standards quotes. *Kansas College and Career Ready Standards.* Kansas State Department of Education. Available at http://community.ksde.org/Default.aspx?tabid=4754

Carse, J. (1986). *Finite and infinite games.* New York, NY: Ballantine Books.

Chadwick, R. (2013). *Finding new ground.* Terrebonne, OR: One Tree.

Chaltain, S. (2014, June 27). Positively deviant school reform? *Democracy. Learning. Voice. [Blog post].*

Costa, A. L., & Garmston, R. J. (2015). *Cognitive coaching: Developing self-directed leaders and learners* (3rd ed.). Lanham, MD: Rowman & Littlefield.

Covey, S. (1989). *The seven habits of highly effective people.* New York, NY: Simon & Schuster.

Crehan, L. (2017). *Cleverlands.* London, United Kingdom: Unbound.

Darling-Hammond, L. (2010). *The flat world and education: How America's commitment to equity will determine our future.* New York, NY: Teachers College Press.

Dewey, J. (1933). *How we think: A restatement of the relation of reflective thinking to the educational process.* Lexington, MA: Health.

Dorsey, D. (2000). Positive deviant. *Fast Company Magazine.* Retrieved from http:// www.childrensaidsociety.org/blog/2013/06/03/positive-deviance-project-finds-keys-school-success

Drago-Severson, E. (1996). *Head-of-school as principal adult developer: An account of one leader's efforts to support transformational learning among the adults in her school.* Unpublished doctoral dissertation, Harvard Graduate School of Education, Cambridge, MA.

Drago-Severson, E. (2004). Becoming adult learners: Principles and practice for effective development. New York, NY: Teachers College Press.

Drago-Severson, E. (2009). *Leading adult learning: Supporting adult development in our schools.* Thousand Oaks, CA: Corwin.

Drago-Severson, E., & Blum-DeStefano, J. (2016). *Tell me so I can hear you.* Watertown, MA: Harvard Education Press.

Drucker, P. F. (1990). Lessons for successful nonprofit governance. *Nonprofit Management and Leadership, 1*(1), 7–14.

Edmonds, R. (1989). History of effective schools. Retrieved from http://www.effectiveschools.com/about-us

Edmondson, A. (2012). *Teaming*. San Francisco, CA: Jossey-Bass.

Frank, C., & Magnone, P. (2011). *Drinking from the fire hose: Making smarter decisions without drowning in information*. London, United Kingdom: Penguin.

Fromm, E. (1994). *The art of listening*. London, United Kingdom: Bloomsbury Academic.

Garmston, R. J., & Wellman, B. (2016). *The adaptive school: A sourcebook for developing collaborative groups*. Lanham, MD: Roman & Littlefield.

Goddard, R., Hoy, W. & Woolfolk Hoy, A. (2000). Collective teacher efficacy: Its meaning, measure and impact on student achievement. *American Educational Research Journal, 37*(2), 479–507.

Goddard, R. Hoy, W. & Woolfolk Hoy, A. (2004, April). Collective efficacy beliefs: Theoretical developments, empirical evidence, and future directions. *Educational Researcher, 33*(3), 3–13.

Goldsmith, M. (2007). *What got you here won't get you there*. New York, NY: Hyperion.

Goldsmith, M. (2015). *Stakeholder centered coaching manual*. Retrieved from http://sccoaching.com/

Grossman, A. (2017, Jan. 28). Using Kohlberg's 6 moral principles in the classroom presentation materials. Retrieved from https://coretaskproject.com/2017/01/28/using-kohlbergs-6-moral-principles-in-the-classroom-presentation-materials/

Hargreaves, A., & Fullan, M. (2012). *Professional capital: Transforming teaching in every school*. Thousand Oaks, CA: Corwin.

Hargreaves, A., & O'Connor, M. (2017). *Collaborative professionalism*. Dyersburg, TN: WISE Foundation.

Hargreaves, A., & O'Connor, M. (2018). *Collaborative professionalism*. Thousand Oaks, CA: Corwin.

Hattie, J. (2012). *Visible learning for teachers: Maximizing impact on learning*. New York, NY: Routledge.

Hattie, J. (2015). *What works best in education: The politics of collaborative expertise*. London, United Kingdom: Pearson.

Heifetz, R. (1994). *Leadership without easy answers*. Cambridge, MA: Belknap Press.

Hord, S. M., Rutherford, W. L., Huling-Austin, L., & Hall, G. E. (1987). *Taking charge of change*. Alexandria, VA: ASCD.

Jones, D. (1999). *Everyday creativity* [Training video]. Minneapolis, MN: Star Thrower Distribution.

Joyce, B., & Showers, B. (2003). Student achievement through staff development. *National College for School Leadership*. Available at https://www.nationalcollege.org.uk/cm-mc-ssl-resource-joyceshowers.pdf

Kegan, R. (1982). *The evolving self: Problem and process in human development*. Cambridge, MA: Harvard University Press.

Kegan, R., & Lahey, L. (2009). *Immunity to change: How to overcome it and unlock the potential in yourself and your organization*. Boston, MA: Harvard Business Press.

Kegan, R., & Lahey, L. (2016). *An everyone culture: Becoming a deliberately developmental organization*. Watertown, MA: Harvard Business Review Press.

Kim, W., & Marbogne, R. (2003). *Fairness*. Watertown, MA: Harvard Business Review Press.

Klein, G. (1998). *Sources of power: How people make decisions.* Cambridge, MA: The MIT Press.

Lambert, L., Zimmerman, D. P., & Gardner, M. E. (2016). *Liberating leadership capacity: Pathways to educational wisdom.* New York, NY: Teachers College Press.

Merrill, D. & Reid, R. (1981). *Personal Styles & Effective Performance.* Boca Raton, FL: CRC Press.

Merrow, J. (2015, June 19). Is teaching a profession, an occupation, a calling, or a job? [Blog post]. Retrieved from http://takingnote.learningmatters.tv/?p=7595

National Council for Accreditation of Teacher Education Glossary. (2017). Professional disposition. Retrieved from http://ncate.org/Standards/UnitStandards/Glossary/tabid/477/Default.aspx#P

Perkins, D. (1992). *Smart schools.* New York, NY: The Free Press.

Pfeffer, J., & Sutton, R. (2000). *The knowing-doing gap: How smart companies turn knowledge into action.* Watertown, MA: Harvard Business School Press.

Rock, D. (2010. *SCARF: A brain-based model for collaborating with and influencing others* (Vol. *1*). *The NeuroLeadership Journal.* Retrieved from https://neuroleadership.com/portfolio-items/scarf-a-brain-based-model-for-collaborating-with-and-influencing-others/

Rowe, M. B. (1986). Wait time: Slowing down may be a way of speeding up! *Journal of Teacher Education, 37,* 43.

Sahlberg, P. (2015). *Finnish lessons 2.0: What can the world learn from educational change in Finland* (2nd ed.)? New York, NY: Teachers College Press.

Sanford, C. (2014). *The responsible entrepreneur.* San Francisco, CA: Jossey-Bass.

Satir, V. (1972). *Peoplemaking.* Palo Alto, CA: Science and Behavioral Books.

Schein, E. (2009). *Helping: How to offer, give, and receive help.* San Francisco, CA: Berrett-Koehler.

Schein, E. (2013). *Humble inquiry: The gentle art of asking instead of telling.* San Francisco, CA: Berrett-Koehler.

Schein, E. (2016). *Humble consulting: How to provide real help faster.* San Francisco, CA: Berrett-Koehler.

Schön, D. (1983). *The reflective practitioner.* New York, NY: Basic Books.

Senge, P. (1990). *The fifth discipline: The art and practice of the learning organization.* New York, NY: Currency.

Sinetar, M. (1991). *Developing a 21st century mind.* New York, NY: Villard Books.

Slap, S. (2010). *Bury my heart at conference room B.* New York, NY: Penguin.

Sommers, W. (2007). Our kids deserve your best. *Journal of Staff Development, 28*(1).

Sommers, W., & Olsen, W. (2016). *Learning omnivores.* Retrieved from www.learningomnivores.com

Stages of Concern. (2015). American Institute for Research. From the SEDL Archive. Retrieved from http://www.sedl.org/cbam/stages_of_concern.html

Sternin, J. (1991). *What is positive deviance? Positive deviance initiative.* Retrieved from https://positivedeviance.org/

Sternin, J. & Choo, R. (2000). The power of positive deviancy. *Harvard Business Review.* Jan-Feb 2000. Retrieved from https://hbr.org/2000/01/the-power-of-positive-deviancy

Tschannen-Moran, M. (2004). Principals' sense of efficacy. *Journal of Educational Administration, 42*(5), 573–585.

Tucker, M. (Ed.). (2012). *Surpassing Shanghai.* Watertown, MA: Harvard Education Press.

York-Barr, J., Sommers, W., Ghere, G., & Montie, J. (2016). *Reflective practice for renewing schools* (3rd ed.). Thousand Oaks, CA: Corwin.

INDEX

Note: Page numbers in *italics* refer to figures and tables.

CORWIN LEADERSHIP

Anthony Kim & Alexis Gonzales-Black

Designed to foster flexibility and continuous innovation, this resource expands cutting-edge management and organizational techniques to empower schools with the agility and responsiveness vital to their new environment.

Jonathan Eckert

Explore the collective and reflective approach to progress, process, and programs that will build conditions that lead to strong leadership and teaching, which will improve student outcomes.

PJ Caposey

Offering a fresh perspective on teacher evaluation, this book guides administrators to transform their school culture and evaluation process to improve teacher practice and, ultimately, student achievement.

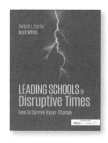

Dwight L. Carter & Mark White

Through understanding the past and envisioning the future, the authors use practical exercises and real-life examples to draw the blueprint for adapting schools to the age of hyper-change.

Raymond L. Smith & Julie R. Smith

This solid, sustainable, and laser-sharp focus on instructional leadership strategies for coaching might just be your most impactful investment toward student achievement.

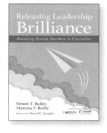

Simon T. Bailey & Marceta F. Reilly

This engaging resource provides a simple, sustainable framework that will help you move your school from mediocrity to brilliance.

Debbie Silver & Dedra Stafford

Equip educators to develop resilient and mindful learners primed for academic growth and personal success.

Peter Gamwell & Jane Daly

Discover a new perspective on how to nurture creativity, innovation, leadership, and engagement.

To order your copies, visit **corwin.com/leadership**

Leadership That Makes an Impact

Steven Katz, Lisa Ain Dack, & John Malloy
Leverage the oppositional forces of top-down expectations and bottom-up experience to create an intelligent, responsive school.

Peter M. DeWitt
Centered on staff efficacy, these resources present discussion questions, vignettes, strategies, and action steps to improve school climate, leadership collaboration, and student growth.

Eric Sheninger
Harness digital resources to create a new school culture, increase communication and student engagement, facilitate real-time professional growth, and access new opportunities for your school.

Russell J. Quaglia, Kristine Fox, Deborah Young, Michael J. Corso, & Lisa L. Lande
Listen to your school's voice to see how you can increase engagement, involvement, and academic motivation.

Michael Fullan, Joanne Quinn, & Joanne McEachen
Learn the right drivers to mobilize complex, coherent, whole-system change and transform learning for all students.

CORWIN LEADERSHIP

A SAGE Publishing Company

CORWIN HAS ONE MISSION: to enhance education through intentional professional learning.

We build long-term relationships with our authors, educators, clients, and associations who partner with us to develop and continuously improve the best evidence-based practices that establish and support lifelong learning.